酒店汉语

主　编　李　洁
副主编　李　群　刘　伟　石佳玉
　　　　王　欢　布　仁

东北师范大学出版社
长　春

图书在版编目（CIP）数据

酒店汉语：汉文、英文／李洁主编. — 长春：东北师范大学出版社，2024.11. --ISBN 978 - 7 - 5771 - 1815 - 4

I.F719.2

中国国家版本馆 CIP 数据核字第 2024HL6211 号

□责任编辑：冯咏艳　□封面设计：创智时代
□责任校对：徐　莹　□责任印制：侯 建 军

东北师范大学出版社出版发行
长春净月经济开发区金宝街 118 号（邮政编码：130117）
电话：010—82893525
传真：010—82896571
网址：http:∥www.nenup.com
东北师范大学音像出版社制版
长春市新颖印业有限责任公司印装
长春市清和街 23 号（邮政编码：130061）
2024 年 11 月第 1 版　2024 年 11 月第 1 次印刷
幅面尺寸：185 mm×260 mm　印张：15　字数：298 千

定价：49.80 元

前　言

近年来，广大留学生以及世界各地的人们表现出对中文学习的极大热爱。为服务国际产能合作，让中文与职业技能共同赋能人才培养，提升中文的国际语言服务能力，编者结合酒店行业特点和职业情景编写了《酒店汉语》一书。

教材充分着眼于语言学习和职业技能，将单纯的语言学习拓展到复合型技能人才培养，将职业技能作为中文的附加能力，实现语言学习的功能价值。教材以服务为导向，以任务为驱动，涵盖了前厅服务、客房服务、餐饮服务、康乐服务、会议服务以及其他服务等主要内容，呈现出酒店服务的具体情景。每个情景由多个具体任务组成，每项任务又包含导言、词库、常用句型、情景对话、补充阅读、练一练六个模块，把学习内容巧妙地融入每个任务之中，环环相扣，逻辑紧密。学习者在教师的引导下，通过完成任务，逐步掌握所学的知识与技能，在一个寓学于实践的教学情境里，充满兴趣地进行学习，真正实现学习者"学中做、做中练、练中熟"的教学循环模式。

教材设计科学，安排合理，语言简洁明了，词汇通俗易懂，兼具专业性、实践性与拓展性，可以作为外国朋友从事酒店行业技能培训的参考书，亦可作为汉语爱好者学习汉语的参考书。

本书编写力求细致，但书中难免存在不足，敬请广大读者在使用过程中，随时批评指正，以便将来更正，更好地服务读者朋友。

编　者
2024 年 3 月

目 录

Chapter 1 前厅服务 Front Office Service ········· 1
    Unit 1 房间预订 Room Reservations ········· 2
    Unit 2 办理入住 Check-in ········· 10
    Unit 3 礼宾服务 Concierge Service ········· 18
    Unit 4 问讯服务 Information Service ········· 27
    Unit 5 总机服务 Operator Service ········· 35
    Unit 6 外币兑换 Foreign Currency Exchange ········· 42
    Unit 7 办理离店 Check-out ········· 47
    Unit 8 处理投诉 Dealing with Complaint ········· 54

Chapter 2 客房服务 Housekeeping Service ········· 63
    Unit 1 清洁服务 Cleaning Service ········· 64
    Unit 2 常规服务 Regular Service ········· 69
    Unit 3 洗衣服务 Laundry Service ········· 74
    Unit 4 维修服务 Maintenance Service ········· 80
    Unit 5 其他客房服务 Other Housekeeping Services ········· 85
    Unit 6 紧急事件 Emergency ········· 92

Chapter 3 餐饮服务 Food & Beverage Service ········· 99
    Unit 1 订餐和领位 Reservations and Seating Guests ········· 100
    Unit 2 点菜 Taking Order ········· 109
    Unit 3 中餐服务 Chinese Food Service ········· 117
    Unit 4 西餐服务 Western Food Service ········· 124
    Unit 5 酒水服务 Drinks Service ········· 132
    Unit 6 结账 Settling the Bill ········· 138

Chapter 4 康乐服务 Health and Recreation Service ········· 145
    Unit 1 歌厅 KTV ········· 145
    Unit 2 水疗服务 SPA Service ········· 151
    Unit 3 健身房 Fitness Center ········· 157
    Unit 4 美容院 Beauty Salon ········· 163

Chapter 5 会议服务 Conference Service ·············· 170
 Unit 1 会议设备 Conference Equipment ·············· 171
 Unit 2 会议接待服务 Conference Reception Service ·············· 180

Chapter 6 其他服务 Other Services ·············· 188
 Unit 1 医疗服务 Medical Service ·············· 188
 Unit 2 购物中心 Shopping Center ·············· 194
 Unit 3 展览服务 Exhibition Service ·············· 202
 Unit 4 订票服务 Ticket Booking Service ·············· 210

练一练参考答案 ·············· 215
参考文献 ·············· 232

Chapter 1　前厅服务 Front Office Service

前厅部是整个酒店服务工作的核心。前厅部是每一位客人抵达、离开酒店的必经之地，是酒店对客服务开始和最终完成的场所，也是客人形成对酒店的第一印象和最后印象之处。

The front office department is the core of the whole hotel service work. It is the place for every guest to pass by when they arrive at and leave the hotel. It is the place where the hotel starts and finally completes the guest service, and the place where guests shape the first impression and final impression of the hotel.

前厅负责与顾客的大部分沟通服务，以确保客人入住期间一切顺利，包括预订、入住、退房、电话服务、财务和出纳、外汇兑换、房间分配、问讯等，向客人提供令其满意的服务，使酒店获得理想的经济效益和社会效益。

The front office manages most of the contact with guests to make sure their stay goes smoothly, including reservation, check-in, check-out, telephone services, financial transactions and cashier duties, currency exchange, room assignments, inquiry, etc., to provide satisfactory services to guests, so that the hotel can obtain ideal economic and social benefits.

Front Office Department（前厅部）:
- Reservation 预订处
- Concierge 礼宾部
- Reception 接待处
- Information 问讯处
- Operator 总机
- Assistant Manager 大堂副理
- Cashier Counter 收银处
- Business Center 商务中心

Unit 1　房间预订 Room Reservations

导言 Preview

　　酒店预订服务是顾客通过在线平台或电话预订酒店房间的过程。顾客可以选择合适的酒店，确定入住和离店日期，并选择房间类型和数量。预订完成后，顾客通常需要支付预订费用或提供信用卡信息作为担保。预订确认后，顾客可以收到预订确认函，其中包含入住日期、房间号和其他细节。酒店预订服务为顾客提供了方便、快捷的预订方式，并确保他们在旅行期间有一个舒适的住宿环境。

　　Hotel reservation service is the process of booking hotel rooms for customers through online platforms or telephone. Customers can choose the suitable hotel, determine the check-in and check-out dates, and select the room type and quantity. After the reservation is completed, customers usually need to pay the booking fee or provide credit card information as a guarantee. Upon reservation confirmation, customers will receive a booking confirmation letter that includes the check-in date, room number, and other details. Hotel reservation service provides customers with a convenient and fast way to book and ensures they have a comfortable accommodation environment during their travels.

词库 Word Bank

酒店房型 Type of room			
汉语 Chinese	英语 English	汉语 Chinese	英语 English
单人间 dān rén jiān	single room	双人间 shuāng rén jiān	double room
三人间 sān rén jiān	triple room	套房 tào fáng	suite
大床房 dà chuáng fáng	queen-size room	标准间 biāo zhǔn jiān	standard room
豪华间 háo huá jiān	deluxe room	商务房 shāng wù fáng	business room
无障碍房 wú zhàng ài fáng	barrier-free room	无烟房 wú yān fáng	non-smoking room
常用词汇 Common vocabulary			
汉语 Chinese	英语 English	汉语 Chinese	英语 English
预订 yù dìng	book	房价 fáng jià	room rate
折扣 zhé kòu	discount	保证 bǎo zhèng	guarantee
高楼层 gāo lóu céng	high floor	低楼层 dī lóu céng	low floor
景观房 jǐng guān fáng	room with a view	安静房间 ān jìng fáng jiān	quiet room
特价 tè jià	special offer	套餐价 tào cān jià	package deal

常用句型 Useful Expressions

提供帮助 Offer One's Help
1. 我能帮您什么忙呢？How can I help you, please?
2. 要我帮忙吗？May I help you, please?
3. 有什么需要帮忙的，先生/女士？Is there anything I can do for you, sir/madam?

预订房间 Book a Room
1. 有空房吗？Are there any rooms available?
2. 我想订一个双人房间，下周五用。I'd like to book a double room for Friday next week.
3. 两个晚上的单人房一间，有吗？Do you have one single room for two nights?
4. 我星期四订一间房。I need to book a room for Thursday.
5. 我想订一个从 4 月 5 日到 4 月 9 日的房间。I would like to reserve a room from April 5th to April 9th.
6. 我想订一个带淋浴的单人间，10 月 4 日下午到 10 月 10 日上午。I'd like to book a single room with a shower from the afternoon of October 4th to the morning of October 10th.
7. 顺便说一下，如有可能我想要一个不临街的安静房间。By the way, I'd like a quiet room away from the street if that is possible.

介绍房间和房价 Introduce a Room and Room Rate
1. 我们有许多不同类型的房间，例如……We have many types of rooms, such as…
2. 您想订哪种类型的房间？What kind of room do you want to reserve?
3. 您想要哪种价位的？What rate do you prefer?
4. 淡季我们房价打 7 折。We can give/offer you 30% off/a 30% discount in the off-season.
5. 团体预订我们优惠 15%。We will give/offer you 15% off/a 15% discount for the group reservation.
6. 双人间每晚 85 美元，另外还要加算 10%的税金和 10%的服务费。A double room is 85 dollars per night, a 10% tax and a 10% service charge extra.
7. 阳面的双人间每晚 160 美元，而阴面的双人间每晚 140 美元。A double room with a front view is 160 dollars per night, and one with a rear view is 140 dollars per night.
8. 房价有何差别？What's the price difference between the rooms?
9. 这个价格包含哪些服务项目呢？What services come with this price?

确认预订 Confirm a Reservation
1. 能告诉我您打算在我们酒店待多长时间吗？Would you tell me how long you will

stay in our hotel?

2. 我们还有满足你们需要的空房。We still have rooms available which meet your requirements.

3. 请问您以谁的名义预订？In whose name will you reserve, please?

4. 除用现金或信用卡担保的预订外，一般预订的房间只保留至当天的晚上6点。The reserved room will be held till 6:00 p.m. on arrival unless a cash or credit card guarantee is made.

5. 我将确认一下您的预订信息。I will confirm your reservation information.

6. 可以再确认一下您的预订吗？王先生，10月20日预订一间超级大床房。我的名字是××，如有任何疑问请与我们联系。Can I reconfirm your reservation? A king-size room for Mr. Wang on Oct. 20th. My name is ××. If you have any questions, please feel free to contact us.

7. 感谢您预订花园酒店，如有任何疑问或需作任何更改，请尽快与我们联系。Thank you for your reservation at Garden Hotel. If you have any questions or changes, please contact us as soon as possible.

8. 期待您的光临。We look forward to your arrival/your coming/seeing you soon.

房间满员时 Fully Booked

1. 抱歉，没有空房。I am sorry. No rooms are available.

2. 您打算来的那天，所有的大床房都被订完了。All the queen-size rooms have been booked on the day you plan to come.

3. 现在是旺季。非常抱歉，可以请您这个周末再打电话过来吗？可能会有人取消预订。It's the peak season now. I'm very sorry, but could you call us again on this weekend? We may have a cancellation.

4. 很抱歉，本周所有的客房已满。I am sorry, but all the rooms are occupied for this week.

5. 恐怕那天晚上各种类型的房间都预订满了。现在是旺季。I am afraid we are fully booked for all types of rooms on that night. It's the peak season now.

变更预订 Change a Reservation

1. 对不起，因为……我不得不取消在贵酒店的预订。Sorry, due to…, I have to cancel the reservation made in your hotel.

2. 我想多延住两晚，直到9号。I'd like to extend it for two more nights until the 9th.

3. 我想更改我的预订信息。I would like to change my reservation information.

4. 我想再延长两个晚上。I want to extend it for two more nights.

5. 我想更改预订。I'd like to change my reservation.

情景对话 Situational Dialogues

对话 1 Dialogue 1 预订房间 Booking a Room

场景：一对夫妻想要预订一个房间。

Scene：A couple would like to book a room.

C：Clerk（前台职员）　G：Guest（宾客）

C：早上好，这是客房预订部，能为您效劳吗？Good morning. This is room reservation department. May I help you?

G：噢，我想预订一个房间。Well, I'd like to reserve a room.

C：好的，要订哪天的？OK. Which date would that be?

G：从 5 月 12 日到 14 日。From May 12th to 14th.

C：住三晚，对吧？Three nights, right?

G：是的。Yes.

C：能告诉我你们一共有多少位客人吗？Would you tell me how many guests there are in your group?

G：我和我太太。Just my wife and me.

C：您喜欢什么样的房间，是一张双人床还是两张单人床的房间呢？What kind of room would you prefer, a double or a twin room?

G：我要一间两张单人床的房间。A twin room, please.

C：请别挂断，我要查查那几天有没有空房。先生，感谢您的等待，我们有 488 元和 588 元的两种房间，您喜欢哪一种呢？Please hold the line. I'll check if there's a room available for those days. Thank you for waiting, sir. We have two types of rooms at RMB 488 and RMB 588. Which one would you prefer?

G：两种房间有什么差别？What's the difference between the two types of rooms?

C：阳面的房间每晚 588 元，而阴面的房间每晚 488 元。A room with a front view is RMB 588 per night, and one with a rear view is RMB 488 per night.

G：我们要订 588 元的房间。We will take the one at RMB 588.

C：好的，先生，请问我可以知道您的名字及其拼写吗？Certainly, sir. May I take your name and spelling, please?

G：好的，我叫王林。W-A-N-G L-I-N。Yes, it's Wang Lin. W-A-N-G L-I-N.

C：谢谢，王先生，请给我您的电话号码好吗？Thanks, Mr. Wang. May I have your phone number, please?

G：好的，号码是 08-123-2622。Yes, the number is 08-123-2622.

C：08-123-2622。这是您家里的电话号码吗？08-123-2622. Is this your home phone number?

G：是的。Yes, it is.

C：先生，您预计什么时候抵达？What time do you expect to arrive, sir?

G：哦，我想是晚上8点左右吧。Oh, around 8 p.m., I suppose.

C：您需要机场接送服务吗？Do you need transportation to and from the airport?

G：谢谢，不需要。No, thanks.

C：好的。我再确定一下您的预订。王先生，您预订一间两张单人床的双人房间，每晚588元，从5月12日到14日三晚。期待能为您服务。OK, I'd like to confirm your reservation again. A twin room for Mr. Wang at RMB 588 per night for three nights from May 12th to 14th. We look forward to serving you.

对话2 Dialogue 2 团体预订 A Group Reservation

场景：一家旅行社的计调为一个20人的团队预订房间。

Scene：The operator of a travel agency plans to book rooms for a group of 20 people.

C：Clerk（前台职员）　　O：Operator（计调）

C：下午好，客房预订部。能为您效劳吗？Good afternoon, room reservation department. May I help you?

O：下午好，我这里是中慧旅行社。请问5月5日到5月10日期间你们酒店有空房间吗？我想要为一个旅游团订房。Good afternoon. I'm calling from Zhonghui Travel Agency. I'd like to know if you have rooms available for the nights from May 5th to May 10th. I'd like to reserve some rooms for a tourist party.

C：我可以问下有多少位客人吗？May I ask how many people will be in your party?

O：一共20人。A total of 20 persons.

C：您要订何种客房呢？What kind of room would you like?

O：要有两张床的双人房。Double rooms with twin beds.

C：请稍等，先生。我可以确认我们在那段时间有10套客房。A moment please, sir. I can confirm 10 rooms for those days.

O：谢谢！请问对团体预订有优惠吗？Thank you. Is there a special rate for a group reservation?

C：是的，可以打九折。Yes, there is a 10 percent discount.

O：很好。That is fine.

C：顺便问一下，您打算如何支付？By the way, how will you settle the account, please?

O：公司将支付所有费用。我们很快寄送你们支票。The company will cover all the

expenses and we'll send you a cheque soon.

C：谢谢您，先生！还有其他需要吗？Thank you, sir! Anything else?

O：5号晚上8点在酒店的中餐厅订一个20人的包间。I'd like to book a private room for 20 persons at the Chinese restaurant at 8 p.m. on the 5th.

C：好的，先生。有什么特殊要求吗？OK, sir. Do you have any special requirements?

O：没有，谢谢，再见。No. Thank you and goodbye.

C：恭候您的光临。再见。We look forward to your arrival. Goodbye.

对话3 Dialogue 3 变更预订 Changing a Reservation

场景：一位预订客人打算更改自己的房间预订。

Scene：A booked guest intends to change his room reservation.

C：Clerk（前台职员）　　G：Guest（宾客）

G：你好，请问我想变更一下房间预订，能帮我办理吗？Hi, I would like to change my room reservation. Can you assist me with that?

C：当然，我可以帮您处理。请问您想要变更为哪种房间类型？Of course, I can help you with that. Which room type would you like to change to?

G：我之前预订的是标准间，但是我想升级为豪华套房。I originally booked a standard room, but I would like to upgrade to a deluxe suite.

C：好的，让我查一下是否还有豪华套房。请稍等片刻。OK, let me check if there is availability for a deluxe suite. Please wait a moment.

G：好的，谢谢。Alright, thank you.

C：非常抱歉，豪华套房已经预订满了，没有可用的房间了。I'm sorry, but all the deluxe suites have been fully booked. There is no available room.

G：那有其他类型的房间可供选择吗？Are there any other room types to choose from?

C：是的，我们还有行政套房和高级房可供选择。您可以选择其中之一。Yes, we still have executive suites and superior rooms available. You can choose one of them.

G：我选择高级房吧。I'll go for the superior room then.

C：好的，让我为您更改预订。请您再次确认您的姓名和预订信息。OK, let me make the change for you. Please confirm your name and reservation details again.

G：我的姓名是王明，预订的是7月15日入住，预订号是123456。My name is Wang Ming, and my reservation is for July 15th, and the reservation number is 123456.

C：好的，已经为您更改预订到高级房了，预订成功。Alright, I have successfully changed your reservation to a superior room. Your reservation is confirmed.

G：谢谢你的帮助。Thank you for your assistance.

C：您的满意是我们最大的追求，有任何其他需求请随时告知我们。Your

satisfaction is our top priority. If you have any other requests, please feel free to let us know.

补充阅读 Supplement Reading

酒店预订通常包括有保证预订和无保证预订两种方式。大多数酒店为客人保留房间到下午六点钟。通常如果客人在下午六点钟前进行入住登记，则无须做有保证客房预订。但如果客人六点钟以后才能到达，则需要做有保证客房预订。有保证客房预订是通过下列方式之一来完成的：

1）预收款保证预订：客人提前支付足额房费。

2）信用卡保证预订：记下客人信用卡号码，如果客人没有按预订要求来酒店办理入住，酒店可向持卡人收取费用。这是最常用的一种有保证预订方式。

3）押金保证预订：客人提前支付一天房费。

4）合同协议保证预订：酒店与公司有协议在先，无论公司预订的客房是否被使用，房费均由公司承担。

在接受客房预订时通常要询问客人的到店时刻，目的是确认客人能否在下午六点钟前到店。如果客人不能在下午六点钟前到店，就要做有保证订房安排。

Hotel reservations usually include two types: guaranteed reservations and non-guaranteed reservations. Most hotels reserve rooms for guests until 6:00 p.m. Generally, if guests check in before 6:00 p.m., there is no need for a guaranteed reservation. However, if guests arrive after 6:00 p.m., a guaranteed reservation is required. Guaranteed reservations can be made through one of the following methods:

1) Prepayment guaranteed reservations: Guests pay the full room rate in advance.

2) Credit card guaranteed reservations: Record the credit card numbers of guests, and if they fail to check in according to the reservation requirements, the hotel can charge them. This is the most commonly used type of guaranteed reservations.

3) Advanced deposit guaranteed reservations: Guests pay one day's rate in advance.

4) Contract agreement guaranteed reservations: The hotel has a prior agreement with a company, and regardless of whether the company's reserved rooms are used or not, the company covers the fee.

When accepting room reservations, it is usually necessary to ask guests about their arrival time to confirm whether they can arrive before 6:00 p.m. If guests cannot arrive before 6:00 p.m., a guaranteed reservation arrangement must be made.

练一练 Activities

一、连线题

单人间　　　　　　Business Room

双人间　　　　　　Deluxe Room

标准间　　　　　　Double Room

三人间　　　　　　Triple Room

商务间　　　　　　Barrier-free Room

豪华间　　　　　　Single Room

无障碍房　　　　　Standard Room

二、请按照预订程序，将下面的句子排序

1. 请别挂断好吗？我来查看一下是否有空房间。（过了一会儿）让您久等了，先生。我们有空余的双床间，现在价格是每晚 180 美元，这样可以吗？

2. 我想预订一个房间。

3. 要订在什么时候？您一行有多少人？

4. 4 月 16 日到 20 日，只有我和我太太。

5. 嗯，是的，是军队的军。

6. 再见。

7. 双人间。

8. 请问您 4 月 16 日大概什么时候到酒店？

9. 您好，客房预订部，请问有什么可以帮助您？

10. 好的，可以，我订了。

11. 没有了。

12. 好的，您有任何需要再联系我们，再次感谢您，再见。

13. 谢谢您，先生。您能告诉我您的姓名和电话号码吗？

14. 李军，电话是 3242-5827。请问您，军是军队的军吗？

15. 4 月 16 日到 20 日，请问您想预订哪种房间？

16. 大约中午 12 点。

17. 李先生，因为现在是旺季，我们酒店预订只能保留到下午 6 点。

18. 谢谢您，李先生。您已经在广州×××酒店办理了预订，从 4 月 16 日到 20 日，预住 5 天。您若不能如期到达，请务必在 16 日下午 6 点前通知我们。感谢您的电话，我们期待能为您服务。请问您还有其他问题吗？

19. 没问题。我叫李军，电话是 3242-5827。

20. 好的，我知道了，我会在6点前到达。

三、翻译下列句子

1. 我想订一个从4月5日到4月9日的房间。

2. 我想订一个带浴室的单人房间，10月4日下午到10月10日上午。

3. 现在是旺季。非常抱歉，您这个周末可以再打电话过来吗？可能会有人取消预订。

4. 恐怕那天晚上各种类型的房间都预订满了。现在是旺季。

5. 对不起，因为……我不得不取消在贵酒店的预订。

Unit 2　办理入住 Check-in

导言 Preview

酒店办理入住是指顾客到达酒店后，完成登记手续并拿到房卡的过程。一般情况下，入住流程包括以下几个步骤：

Hotel check-in is the process by which a guest arrives at a hotel, completes the registration procedure, and obtains the room card. Generally, the check-in process includes the following steps：

●填写登记表：顾客需要提供个人信息，如姓名、身份证号码、联系方式等，填写登记表格。

Fill out the registration form：Guests are required to provide personal information such as their names, ID numbers, contact details, etc., by filling out the registration form.

●辨认身份：酒店会核对顾客身份证件，以确保信息准确。

Verify identity：The hotel will verify guests' identification documents to ensure accuracy of information.

●确定入住时间和房间类型：顾客需要告知酒店入住的具体时间，并选择所需的房间类型，如单人间、双人间或套房等。

Determine check-in time and room type：Guests need to inform the hotel about their specific check-in time and choose the desired room type, such as single room, double room, or suite.

●登记付款方式：顾客需要选择付款方式，如现金、信用卡或支付宝等，并进行相关登记。

Register the payment method：Guests need to choose a payment method, such as cash, credit card, or Alipay, and complete the relevant registration.

●交付房卡：完成以上步骤后，酒店会提供房卡，顾客可以凭借房卡进入自己的房间。

Issue the room card：After completing the above steps, the hotel will provide a room card, which allows guests to access their assigned room.

词库 Word Bank

登记材料 Registration materials			
汉语 Chinese	英语 English	汉语 Chinese	英语 English
表格 biǎo gé	form	护照 hù zhào	passport
身份证 shēn fèn zhèng	ID card	签证 qiān zhèng	visa
国籍 guó jí	nationality	职业 zhí yè	occupation
地址 dì zhǐ	address	性别 xìng bié	gender
男 nán	male	女 nǚ	female
常用词汇 Common vocabulary			
汉语 Chinese	英语 English	汉语 Chinese	英语 English
签字 qiān zì	sign	填写 tián xiě	fill in
登记 dēng jì	registration	房卡 fáng kǎ	room card
押金 yā jīn	deposit	到客名单 dào kè míng dān	the arrival list
未预订客人 wèi yù dìng kè rén	walk-in guest	办理入住 bàn lǐ rù zhù	check in
淋浴 lín yù	shower	浴缸 yù gāng	bath

常用句型 Useful Expressions

接待 Reception

1. 欢迎光临我们酒店。Welcome to our hotel.
2. 接待处就在正前方。The reception desk is straight ahead.
3. 您先请。After you, please.
4. 请稍坐一会儿，我将会为您办理入住手续。Please have a seat for a while. I'll help you with the check-in procedure.

办理入住手续 Check-in Procedure

1. 可以把您的护照或身份证以及信用卡交给我吗？我帮您填表格。Would you please give me your passport or ID card and credit card? I'll help you to fill in the form.
2. 这次您住几天？How many days will you stay this time?
3. 您要哪种房间？我们有以下种类的房间……Which type of room would you like?

We have these types of rooms...

4. 先生/女士，不好意思，打扰一下。请问您如何付押金？付现金还是刷卡（分开付还是一起付）呢？Excuse me, sir/madam. How would you like to pay the deposit, in cash or by credit card (separately or together)?

5. 这是您的房卡和早餐券。请您在这里签个名好吗？Here is your room card and the breakfast coupon. Would you please sign here?

6. 这是您的护照和信用卡。现在您可以去房间了。希望您在这里住得愉快。Here is your passport and credit card. You can go up to the room now. I hope you enjoy your stay here.

信息登记 Information Registration

1. 请填写这份表格。Please fill in this form.

2. 请签上您的姓名。Please sign your name.

3. 请把护照给我，我们登记时需要。Give me your passport, please. We need it for registration.

4. 您有任何有效的身份证明吗？Have you got any valid identification?

5. 请您填写这张登记表，好吗？Would you please complete this registration form?

6. 请问您的职业？What's your occupation, please?

7. 请问您的国籍？What's your nationality, please?

8. 请问您在自己国家的住址？What's your address in your native country, please?

9. 请把护照给我。Please give me your passport.

10. 请在右下角签名。Please sign at the bottom on the right hand side.

房间安排 Room Arrangement

1. 您的房间是二楼的208。Your room is 208 on the second floor.

2. 208房间是带淋浴的空调房。Room 208 is an air-conditioned room with a shower.

3. 这是您的房卡。Here's your room card.

4. 这是您208号房的房卡。Here's your card to Room 208.

5. 我会叫行李员把您的行李搬上去。I'll get the porter to take your luggage up.

6. 这里的行李员会为您提行李，并为您带路。The porter here will take your luggage and show you the way.

情景对话 Situational Dialogues

对话1 Dialogue 1 常规入住登记 Normal Check-in

场景：一辆出租车停在建国宾馆门前，一名行李员上前迎接客人，并将他们引导到前台。

Scene: A taxi pulls up in front of Jianguo Hotel and a porter goes forward to meet the guests and guides them to the reception desk.

R：Receptionist（前台接待员）　　G：Guest（客人）

R：晚上好！先生，有什么能为您效劳的？Good evening. What can I do for you, sir?

G：两周前我订了一间带淋浴的超级大床房。我叫王林。I booked a king-size room with a shower two weeks ago. I'm Wang Lin.

R：请稍等，王先生。我查一下到客名单。抱歉让您久等了，先生。是的，您预订了一间从今天到15日的超级大床房。请出示一下您的护照，好吗？Just a moment, please, Mr. Wang. I'll check the guest arrival list. Sorry to have kept you waiting, sir. Yes, you have reserved a king-size room from today to the 15th. Could I see your passport, please?

G：好的，给你。Yes, here you are.

R：谢谢您，先生。请填一下登记表好吗？Thank you, sir. And would you please fill in the registration form?

G：当然。（填表）给你。这样可以吗？Sure.（Fill in the form）Here you are. Is this all right?

R：是的，谢谢。您打算如何付款，用现金、信用卡还是旅行支票？Yes, thanks. How are you going to pay, in cash, by credit card or with traveler's check?

G：现金。In cash.

R：我明白了。可以给我3000元人民币押金吗？I see. May I have RMB 3,000 as a deposit?

G：给你。Here you are.

R：谢谢。请保管好押金收据。这是1015房间的房卡。请保管好。Thank you. Please keep the deposit receipt. Here's the card to Room 1015. Please keep it.

G：谢谢。Thank you.

R：如果您有贵重物品，请将它们存放在我们这里或使用您房间的保险箱。If you have any valuables, please deposit them with us or use the safe in your room.

G：我明白了。I see.

R：行李员会带您去的。祝您晚上愉快，先生。The porter will show you up. Have a nice evening, sir.

对话2 Dialogue 2 团队办理登记手续（1）Checking in a Group（1）

场景：奥地利教育代表团团长正在接待处办理入住手续。

Scene：The leader of the Austrian Education Delegation is checking in at the reception desk.

R：Receptionist（前台接待员）　　L：Leader（团长）

R：早上好，先生！有什么能为您效劳的？Good morning, sir! May I help you?

L：我是王林，奥地利教育代表团团长。我们在你们酒店预订了12个房间。这是确认信。I'm Wang Lin, the leader of the Austrian Education Delegation. We have 12 rooms reserved at your hotel. Here is the confirmation letter.

R：是的，王先生。所有的团员都在外面等着吗？Yes, Mr. Wang. Are all the group members waiting outside?

L：是的。他们还在大巴车上。Yes. They are still in the coach.

R：好的，王先生。我们已经为贵国代表团准备好了登记材料。您预订了12间标准客房，其中包括一间无障碍房，并且您希望所有的房间都安排在9楼。有什么变化吗？Very well, Mr. Wang. We have got the registration materials ready for your delegation. You've reserved 12 standard rooms, including a barrier-free room. And you want all the rooms arranged on the 9th floor. Are there any changes?

L：没有。No.

R：可以出示一下您的护照和团体签证吗？Could I see your passport and the group visa?

L：好的，给你。Yes, here you are.

R：谢谢。您能在登记表上填写您的个人信息吗？Thank you. Would you fill in the registration form with your personal information?

L：好的，给你。OK. Here you are.

R：谢谢。这是房卡。Thank you. Here are the room cards.

L：好的。我来给团员分配房间。OK. I'll assign rooms among my members.

R：行李员会把行李送到各位的房间。我会安排一位行李员陪同那位身体不便的先生上楼。The porter will carry the baggage up to your rooms. And I will arrange a porter to help the disabled gentleman upstairs.

L：你真贴心！还有一件事，根据行程安排，我们15日将有一次会议。有可容纳60人的会议室吗？That's very considerate of you! One more thing, according to the schedule, we'll have a meeting on the 15th. Have you got a meeting room for about sixty people?

R：是的，我们有设备齐全的会议室，可容纳约100人。每天1800元人民币。Yes, we have a fully equipped meeting room for about 100 people. It costs RMB 1,800 per day.

L：太好了。晚饭后我会来找你的。这样可以吗？That's great. I will come to you for it after dinner. Would that work for you?

R：没问题。如果您还有任何问题或要求，请随时咨询。No problem. If you have any more questions or requests, please don't hesitate to ask us.

对话3 Dialogue 3 团队办理登记手续（2） Checking in a Group (2)

场景：一个旅行团抵达酒店，准备办理入住手续。

Scene：A tour group arrives at the hotel. They are going to check in.

R：Receptionist（前台接待员）　　L：Local Guide（地陪）

R：下午好。欢迎来到花园酒店。有什么可以为您效劳的吗？Good afternoon. Welcome to Garden Hotel. May I help you?

L：是的。我来自中慧旅行社。我们为15位游客预订了两间套房和5间双人间。Yes. I come from Zhonghui Travel Agency. We have booked two suites and five double rooms for 15 tourists.

R：请稍等。我查看一下到客名单。谢谢您的等候。是的，您预订的是两间套房和5个双人间，住4晚。贵团人数有变动吗？Just a moment, please. Let me check the guest arrival list. Thank you for waiting. Yes, your reservation is two suites and five double rooms for four nights. Is there any change in the number of your group?

L：没有。No.

R：很好。您能填一下登记表吗？Good. Could you please fill out the registration form?

L：当然。Sure.

R：有团体签证吗？Do you have a group visa?

L：有，给你。这些是护照。Yes, here you are. And these are our passports.

R：谢谢。能不能给我一份团体分房名单呢？Thank you. May I have a group rooming list, please?

L：没问题。No problem.

R：给您房卡和早餐券。行李员会带你们去房间。Here are the room cards and breakfast vouchers. The porter will show you to your rooms.

L：多谢。Thanks.

R：我可以再确认一下您的退房时间吗？May I reconfirm your check-out time?

L：26号退房。我们需要订一个6点叫早服务。We will leave on the 26th. And we need a wake-up call at 6:00 a.m.

R：没问题。还有别的吗？No problem. Anything else?

L：没了，谢谢。No. Thank you.

R：这是我的荣幸。祝您入住愉快。My pleasure. Enjoy your stay.

对话4 Dialogue 4 接待散客入住 Receiving a Walk-in Guest

场景：一位男士走了进来，希望能找一个房间过夜。

Scene：A gentleman steps in, trying to find a room for the night.

R：Receptionist（前台接待员）　　G：Guest（客人）

R：早上好，先生，有什么能为您效劳的？Good morning, sir. May I help you?

G：你好，我刚刚抵达北京，想要订一间房间。Yes, please. I've just arrived in Beijing. I want to book a room.

R：先生，您有预订吗？Have you made a reservation, sir?

G：没有。I am afraid not.

R：请问您几位？How many people do you have, please?

G：就我一位。Just me.

R：请稍等。我看看有没有空房。抱歉，先生，目前房间全满。但是下午两点可以给您安排一间房间。如果您现在就需要的话，您愿意让我帮您联系其他酒店吗？Just a moment, please. I have to check if there's a room available. Oh, sorry sir. All the rooms are booked up now. But I think we'll be able to arrange for you a room after 2 o'clock this afternoon. If you need a room right now, would you like me to get in touch with some other hotels for you?

G：不用了，谢谢。我想我更愿意住在这里。我的一位朋友强烈推荐你们酒店。我在这里等到2点。No, thanks. I should say I prefer to stay here. A friend of mine highly recommended your hotel to me. I'll just wait here till 2 p.m.

R：不客气，先生。也许在经历了一段疲惫的旅程后，您在我们的大堂酒吧休息会更舒服。如果您有任何需要，一定要告诉我们。You are welcome, sir. Perhaps you might feel more comfortable to rest in our lobby bar after a tiring journey. And if you have any requests, do let us know.

G：谢谢了。Thank you.

补充阅读 Supplement Reading

外国人临时住宿登记表
Registration Form of Temporary Residence for Foreigners

全名 Full Name		房间号 Room No.	
国籍 Nationality	性别 Gender	出生日期 Date of Birth	职业 Occupation
签证号或旅行文件号 Visa or Travel Document No.		有效时间 Date of Validity	
停留事由 Object of Stay		入境日期 Date of Entry	
何处来去何处 Where from & to		抵达日期 Arrival Date	

续表

接待单位 Received by	离开日期 Departure Date
地址 Address	宾客签名 Guest Signature
结账方式 ON CHECKING OUT MY ACCOUNT WILL BE SETTLED BY □现金 CASH □信用卡 CREDIT CARD □旅行社 AGENCY	请注意 PLEASE NOTE 酒店结账时间以当天中午 12:00 为限。Hotel check-out time is until 12:00 noon on the day of departure. 房费不包含房间中的饮料。Room rate does not include beverage in your room. 钱、珠宝等贵重物品必须存放在酒店的保险箱里。否则，遗失概不负责。Valuables such as money and jewelry must be deposited in the hotel safe. Otherwise, the hotel will not be responsible for any loss.

练一练 Activities

一、请选择对应的答案

性别　　　　　　美国

国籍　　　　　　身份证

职业　　　　　　男

证件　　　　　　教师

二、请按照登记程序，将下面的句子排序

好的，谢谢。

您好！请问您有预订吗？

李先生，预订信息显示，您是预订了一间标间，4月16日到20日，预住5天，是吗？

嗯，是的。

是的，我有预订。

我给您登记了8215房间，房间在2楼，您可以向前走，有电梯。这是房卡，请您收好。早餐是早上五点到九点，如果您有问题可以拨打总台电话8888。

请您稍等，我给您登记一下，请您看摄像头（摄像头采集信息）。您需要预交押金1000元，押金收据退房时需要您出示。

好的，我划卡。

这是您的押金收据，请您收好。

请出示一下您的身份证，我查一下订单。

请问您是划卡还是交现金？

好的。

17

三、翻译下列句子

1. 请稍坐一会儿，我将会为您办理入住手续。
2. 请把您的护照或身份证以及信用卡交给我，我帮您填表格。
3. 请把护照给我，我们登记时需要。
4. 我会叫行李员把您的行李搬上去。
5. 这里的行李员会为您提行李，并为您带路。

Unit 3　礼宾服务 Concierge Service

导言 Preview

礼宾服务是许多酒店不可或缺的组成部分，为客人提供个性化的协助，确保他们有一个难忘且无忧的入住体验。以下是对酒店礼宾服务的简要介绍：

Concierge service is an integral part of many hotels, providing guests with personalized assistance and ensuring them a memorable and hassle-free stay. Here is a brief introduction to hotel concierge service：

●接待和问候 Reception and Greeting

抵达酒店时，礼宾人员会热情地迎接客人并协助其完成入住手续，同时提供热情友好的接待。他们会提供有关酒店设施、服务和当地景点的信息。

Upon arrival, guests are warmly welcomed by the concierge staff members, who assist with check-in procedures and provide a warm and friendly greeting. They offer information about hotel facilities, services, and local attractions.

●行李协助 Luggage Assistance

礼宾人员负责处理客人的行李，包括入住和退房。他们帮助搬运行李，并在需要时安全存放行李。

Concierge staff members are responsible for handling guests' luggage, both during check-in and check-out. They assist with transporting luggage to and from the room, as well as storing it securely if needed.

●信息与推荐 Information and Recommendations

礼宾人员对当地情况非常了解，可以为客人提供有关附近的景点、餐厅、购物区、交通和文化活动的信息。他们还可以为客人预订餐厅或演出和活动的门票。

Concierge staff members are knowledgeable about the local area and can provide guests with information regarding nearby attractions, restaurants, shopping areas, transportation, and cultural events. They can also make reservations for restaurants or tickets to shows and events for guests.

●交通安排 Transportation Arrangements

礼宾人员通常会协助客人进行交通安排，如安排机场接送、出租车或租车服务。他们可以提供指引或安排私人交通。

Concierge staff members often assist guests with transportation arrangements, such as arranging airport transfers, taxi or rental cars services. They can provide directions or arrange for private transportation.

酒店礼宾服务旨在为客人提供顺畅愉快的入住体验，满足他们的个性化需求，确保在酒店期间始终享受愉快的体验。

Hotel concierge service aims to provide guests with a seamless and enjoyable stay, cater to their personalized needs and ensure them a pleasant experience throughout their time at the hotel.

词库 Word Bank

常用词汇 Common vocabulary			
汉语 Chinese	英语 English	汉语 Chinese	英语 English
门童 mén tóng	doorman	行李员 xíng li yuán	bellman
礼宾部 lǐ bīn bù	Concierge	大堂副理 dà táng fù lǐ	assistant manager
行李 xíng li	luggage/baggage	行李车 xíng li chē	baggage trolley
行李牌 xíng li pái	luggage tag	行李架 xíng li jià	luggage rack
行李存放处 xíng li cún fàng chù	luggage depository	寄存牌 jì cún pái	storage tag
打扰 dǎ rǎo	disturb	插入 chā rù	insert
寄存 jì cún	deposit	电梯 diàn tī	lift
接机服务 jiē jī fú wù	pick-up service	出租车 chū zū chē	taxi
签名 qiān míng	signature	服务指南 fú wù zhǐ nán	the service guide
拿 ná	take	营业时间 yíng yè shí jiān	the service time

常用句型 Useful Expressions

取送行李 Pick up & Drop off Luggage

1. 这是您的行李吗？Is this your baggage?

2. 这是全部东西吗，先生？Is this everything, sir?

3. 我来帮您拿好吗？/让我来帮您拿行李吧。May I take them for you? / Let me help you with your luggage.

4. 我希望没有打扰您。I hope I'm not disturbing you.

5. 等一会儿，先生。我马上送来。Just a moment, sir. I'll bring them to you right away.

6. 夫人，行李员会送您到房间的。The bellboy will show you to your room, madam.

7. 您可以把行李放在礼宾部。You may leave your luggage at the concierge.

8. 您要在这里寄存行李吗？Would you like to deposit your luggage here?

9. 别担心，您的行李很快就会送上去的。Don't worry, your luggage will be sent up at once.

10. 如果您要退房，请致电 9234，我们将马上帮您运送行李。When you check out, please call 9234 and we'll help you with your luggage immediately.

11. 我乘另一部电梯把行李送上去。I'll send the luggage up by another lift.

12. 我把您的行李放在这里好吗？Do you mind if I put your luggage here?

13. 我马上派人来替您取行李。I'll have somebody to collect your luggage right away.

14. 您能在房间里稍等会儿吗？我们马上来。Could you wait a moment in your room, please? We'll come at once.

带客人进房间 Show a Guest to the Room

1. 我带您去 1206 房。I'll show you to Room 1206.

2. 请您在这里签名。Please sign your name here.

3. 给您房间钥匙。Here is your room key.

4. 请稍等，我去推辆行李车来。Just a moment, please. I will bring a luggage cart.

5. 这边请。This way, please.

6. 您先请。After you, please. /You first, please.

7. 您的包/公文包/手提箱里有什么贵重或易碎物品吗？Is there anything valuable or breakable in your bag/briefcase/suitcase?

8. 先生，1101 房到了。Here we are, sir, Room 1101.

9. 让我带您到房间，这边请。Let me show you to your room. This way please.

10. 请小心脚下，先生。Watch your step, sir.

11. 请稍等，电梯马上就下来了。Just a moment, please. The elevator will be here soon.

12. 电梯在这边。Here we go to the elevator.

提供服务 Offer Services

1. 您能告诉我您的房间号吗？May I know your room number？/ What's your room number, please?

2. 您什么时候来取行李呢？What time will you pick up your luggage?

3. 请在行李牌上签上名。Please sign your name on the luggage tag.

4. 我可以看一下您的房卡吗？May I have a look at your room card?

5. 需要我为您叫一辆出租车吗？Would you like me to call a taxi for you?

6. 从这里乘出租车到机场大概需要 20 分钟。It's about 20 minutes by taxi from here to the airport.

7. 对不起，让您久等了。I'm sorry to have kept you waiting for such a long time.

8. 您能告诉我您的电话号码吗？Would you please tell me your phone number?

9. 还有什么事我能帮您做吗？Is there anything else I can do for you?

10. 我了解您的意思。I see what you mean.

客房设施和服务介绍 Introduce the Room Facilities and Services

1. 这是您的房间，先生。This is your room, sir.

2. 我可以把您的包放这儿吗？May I put your bag here?

3. 我替您打开窗帘，好吗？Shall I open the curtains for you?

4. 插入电源钥匙卡。Insert the key card for electricity.

5. 请将钥匙标签插入墙上的钥匙标签槽中，打开灯。Please insert the key tag into the key tag slot on the wall to switch the lights on.

6. 如果您不想被打扰，您可以按下这个按钮，打开"请勿打扰"标志。If you don't want to be disturbed, you can turn on the "Do Not Disturb" sign by pushing this button.

7. 这里有个介绍酒店各项服务的小册子。Here is a brochure explaining various hotel services.

8. 这是电视的遥控器。Here is the remote control for the TV.

9. 您可以用这个空调控制器调节室温。You can adjust the room temperature with this air conditioner control.

10. 您房间的电压是 220 伏。The voltage in your room is 220 volts.

11. 这是您的房卡。您可以一直保存到退房。出门时记得带上它。Here is your room card. You can keep it until you check out. Remember to take it with you when you go out.

12. 假如您有任何问题，请拨打客房服务中心电话"9"。If you have any question, you can dial "9", and it is housekeeping service center.

13. 如果您需要任何东西或任何帮助，您可以打电话给管家或前台。If you require anything or help, you can call the housekeeper or the front desk.

14. 我们酒店是我市第一家接待海外代表团的五星级酒店。Our hotel is the first 5-star hotel in this city that caters to oversea delegations.

15. 本酒店被誉为"花园酒店"，景色宜人，风景秀丽。It is well-known as a "Garden Hotel", featuring fantastic scenery and beautiful landscapes.

16. 客房配有宽带互联网接入和视频点播电影系统。酒店拥有 16 间大小不等的会议室，以及 23 间中西式餐厅。Rooms come with broadband Internet access and VOD movie system. The hotel has 16 meeting rooms in different sizes as well as 23 dining halls of Chinese and Western style.

17. 酒店拥有各种娱乐设施，如室内外网球场、室内温水游泳池、按摩中心、水疗中心、购物中心、理发室、茶室、酒吧、咖啡馆和夜总会等。The hotel has various recreational facilities such as indoor & outdoor tennis courts, an indoor heated swimming pool, a massage center, a SPA center, a shopping center, a barber shop, a tea room, a bar, a café and a nightclub, etc.

18. 餐厅的开放时间是从早上 7 点到晚上 10 点，但客房送餐提供 24 小时服务。The opening time of the dining room is from 7:00 a.m. till 10:00 p.m., but room service is available 24 hours.

19. 您可以把贵重物品存放在酒店的保险柜里。You can store your valuables at the hotel's safe.

20. 所有文具都在书桌抽屉里。All stationery is in this desk drawer.

情景对话 Situational Dialogues

对话 1 Dialogue 1 接机服务 Pick-up Service

场景：花园酒店的行李员前往机场接王林先生。他在机场出口处举着"王林"的接机牌。

Scene: A bellman from Garden Hotel goes to the airport to pick up Mr. Wang Lin. He holds the pick-up sign "Wang Lin" at the airport exit area.

B：Bellman（行李员）　W：Wang Lin（王林）

B：打扰了，请问您是来自法国的王林先生吗？Excuse me. Are you Mr. Wang Lin from France?

W：是的，我是王林。Yes, my name is Wang Lin.

B：见到您很高兴。我是花园酒店的行李员。Nice to meet you. I am a bellman from Garden Hotel.

W：见到您也很高兴。Nice to meet you, too.

B：欢迎来到北京。旅途顺利吗？Welcome to Beijing. Did you have a nice trip?

W：是的，旅途很愉快。Yes, I had a pleasant trip.

B：这是您所有的行李吗？Is this all your luggage?

W：是的。Yes.

B：让我帮您搬行李吧。Let me carry the luggage for you.

W：太感谢啦。Thank you very much.

B：您之前来过北京吗？Have you been to Beijing before?

W：没有。这是我第一次到这里。No. It is my first time here.

B：北京是一座历史文化名城。拥有很多名胜古迹，比如故宫、天坛、颐和园等等。希望您在这里过得愉快。Beijing is a famous historical and cultural city. It has many ancient historical sights, including the Palace Museum, the Temple of Heaven, and the Summer Palace, etc. I hope you enjoy your stay here.

W：谢谢。Thanks.

B：请这边走。我们已经备好车送您去酒店。This way, please. The car is ready to take you to the hotel.

对话2 Dialogue 2 接待客人 Receiving a Guest

场景：行李员正在接待一位客人。

Scene：The bellman is receiving a guest.

B：Bellman（行李员）　　G：Guest（客人）

B：早上好，先生。欢迎来到花园酒店。Good morning, sir. Welcome to Garden Hotel.

G：早上好。Good morning.

B：您有几件行李？How many pieces of luggage do you have?

G：三件。Three.

B：两个包和一个手提箱。对吗？Two bags and a suitcase. Is that right?

G：是的。Yes.

B：我带您去前台。请这边走。我会把您的行李放在那边的柱子旁边。I'll show you to the front desk. This way, please. I'll put your luggage by the post over there.

G：谢谢。Thanks.

（当客人办理入住手续时，行李员与客人保持一定距离，并在存放前在每件行李上贴上行李标签。行李员从接待员手中接过房卡，并在行李牌上写下房间号码，然后引导客人进入房间。When the guest is checking in, the bellman keeps a certain distance from the guest and puts a luggage tag on each luggage before storing it. The bellman takes the room card from the receptionist, writes the room number on the luggage tag, and guides the guest to get into the room.）

B：您办理完入住手续后，我带您去房间。I will show you to your room when you have finished checking in.

G：好的。OK.

对话3 Dialogue 3 搬运行李 Carrying Luggage

场景：行李员正在帮助一对夫妇。

Scene：The bellman is helping a couple.

B：Bellman（行李员）　　G：Guest（客人）

B：先生，女士，下午好！我是本酒店的行李员，帮你们拿行李。Good afternoon, madam and sir. I am the bellman and I'm here to help you with your luggage.

G：哦，谢谢。Oh. Thank you.

B：让我来搬行李吧。这是所有的行李吗？Let me carry your luggage. Are these pieces of luggage all yours?

G：是的。这三件行李是我们的。Yes. These three pieces of luggage are ours.

B：好的。我会处理好的。OK. I'll take care of them.

G：谢谢。Thanks.

B：这是我的荣幸。请这边走。乘电梯到五楼，楼层服务员会带你们去506房间。我将乘行李电梯把行李送到你们的房间。It's my pleasure. This way, please. Please take the lift to the fifth floor. The floor attendant will show you to Room 506. I'll take the baggage lift and get your baggage up to your room.

G：好的，一会儿见。OK. See you then.

B：回见。See you.

对话 4 Dialogue 4 引客入房 Showing a Guest to the Room

场景：行李员带客人林先生进入房间。

Scene: The bellman shows the guest Mr. Lin to his room.

B：Bellman（行李员）　　L：Mr. Lin（林先生）

B：先生，这是您所有的行李吗？Is this all your luggage, sir?

L：是的。所有的行李都在这里。Yes, that's all.

B：好的，能让我看一下您的房卡吗？OK, may I have a look at your room card?

L：好的。我的房号是1335。Oh, yes. Room 1335.

B：好的。请跟我来。我将带您进房间。I see. Now please follow me. I'll show you to your room.

L：顺便问一下，西餐厅在哪里？By the way, where is the Western restaurant?

B：在一楼，出电梯后向右转，先生。Oh, it's on the first floor. Turn right when you get out of the elevator, sir.

L：开餐时间几点？When will it open?

B：开餐时间是早上7点到晚上10点。The opening time is from 7:00 a.m. to 10:00 p.m.

L：好的。酒店有游泳池吗？OK. Do you have a swimming pool?

B：是的。游泳池在五楼。同一楼层还有娱乐中心，您可以去打乒乓球和保龄球。Yes, the swimming pool is on the fifth floor. There is also a recreation center there. You can play table tennis, and go bowling.

B：先生，我们到了。1335室。让我帮您开门。Here we are, sir. Room 1335. Let me help you to open the door.

［开门 Open the door…］

B：先生，您先请。介意我把您的行李放在这里吗？After you, sir. Do you mind if I put your luggage here?

L：没关系。非常感谢。It's OK. Thank you very much.

B：这是我的荣幸。您觉得房间怎么样？It's my pleasure. How do you like this room?

L：非常舒适。我非常喜欢。It's very cozy. I like it very much.

B：听您这么说真是太好了！我还能为您做什么吗？That's wonderful to hear that! Is there anything else I can do for you?

L：没有。谢谢。No, thank you.

B：好的。晚安！OK, good night.

对话5 Dialogue 5 介绍设施和服务 Introducing the Facilities and Services

场景：行李员给林先生介绍酒店设施及餐厅。

Scene：The bellman introduces the facilities and the restaurant to Mr. Lin.

B：Bellman（行李员） L：Mr. Lin（林先生）

B：林先生，这是您的房间。您请进。Here's your room, Mr. Lin. After you, please.

L：谢谢。Thank you.

B：我帮您拉窗帘好吗？Shall I draw the curtains for you?

L：好的。我的房间是海景房！OK. Oh, my room has a sea view!

B：很高兴您喜欢。I'm glad you like it.

L：酒店有游泳池吗？Is there a swimming pool in your hotel?

B：是的，在三楼。它开放时间是上午9点到晚上11点。您在酒店做任何事情都出示一下您的房卡。我还能为您做什么吗？Yes, it is on the third floor. It opens from 9:00 a.m. to 11:00 p.m. You should show your room card whatever you do at the hotel. Is there anything else I can do for you?

L：我想了解一下中餐厅。I want to know something about the Chinese restaurant.

B：我们酒店以上海菜闻名。对了，端午节就要到了。您可以试试粽子，这是这个节日的传统食物。We are known for our Shanghai Cuisine. By the way, the Dragon Boat Festival is around the corner. You can try Zongzi, the traditional food for the festival.

L：非常感谢。酒店的服务指南在哪里？我想了解更多关于酒店的信息。Thank you very much. Where is the service guide located? I want to get more information about the hotel.

B：它在梳妆台的第二个抽屉里。我还能为您做什么吗？It is in the second drawer of the dresser. Is there anything else I can do for you?

L：没有啦。非常感谢。No. Thank you very much.

B：这是我的荣幸。我把您的房卡放在桌子上。祝您入住愉快！It's my pleasure. I'll leave your room card on the desk. Enjoy your stay.

补充阅读 Supplement Reading

"金钥匙"源自十九世纪初期欧洲酒店的"门房"(concierge)。而古代的门房是指宫廷、城堡的"钥匙保管人"。国际"金钥匙"是一个全球性的协会,已分布在全球40多个国家和地区,拥有数千名会员,于1995年正式引入中国。

"金钥匙"的口号是:"先利人,后利己;用心极致,满意加惊喜。在客人的惊喜中,找到富有乐趣的人生。"对中外商务旅游者而言,"金钥匙"是酒店内外综合服务的总代理,就像一个在旅途中可以信赖的人,一个充满友谊的忠实朋友,一个解决麻烦问题的人,一个个性化服务的专家。在中国"金钥匙"的蓝图中,始终有一个明晰的目标:让中国酒店业符合国际标准,同时在国际上建立声誉,证明中国的酒店服务质量上乘。

The Golden Key is derived from the "concierge" of European hotels in the early 19th century. In ancient times, the concierge referred to the "key guardian" of palaces and castles. The international "Golden Key" is a global association with more than 40 countries and regions, with thousands of members. It was officially introduced to China in 1995.

The motto of the Golden Key is that "First serve others, and then serve oneself; provide exceptional service with dedication, resulting in satisfaction and surprises. Find a joyful life in the delight of guests." For business travelers at home and abroad, the Golden Key is the overall agent for comprehensive services both inside and outside the hotel, like a trusted person during their journey, a loyal friend full of friendship, a problem solver, and an expert in personalized services. The blueprint of the Golden Key in China always has a clear goal that enables the Chinese hospitality industry to align with international standards and establish a reputation internationally, proving that hotel services in China are of high quality.

练一练 Activities

一、请写出以下名称

(　　)　　(　　)

二、请排序

向宾客问好，表示欢迎。

记下出租车的车号，引导车辆离开。

将宾客乘坐的车辆引领至适当的停车位。

主动上前为宾客开启车门，并用手挡在车门上方，以免宾客碰头。

及时拉开酒店大门，方便宾客进入大厅。

协助行李员卸行李，并确认件数，以免有遗漏。

三、翻译下列句子

1. 我乘另一部电梯把行李送上去。
2. 让我带您到房间，这边请。
3. 需要我为您叫一辆出租车吗？
4. 您房间的电压是220伏。
5. 您可以把贵重物品存放在酒店的保险柜里。

Unit 4　问讯服务 Information Service

导言 Preview

前厅问讯服务是酒店服务中至关重要的一环。它不仅为客人提供了酒店的基本信息，解决了他们在酒店中可能遇到的问题，还提供了受理客人留言、处理宾客邮件、完成委托代办以及负责钥匙分发等服务。

Front desk information service is an essential part of hotel services. It not only provides guests with basic information about the hotel and resolves the issues they may encounter during their stay, but also offers services such as taking messages, handling guest emails, carrying out delegated tasks, and managing key distribution, etc.

前厅问讯员的基本职责包括：

The basic responsibilities of front desk information staff members include：

● 掌握本酒店的一切设施及酒店所在城市的其他大酒店、娱乐场所、游览胜地的一些情况；

Familiarizing themselves with all the hotel facilities and information about other major hotels, entertainment venues, and tourist attractions in the city.

● 管理好客房钥匙，做好保管和收发工作；

Managing room keys, ensuring proper storage, and handling key distribution and collection.

●熟悉电脑查询操作；

Being proficient in computer query operations.

●帮助客人安排会客。将来访者的姓名等情况传达给客人，再根据客人的意见安排会面事宜；

Assisting guests with arranging meetings. Communicating the names and other information of visitors to guests and arranging meetings according to their preferences.

●负责办理客人委托的相关事宜。包括为客人办理订房、购买机票和车（船）票、办签证、取送物品、购物等各项事宜。

Handling delegated tasks on behalf of guests. These tasks may include making room reservations, purchasing flight tickets and transportation tickets, processing visas, retrieving and delivering items, and assisting with shopping, etc.

词库 Word Bank

酒店部门 Hotel department			
汉语 Chinese	英语 English	汉语 Chinese	英语 English
前厅部 qián tīng bù	Front Office Department	餐饮部 cān yǐn bù	Food & Beverage Department
房务部 fáng wù bù	Housekeeping Department	人力资源部 rén lì zī yuán bù	HR Department
营销部 yíng xiāo bù	Marketing Department	财务部 cái wù bù	Finance Department
商务中心 shāng wù zhōng xīn	Business Center	工程部 gōng chéng bù	Engineering Department
康体中心 kāng tǐ zhōng xīn	Fitness Center	安保部 ān bǎo bù	Security Department
常用词汇 Common vocabulary			
汉语 Chinese	英语 English	汉语 Chinese	英语 English
地铁 dì tiě	subway	走廊 zǒu láng	corridor
对面 duì miàn	opposite	娱乐 yú lè	recreation
软饮料 ruǎn yǐn liào	soft drinks	欣赏 xīn shǎng	appreciate
古典音乐 gǔ diǎn yīn yuè	classical music	营业 yíng yè	open
旅游 lǚ yóu	tour	出租车 chū zū chē	taxi
专车 zhuān chē	a private car	咨询 zī xún	consult
一日游 yí rì yóu	one-day tour	预算 yù suàn	budget
旅游团 lǚ yóu tuán	tour group	品尝 pǐn cháng	taste

常用句型 Useful Expressions

指路 Show the Direction for the Guest

1. 一直往前走。Walk straight ahead.

2. 往左/右转。Turn left/right.

3. 上/下楼。Go upstairs/downstairs.

4. 乘电梯到三楼。Take the lift to the third floor.

5. 电梯间在大厅靠大门处。The lifts are in the lobby near the main entrance.

6. 酒店服务员将领您去宴会厅。The hotel attendant will show you the way to the banquet hall.

7. 洗手间在走廊尽头。There is a washroom at the end of the corridor.

8. 购物中心在大堂吧对面。The shopping center is opposite the lobby bar.

9. 打扰啦，请问收银处在哪里？Excuse me, where is the cashier's office?

10. 打扰一下，能告诉我电梯在什么地方吗？Excuse me, could you please show me where the lift is?

酒店提供服务 Offer Services in a Hotel

1. 酒店里有娱乐场所吗？Is there any place in the hotel where we can amuse ourselves?

2. 如果您想散步，可以去位于30楼的顶层花园。If you want to take a walk, you can go to the roof garden on the 30th floor.

3. 一楼有个娱乐中心。There is a recreation center on the ground floor.

4. 您可以去打台球、乒乓球、桥牌和保龄球。You can play billiards, table tennis, bridge, and go bowling.

5. 有听音乐的地方吗？Is there a place where we can listen to some music?

6. 有个音乐茶座，您可以一边欣赏古典音乐和现代音乐，一边品尝中国茶或者其他软饮料。There is a music teahouse where you can enjoy both classical music and modern music, while having some Chinese tea or other soft drinks.

7. 请告诉我餐厅每天的服务时间，好吗？Would you please tell me the daily service hours of the dining room?

8. 从早上七点一直到晚上十点。From 7:00 a.m. till 10:00 p.m.

9. 酒吧和咖啡馆什么时间营业？When will the bar and café open?

10. 从下午三点到午夜。From 3:00 p.m. till midnight.

11. 酒店还提供其他服务吗？Does the hotel offer any other services?

12. 我们有美容院、洗衣房、商店、邮政和传真服务、台球、乒乓球和电子游戏等。We have a beauty parlor, a laundry, a store, post and fax services, billiards, table tennis, video games and so on.

13. 请问我去哪里洗衣服呢？Where can I have my laundry done?

14. 我想了解关于游览北京的信息。I need some information about touring Beijing.

15. 为何不去王府井大街呢？那是购物天堂。Why not go to Wangfujing Street? It is a paradise for shopping.

16. 你能否卖给我三张今晚的车票？Could you sell me three tickets for tonight?

情景对话 Situational Dialogues

对话 1 Dialogue 1 指路 Showing the Way

场景：住在建国饭店的约翰·布朗打算去全聚德吃烤鸭。他正在前台问路。

Scene: John Brown staying at Jianguo Hotel is going to have roast duck at Quanjude. He is asking for directions at the information desk.

S：Front Desk Staff（前台职员） J：John Brown（约翰·布朗）

S：先生，早上好，有什么能为您服务的？Good morning, sir. What can I do for you?

J：您好，请问我想从建国饭店到全聚德烤鸭店怎么走？Hello, how can I get from Jianguo Hotel to Quanjude Roast Duck Restaurant?

S：如果您想乘坐公共交通工具的话，您可以在酒店附近搭乘地铁一号线，乘坐7站到天安门东站下车。If you want to take public transportation, you can take Subway Line 1 near our hotel and ride for 7 stops until you reach Tian'anmen East Station.

J：然后呢？And then?

S：从天安门东站出来后，您可以步行约700米，大约15分钟就能到达全聚德烤鸭店。After exiting from Tian'anmen East Station, you can walk for about 700 meters, approximately 15 minutes, to reach Quanjude Roast Duck Restaurant.

J：非常感谢！还有其他交通方式吗？Thank you very much! Are there any other transportation options?

S：是的，如果您不想步行，您也可以搭乘出租车或预约专车，大约需要20分钟的车程。Yes, if you don't want to walk, you can also take a taxi or book a private car, which would take around 20 minutes.

J：非常感谢您的帮助！Thank you for your help!

S：不客气，祝您用餐愉快！You're welcome. Enjoy your meal!

对话 2 Dialogue 2 一日游咨询 Consultation on the One-Day Tour

场景：一对外国夫妇向前台的工作人员咨询杭州一日游项目。

Scene: A foreign couple consults with the front desk staff about the one-day tour in Hangzhou.

FC：Foreign Couple（外国夫妇）　　S：Front Desk Staff（前台工作人员）

S：女士、先生，下午好！请问有什么需要帮助的？Good afternoon, madam and sir! What can I do for you?

FC：您好！我们想了解一下杭州的一日游项目。Hello! We would like to inquire about the one-day tour options in Hangzhou.

S：很高兴为你们提供信息。我们合作的旅行社有多种杭州一日游的选择，你们对这次旅行有什么具体要求吗？I am glad to provide you with information. The travel agencies we are partnering with offer various options for the one-day tour in Hangzhou. Do you have any specific requirements for the tour?

FC：我们希望能参加一个全天的导游团，能够体验到杭州的文化和自然景观。We would like to join a full-day guided tour that allows us to experience the cultural and natural scenery of Hangzhou.

S：非常好！我们可以为你们安排参观杭州市区的著名景点，比如西湖、岳王庙，还可以品尝当地美食。还有其他特别的需求吗？Great! We can arrange for you to visit famous attractions in downtown Hangzhou, such as West Lake and Yuewang Temple. You can also taste local cuisine. Do you have any other special requests?

FC：感谢您的建议！我们预算有限，能告诉我们一下导游团的价格吗？Thank you for your suggestions! We have a limited budget. Could you inform us about the price for the guided tour?

S：导游团的价格根据你们选择的套餐不同而有所变化，一般在每人800元到1200元之间。The price for the guided tour varies depending on the package you choose, generally ranging from 800 to 1,200 yuan per person.

FC：这个价格在我们的预算范围内。请为我们预订导游团。This price fits within our budget. Please make a reservation for the guided tour.

S：当然可以！我会帮你安排好一切。明天早上8点旅游团会在酒店接你们出发，可以吗？Of course! I will help you arrange everything. The tour group will pick you up from the hotel at 8 o'clock tomorrow morning. Is that OK with you?

FC：太好了！非常感谢您的帮助。That's great! Thank you very much for your assistance.

S：不客气！希望你们在杭州度过一个难忘的旅行！You're welcome! I hope you have an unforgettable trip in Hangzhou!

对话3 Dialogue 3 介绍景点 Introducing Some Scenic Spots

场景：一对外国夫妇打算今天在呼和浩特市内逛逛。酒店前台工作人员给了他们一些建议。

Scene：A foreign couple plans to go around downtown in Hohhot. The front desk staff gives them some suggestions.

FC：Foreign Couple（外国夫妇）　　S：Front Desk Staff（前台工作人员）

S：先生女士，早上好。有什么能为你们效劳的？Good morning, sir and madam. May I help you?

FC：早上好！今天我们要花一整天的时间去游览一下。这是我们第一次来呼和浩特。能给我们推荐一下这里的历史景点吗？Good morning. Today we are going to spend the whole day sightseeing. It is our first trip in Hohhot. Could you recommend us some historical sights here?

S：推荐去昭君博物馆、大召寺和内蒙古博物馆。My recommendations would be the Zhaojun Museum, the Dazhao Temple, and the Inner Mongolia Museum.

FC：我们对寺庙不感兴趣。We are not interested in the temple.

S：好的，如果你们只有去一个地方游览的时间，我建议去内蒙古博物馆。那里有古生物化石、历史遗迹、民俗文化等很多展览。馆内2层和3层共有8个综合性展览，4层共有6个专题展览。所有14个展览都围绕着一个共同的主题——草原文化。Well, if you only have time for one place, I suggest the Inner Mongolia Museum. It has a lot of exhibitions of ancient biology fossils, historical relics, folk culture and so on. There are 8 general displays on the 2nd and the 3rd floors, and 6 thematic displays on the 4th floor in the museum. All the 14 displays share the common theme of grassland culture.

FC：听起来很有趣。能告诉我们怎么去那里吗？It sounds interesting. Could you tell us how to get there?

S：你们可以在酒店门口乘坐3路公交车在内蒙古博物馆下车。博物馆就在街对面。绝对不会错过。You can take No. 3 Bus at the hotel entrance and get off at the Inner Mongolia Museum. The museum is just across the street. It's impossible to miss.

FC：好的，非常感谢。OK. Thank you very much.

S：这是我的荣幸。It's my pleasure.

补充阅读 Supplement Reading

前台接待人员应如何处理客人的问讯？来看看五星级酒店的问讯工作标准操作流程：

1）仔细聆听。在给客人做任何解答前，必须先弄清客人究竟想了解什么。

如果是面对面的情况，接待人员应该专心地倾听客人的问讯，不要轻易打断客人；学会利用眼神的交流来表达你的想法或感受；必要时，可以加入一些合适的身体语言。

如果是通过电话来咨询,接待人员要仔细倾听客人的问讯内容,并在通话过程中使用简单的确认语,使客人知道你正在听其说话。

2)及时回应。使客人感受到酒店工作人员对其所提出的问题的重视。

在客人陈述完问题后,接待人员应在2至3秒钟内,迅速地对客人所问的问题予以回应,可以对客人说:"哦,×××先生,我已经理解了,你的问题是……"或"请您稍等一下,让我做一个简要的记录……"

3)采取适当的行动。尽量快速地解决客人的问题。

根据客人问题实际性质给出必要的处理措施,或是帮客人转接一个电话,或是提供一些酒店信息或当地旅游指导。

4)对客人问题作跟踪处理,确保客人提出的所有问题都可以得到足够的重视和解决。

有时,一些客人的问题无法立即得到解决。在这种情况下,接待人员必须帮助客人对问题进行跟踪处理并及时将结果通知客人。为此,应至少获取以下必要信息:

对所述问题做一个简要的记录;

联系相关的部门并将信息反馈给他们;

争取获得客人的联系地址或电话号码。

可以对客人说:"×××先生,我可否记录下您的电话号码或其他的联系方式?我将尽快给您答复。"

How do receptionists handle guest inquiries at the front desk? Let's take a look at the standard operating procedures for inquiries in a five-star hotel:

1) Listen carefully. Before providing any answers to the guest, it is important to understand what exactly the guest wants to know.

If it's a face-to-face inquiry, receptionists should listen to the guest's inquiry attentively, without interrupting him or her unnecessarily. Use eye contact to express your thoughts or feelings, and if necessary, utilize appropriate body language.

If it's a phone inquiry, receptionists should listen to the guest's query carefully and use simple acknowledgements during the call to let the guest know you are listening to him or her.

2) Timely responses. Make the guest feel that the hotel staff values his or her questions.

After the guest has stated his or her question, receptionists should respond promptly within 2 to 3 seconds. You can say, "Oh, Mr. ×××, I understand your question is…" or "Please hold on for a moment while I make a brief note…"

3) Take appropriate actions. Resolve the guest's issue as quickly as possible.

Take necessary actions based on the nature of the guest's question, whether it is transferring a call, providing hotel information, or offering local tourism guidance.

4) Follow up on guest inquiries to ensure that all questions are given sufficient attention

and resolved.

Sometimes, certain guest issues cannot be solved immediately. In such cases, receptionists should help the guest track the progress of the issue and inform him or her of the result in a timely manner. To do this, at least obtain the following necessary information:

Make a brief record of the problem discussed;

Contact relevant departments and provide them with the relevant information;

Try to obtain the guest's contact address or phone number.

You can say, "Mr. ×××, may I take down your phone number or other contact information? I will get back to you as soon as possible."

练一练 Activities

一、请将下列句子翻译成汉语

1. A：I want to change some money, and where is the bank?

    B：Go upstairs from here and then turn left. It's next to the post office.

2. You can get your money changed at the cashier's office.

3. There is a coffee shop on the second floor and snacks are served there all day.

4. For all enquiries just lift your telephone receiver and ask for the reception desk.

5. Apart from the recreation centre, we also have a health club on the second floor.

6. A：Could you direct us to the restaurant?

    B：Yes, I'll show you the way myself.

    A：Where's the coffee shop, please?

    B：Go straight through the cafeteria and restaurant and you'll find it just in front of you.

7. A：Is this the right way for the souvenir shop?

    B：Yes, it is. Along the corridor, past the newsstand and the library.

8. A：I'm looking for the Conference Room 4.

    B：The conference rooms are all facing the open lounge. Along to your right, past the elevators and up the stairs.

9. A：What is the basic rate for taxis here?

    B：It's about 1.2 yuan each kilometer, but the rate doubles when exceeding 10 kilometers, and there is night rate after 10 o'clock at night.

二、翻译下列句子

1. 电梯在大厅靠大门处。

2. 打扰啦，请问收银处在哪里？

3. 顺便告诉我一下电梯在什么地方？
4. 请告诉我餐厅每天的服务时间，好吗？
5. 你能否卖给我两张明天的车票？

Unit 5　总机服务 Operator Service

导言 Preview

电话总机服务是酒店内外联系的通信枢纽，是酒店与宾客交流信息的桥梁，是反映酒店服务质量的窗口。总机话务员直接为宾客提供各种话务服务，其服务质量直接影响着宾客对酒店的评价，甚至影响到酒店的经济效益。

The operator service serves as the communication hub for internal and external connectivity in hotels. It acts as a bridge for information exchange between the hotel and guests, and serves as a window reflecting the quality of hotel service. The telephone operators at the switchboard provide various telecommunication services directly to guests, and the quality of their service directly impacts guests' evaluation of the hotel, and even affects the hotel's financial performance.

如今，由于移动通信的发展及短信服务的引入，电话总机的服务范围因酒店的类型、规模及程控电话交换机的功能等有所不同。常见的服务有：

With the development of mobile communication and the introduction of text messaging services nowadays, the scope of services provided by the telephone switchboard varies depending on the type and scale of the hotel, as well as the functionality of the PBX (private branch exchange) system. Common services include：

●长途电话及计费服务；

Long-distance call and billing service；

●电话转接服务；

Call forwarding service；

●电话叫醒服务；

Wake-up service；

●电话查询、留言服务；

Telephone inquiry and message service；

●房间预订和咨询服务；

Room reservation and consultation service；

●应急话务服务等。

Emergency phone service, etc.

词库 Word Bank

总机服务类型 Type of operator service			
汉语 Chinese	英语 English	汉语 Chinese	英语 English
国内长途电话 guó nèi cháng tú diàn huà	domestic long-distance call	电话转接 diàn huà zhuǎn jiē	connect/transfer
叫早服务 jiào zǎo fú wù	wake-up call service	留言 liú yán	leave a message
咨询服务 zī xún fú wù	consultation service	国际电话 guó jì diàn huà	an international call
付费电话 fù fèi diàn huà	a paid call	市内电话 shì nèi diàn huà	a city call
常用词汇 Common vocabulary			
汉语 Chinese	英语 English	汉语 Chinese	英语 English
通话中 tōng huà zhōng	the line is busy	区号 qū hào	area code
国家代码 guó jiā dài mǎ	country code	无人接听 wú rén jiē tīng	no answer
稍后再拨 shāo hòu zài bō	call back later	对方付费电话 duì fāng fù fèi diàn huà	a collect call
分机 fēn jī	extension	别挂机 bié guà jī	hold the line

常用句型 Useful Expressions

电话询问 Inquire by Phone

1. 请问能帮我接通618房间吗？Could you put me through to Room 618, please?

2. 我想和林先生通话。I'd like to speak with Mr. Lin.

3. 请问是假日大酒店吗？Is this the Holiday Hotel?

打错电话 Have the Wrong Number

1. 抱歉，我打错电话了。I'm sorry I have the wrong number.

2. 这里是02-2718-5398吗？Is this 02-2718-5398?

3. 很抱歉，打扰你了。Sorry to have bothered you.

4. 很抱歉。我想我一定是打错电话了。I'm sorry. I think I must have dialed the wrong number.

5. 我可以核对一下电话号码吗？是不是2211-5588？Could I check the number? Is it 2211-5588?

要求转分机 Ask for Extension

1. 可以帮我转分机211吗？May I have extension two-one-one?

2. 能帮我转分机 211 吗？Can I have extension two-one-one, please?

3. 我可以找 211 分机的约翰吗？May I speak to John, extension two-one-one?

4. 请转 211。Extension two-one-one, please.

5. 请帮我转分机 211。Please connect me with extension two-one-one.

6. 请帮我接人事部好吗？Could you put me through to the HR department, please?

信息咨询 Information Consultation

1. 请再试一次好吗？Could you try again?

2. 请帮我广播叫他好吗？Could you page him for me?

3. 这是已付费电话吗？Is this a paid call?

4. 我想打一通国际电话。I'd like to make an international call.

5. 能不能告诉我打电话到美国的费用呢？Could you tell me the rates for calls to the US?

接线员回复 Operator's Response

1. 请问您叫什么？May I have your name? / Would you give me your name?

2. 请拼出客人的名字，好吗？Could you spell the guest's name, please?

3. 对不起，因线路问题我听不清楚您说话，请重新打一次好吗？I'm very sorry. I can't hear clearly because of the line. Could you call again, please?

4. 能告诉我客人是哪里人吗？Would you tell me where the guest comes from?

5. 能告诉我客人是哪家公司的吗？Would you tell me which company the guest is from?

6. 对不起，我们在酒店的名单上找不到客人的名字。I'm sorry. We can't find the guest's name on our hotel list.

7. 介意我把电话转接到接待处让他们为您查一下吗？Would you mind my connecting the line to the reception desk to check it?

8. 我再帮您查一下，请稍等。I will check it for you again. One moment, please.

9. 很抱歉，让您久等了。I am sorry to have kept you waiting.

10. 请重复一遍您说的，好吗？Could you repeat what you said? / I beg your pardon?

11. 510 号房没人接电话。I'm afraid there is no reply from Room 510.

12. 您要留言吗？Would you like to leave a message?

13. 这是接听人付费的电话。It's a collect call.

14. 要打外线的话，请先拨"9"，然后拨电话号码。If you need an outside call, please dial "9" first, and then the number.

15. 电话占线，您待会再打来可以吗？The line is busy. Would you mind calling back later?

16. 我给您转接，请别挂机。I'll transfer your call. You hold the line, please.

17. 对不起，先生，林先生不在，您需要留口信吗？I'm sorry, sir. Mr. Lin is not in. Would you like to take a message to him?

18. 请别担心，他回来后我们一定会把口信转达给他。We must take the message to him when he comes back. Please don't worry about this.

19. 请稍等！Hold on, please!

20. 对不起，电话占线，请您稍后再拨。Sorry, the line is busy. Please call back later.

21. 我将帮您把电话转到问讯处。I'll put you through to the information desk.

22. 史密斯先生，有人打电话给您。您想接听这个电话吗？Mr. Smith, someone wants to speak to you. Would you like me to put the call through for you?

情景对话 Situational Dialogues

对话1 Dialogue 1 留言服务 Message Service

场景：接线员马莉接听电话并为客人留言。

Scene：Ma Li, the operator, answers a call and takes a message for a guest.

M：Ma Li（马莉）　　G：Guest（客人）

M：早上好，这里是花园酒店。我叫马莉。有什么能为您效劳的吗？Good morning, Garden Hotel. Ma Li speaking. May I help you?

G：是的，请帮我接通2106号房间电话。Yes, I want Room 2106.

M：好的。请问客人的姓名及其拼写？Yes. May I ask the guest's name and spelling?

G：我找孙先生。S-U-N。I'm looking for Mr. Sun. S-U-N.

M：现在我将为您转接。（过了一会儿……）I'll connect your call now. (After a moment…)

G：您好，我刚才打过电话让转接孙先生房间的电话，但是无人接听。Hello, I just called and asked for Mr. Sun, but there was no answer.

M：您要留言吗？Would you like to leave a message?

G：是的，请告诉他林先生晚饭时不能和他见面了。就是这些。Yes, please tell him that Mr. Lin can't meet him for dinner. That's it.

M：好的。我们将会把留言写下来。请问您的姓名是什么？OK. We will write down the message on paper. May I have your name, please?

G：王林，W-A-N-G L-I-N。Wang Lin, W-A-N-G L-I-N.

M：好的，王先生。我会把它放到他的房间。OK, Mr. Wang. I'll leave it in his room.

对话2 Dialogue 2 叫醒服务 Wake-up Call Service

场景：一位客人来到前台，预订叫醒服务。

Scene: A guest comes to the front desk to book a wake-up call.

G: Guest（客人）   R: Receptionist（前台接待员）

R: 晚上好，先生。有什么能为您效劳的吗？Good evening, sir. How may I help you?

G: 我要预订叫醒服务。I need to book a wake-up call.

R: 好的，先生。请问您的房间号码是多少？Certainly, sir. May I have your room number?

G: 821房。Yes, it's 821.

R: 您想我们几点叫您起床，先生？What time would you like us to wake you up, sir?

G: 上午八点要赶一个航班。你觉得我应该几点离开酒店呢？I have a flight at 8:00 a.m. What time do you think I should leave the hotel?

R: 到达机场要花一个小时，两小时办理登机手续，因此您应该五点出发。It takes an hour to get to the airport. And allowing for a two-hour check-in, you should leave here by 5:00 a.m.

G: 好的。那么4点半叫醒我吧。That's fine, so wake me up at 4:30 a.m.

R: 没问题，先生。我为您设定的时间是早上四点半。No problem, sir. I have set it for 4:30 a.m.

G: 谢谢。我睡觉很沉，你一定要在四点半叫醒我。Thank you. I am a heavy sleeper; please make sure that you wake me up at 4:30 a.m.

R: 为了以防万一，您需要二次叫醒服务吗？Would you like a second call, just in case?

G: 这当然好。四点四十分再叫我一次。Sure, that's a good idea. Please call me again at twenty to five.

R: 好的，先生。我已经设定好了另一个时间。您需要安排去机场的车吗？我可以给您安排一辆车。OK, sir. I have set another one as well. Do you need a car to the airport? I can arrange a car for you.

G: 好的，请安排一辆车，五点出发。Yes, please arrange a car to depart at five o'clock.

R: 好的，已经帮您预订好了。OK. That is booked.

G: 谢谢。Thank you.

R: 乐意效劳。您还有其他事情吗？My pleasure. Is there anything else I can do for you?

G: 没有了，谢谢。晚安。No, thank you. Good night.

R: 晚安，先生。睡个好觉。Good night, sir. Have a good sleep.

对话3 Dialogue 3 咨询服务 Consultation Service

场景：一位客人打电话咨询酒店的设施设备使用服务。

Scene: A guest calls to inquire about the facilities and equipment usage services at the hotel.

O：Operator（总机）　G：Guest（客人）

O：您好，欢迎致电酒店总机，有什么可以帮助您的？Hello, welcome to call the hotel operator. How can I assist you?

G：您好，我想问一下关于酒店的设施设备使用服务。Hello, I would like to inquire about the facilities and equipment usage services at the hotel.

O：当然，酒店提供各种设施和设备供客人使用。请问您有具体的需求吗？Certainly, the hotel provides various facilities and equipment for guests to use. Do you have any specific needs?

G：我想知道酒店是否提供健身房？I would like to know if the hotel has a fitness center.

O：是的，我们酒店设有健身房，供客人免费使用。健身房设备齐全，包括跑步机、哑铃等。Yes, we have a fitness center available for guests to use free of charge. The fitness center is well-equipped, including treadmills, dumbbells, and more.

G：酒店是否提供免费 Wi-Fi？Does the hotel provide free Wi-Fi?

O：是的，我们提供免费的无线网络服务，每间客房都可以免费连接。Yes, we provide free wireless Internet service, and every guest room has free access.

G：我还想知道酒店是否有游泳池。I also want to know if the hotel has a swimming pool.

O：是的，我们酒店设有室内游泳池和室外游泳池，供客人使用。Yes, we have both indoor and outdoor swimming pools for guests to enjoy.

G：非常感谢您的解答。Thank you very much for your answer.

O：不客气，如果您还有其他问题，随时联系我们。祝您有个愉快的入住体验！You're welcome. If you have any other questions, feel free to contact us. We wish you a pleasant stay!

补充阅读 Supplement Reading

酒店常用电话英语的应答

1. 接电话

接电话时不可以简单地回答"您好"，而应报上自己的公司或所属单位的名称。例如："您好，这里是问讯处。"或者"您好，问讯处，请问您需要什么服务吗？"

2. 打错电话

如果是外线打错时，可以回答："不好意思，您打错电话了。"或者"这里是丽佳酒店，电话是 2234-1156。"

如果是总线转接内线时，可以回答："这里是客房预约处，我帮您转接到餐厅预约柜台。""不好意思，这是直拨电话。我们无法为您转接中餐厅。请您改拨 2234-1156 好吗？"

3. 负责的工作人员不在

"不好意思，林先生现在外出。他应该会在下午 5 点左右回来。"

"不好意思，郝先生正在讲电话。请您在线稍候好吗？"

"他回来时，我会请他回电。"

"请告诉我您的姓名和电话，好吗？"

4. 会话结束

结束电话中的对话时，不可以简单说"再见"，要更礼貌周到。例如："感谢您的来电。""先生，不客气。""我们静候您的佳音。""如果您有任何其他问题，请随时与我联系。"

Common English Responses to Phone Calls in the Hotel

1. Answer the phone

When answering the phone, you should not simply answer "Hello", but should provide the name of your company or affiliated unit. For example, "Hello, this is the information desk." or "Welcome to the information desk. What can I do for you?"

2. Wrong phone number

If it's a wrong call from an outside line, you can answer: "Sorry, you have the wrong number." or "This is Lijia Hotel, and the phone number is 2234-1156."

If it's a wrong inside call transferring from the main line, you can answer: "This is the room reservation office. I will transfer you to the restaurant reservation office." "Sorry, this is a direct call. We cannot transfer you to a Chinese restaurant. Please dial 2234-1156."

3. The responsible staff is not present.

"Sorry, Mr. Lin is out now. He should be back around 5 p.m."

"Sorry, Mr. Hao is on the phone. Could you please wait online?"

"When he comes back, I will ask him to call back."

"Could you please tell me your name and phone number?"

4. End a conversation

When ending a conversation on the phone, you should not simply say "bye-bye", but be more polite and thoughtful. For example, "Thank you for calling." "Sir, you are welcome." "We are waiting for your good news." "If you have any other questions, please contact me."

练一练 Activities

一、请写出汉语

an international call   leave a message   a paid call

wake-up call service   connect/transfer   hold the line

二、请将下列句子翻译成汉语

1. This is the operator. May I help you?

2. Excuse me for asking which country you are calling to.

3. Which country are you calling to, please?

4. Could you please tell me the telephone number?

5. What's your name and room number, please?

6. Would you like me to place the call for you?

7. May I know who is calling, please?

8. I'll switch you to Room 333 right now.

9. I'm sorry. The line is busy. Would you like to hold on or call back later?

10. Sir, there is no answer. Would you like to leave a message?

三、翻译下列句子

1. 请问能帮我接通618房间吗？

2. 很抱歉打扰你了。

3. 可以帮我转分机211吗？

4. 我想打一个国际电话。

5. 对不起，我们在酒店的名单上找不到客人的名字。

Unit 6　外币兑换 Foreign Currency Exchange

导言 Preview

酒店提供外币兑换服务，方便客人将本国货币兑换成目的地所需的外币。客人可以通过前台或指定的兑换窗口进行操作。酒店会根据当天的汇率进行兑换，并收取一定的手续费。一般来说，酒店接受各种常见的货币兑换，如美元、欧元、英镑等。兑换服务的目的是方便客人在陌生的地方进行消费，并确保他们拥有足够的外币付款。酒店的外币兑换服务通常是安全、方便且可靠的。

The hotel offers foreign currency exchange service, which allows guests to convert their home currency into the foreign currency they need in their destination. Guests can do the exchange at the front desk or designated exchange counters. The hotel will provide the exchange based on the current exchange rate and charge a certain handling fee. Generally, the hotel accepts common currencies such as US dollars, Euros, and Pounds Sterling. The purpose of the exchange service is to facilitate guests' spending in unfamiliar places and ensure they have enough foreign currency for payment. The hotel's foreign currency exchange service is typically safe, convenient, and reliable.

词库 Word Bank

常用货币类型 Type of currency			
汉语 Chinese	英语 English	汉语 Chinese	英语 English
人民币 rén mín bì	RMB	港币 gǎng bì	HK Dollar
欧元 ōu yuán	Euro	美元 měi yuán	US Dollar
日元 rì yuán	Japanese Yen	德国马克 dé guó mǎ kè	Deutsche Mark
英镑 yīng bàng	Pound Sterling	法郎 fǎ láng	Franc
泰铢 tài zhū	Thai Baht	韩元 hán yuán	Korean Won
常用词汇 Common vocabulary			
汉语 Chinese	英语 English	汉语 Chinese	英语 English
本地货币 běn dì huò bì	local currency	外币 wài bì	foreign currency
兑换汇率 duì huàn huì lǜ	exchange rate	兑换水单 duì huàn shuǐ dān	exchange memo
小面额 xiǎo miàn é	small bills	大面额 dà miàn é	large bills
手续费 shǒu xù fèi	commission	现金 xiàn jīn	cash

常用句型 Useful Expressions

1. 我想把这些美元换成人民币。I'd like to change these US dollars into RMB.

2. 请您填一下这张表，好吗？Could you fill out this form, please?

3. 美元兑人民币的汇率是100∶720，您可以换7200元。The exchange rate of US dollar to RMB is 100∶720, and you will get 7,200 yuan.

4. 您要小面额还是大面额？Would you like it in small or large bills?

5. 请保留好收据。当您想换回本币时必须出示它。Please keep the receipt. You'll have to produce it when you want to change your money back.

6. 您想换多少钱？How much would you like to change?

7. 在晚上9点到早上8点之间，我们有×××美元的兑换限额。We have a change limit of US dollars ××× between 9 p.m. and 8 a.m.

8. 您可以去中国银行换钱。You may go to the Bank of China to change your money.

9. 如果兑换了大量现金，我们的现金就会用完，就无法满足其他客人的要求。If we exchange large amounts, our cash supply will run out and we will be unable to oblige our other guests.

10. 我们希望您能理解。We hope you understand.

11. 你能告诉我今天美元的兑换汇率是多少吗？Could you tell me what today's exchange rate for US dollars is?

12. 请您在兑换单上签字，写上您的姓名和地址好吗？Would you kindly sign your name and address on the exchange memo?

13. 按照今天的汇率，您的钱兑换成人民币是2200元。According to today's rate, your money converted into RMB will be 2,200 yuan.

14. 顺便说一句，保管好您的兑换水单。离开中国时，您可以将未使用的人民币兑换回外币。By the way, keep your exchange memo safe. You may convert the unused RMB back into foreign currency when you leave China.

15. 这是免费服务。It's a free service.

16. 您要换哪种货币？Which kind of currency do you want to change?

17. 可以把50美元换成小钞，10美元换成零钱吗？Can you give me fifty dollars in small bills and ten dollars in change?

18. 我想知道能否帮我把这笔钱兑回美元？I'd like to know if you could change this money back into US dollars for me.

情景对话 Situational Dialogues

对话1 Dialogue 1 外币兑换服务（1）Foreign Currency Exchange Service (1)

场景：马先生来到收银处兑换外币。

Scene：Mr. Ma comes to the cashier's desk to exchange foreign currency.

M：Mr. Ma（马先生）　C：Cashier（收银员）

M：你好，我想换点本地货币。Hi. I need to get some local currency.

C：没问题，您要换美元吗？Certainly. Do you want to exchange some dollars?

M：不是的，我换欧元，可以吗？No, I have Euros. Is that OK?

C：当然。这是今天的汇率。您打算换多少？Sure. Here is today's exchange rate. How much would you like to change?

M：哦！看样子汇率有点儿高。Wow! That rate seems a little high.

C：我们一天核查两次汇率，基本上和银行的汇率一样高。We check the exchange rates twice a day, and they are basically as high as the bank exchange rates.

M：好的，先换200欧元吧。OK. I will exchange 200 Euros.

C：好的，您的房间号是多少？OK. May I have your room number, please?

M：1602。It is 1602.

C：谢谢您，马先生。请确认您所要兑换的外汇总额、汇率和人民币总额，然后在这里签字。Thank you, Mr. Ma. Please check the amount of foreign currency you want to exchange, the rate and the total amount of RMB, and then sign here.

M：好的。给。OK, here you are.

C：谢谢。这是您的人民币和兑换单据。请再次检查一下是否正确。Thank you. Here is your RMB and the exchange memo. Please double-check if it's correct.

M：非常感谢。Thank you very much.

C：不客气，还有什么需要帮忙的吗？You are welcome. Is there anything else I can do for you?

M：没有了，谢谢。再见。No, thanks. Goodbye.

C：再见，马先生。祝您度过美好的一天！Goodbye, Mr. Ma. Have a good day!

对话2 Dialogue 2 外币兑换服务（2）Foreign Currency Exchange Service（2）

场景：住在花园宾馆的唐先生想把美元换成人民币。

Scene：Mr. Tang who stays in Garden Hotel wants to change US dollars into RMB.

C：Cashier（收银员）　　T：Mr. Tang（唐先生）

C：下午好。有什么需要帮助的？Good afternoon. May I help you?

T：是的。能帮我把一些美元换成人民币吗？Yes. Could you change some US dollars into RMB for me?

C：当然可以，先生。您想换多少钱？Certainly, sir. How much would you like to change?

T：大约三千元人民币。顺便问一下，今天美元的汇率是多少？Three thousand yuan, please. By the way, what is the exchange rate for US dollars today?

C：按照目前的汇率，一美元现金相当于7.2人民币。According to the present rate, one US dollar in cash is equivalent to 7.2 Chinese yuan.

T：好的，这是500美元。OK, here are the 500 US dollars.

C：请出示您的护照好吗？Would you please show me your passport?

T：给你。Here you are.

C：谢谢。我们马上就准备好了。请您在这份兑换单上签名好吗？这是您的钱。请查收。保留这份兑换单。当您离开中国时，需要它来兑换回您未用完的人民币。Thank you. We'll be ready in just a second. Will you please sign your name on this exchange memo? Here is your money. Please check it. Keep this exchange memo. You will need it to convert unused RMB when you leave China.

T：谢谢。我该怎么处理剩下的人民币呢？Thank you. What should I do with some remaining RMB?

C：您可以去银行、机场或火车站的兑换柜台，在那里可以兑换。You can go to the money exchange counter in the bank, airport or railway station and exchange it there.

T：好的，谢谢。OK. Thank you.

C：不客气。You are welcome.

补充阅读 Supplement Reading

海外游客来华时没有兑换外汇和携带外币金额的限制，但数额大时需要入境时据实申报。在中国境内，海外游客可持外汇到中国银行各兑换点（机场、饭店或指定商店）兑换成人民币。

兑换外币后，游客应妥善保管银行出具的外汇兑换证明（俗称"水单"），该证明有效期为6个月。游客若在半年内离开中国，而兑换的人民币没有花完，可持护照和水单将其兑换成外币，但不得超过水单上注明的金额。

There is no limit on the amount of foreign exchange and bills brought by foreign tourists when they come to China, but when the amount is large, they need to declare it truthfully upon entry. Within China, overseas tourists can exchange foreign currency into RMB at various exchange points (airports, restaurants, or designated stores) of the Bank of China.

After exchanging foreign currency, tourists should properly keep the foreign exchange certificate (It is commonly known as the exchange memo.) issued by the bank, which is valid for 6 months. If tourists leave China within six months and have not spent all the exchanged RMB, they can exchange it into foreign currency with their passport and the exchange memo, but the amount stated on the memo must not exceed.

外币兑换单

Exchange Memo

No：

国　籍 Nationality _____	护照号码 Passport No. _____	日期/时间 Date/Time _____
姓　名 Name _____	房　号 Room No. _____	收银代码 Cashier Code _____

外币金额 Foreign Currency Amount	扣贴息 Interest Discount	净额 Net Amount	牌价 Rate	实付人民币金额 Net Amount in RMB
摘要 Remark				

签字　　　　　　　　　　　经办人
Signature _____　　　　Prepared by _____

在你离开柜台之前，请你仔细核对。
Please check carefully before you leave the counter.

练一练 Activities

一、连线题

外币　　　　　　兑付旅行支票时，银行垫付资金而产生的利息

外币兑换　　　　住店客人（境内或境外）持除人民币外的可兑换货币到前台，将其换成人民币

牌价　　　　　　一个国家除本国货币以外的货币

兑付贴息　　　　各国货币之间相互交换时换算的比率

二、写出汉语

Euro　　　　　　RMB　　　　　　Franc　　　　　　Pound Sterling

HK Dollar　　　Deutsche Mark　　Japanese Yen　　　Thai Baht

三、翻译下列句子

1. 请您填一下这张表，好吗？
2. 如果兑换了大量现金，我们的现金就会用完，就无法满足其他客人的要求。
3. 您想换多少钱？
4. 请您在兑换单上签字，写上您的姓名和地址好吗？
5. 这是免费服务。

Unit 7　办理离店 Check-out

导言 Preview

办理退房手续时，客人应当结清他的账单。由于大多数酒店账单都是计算机化的，所以手续应非常快速且顺利。客人通常已经支付了预订押金。如果是这样，收银员应将押金的金额从账单中扣除。如果客人用旅行支票结账，请确保他在收银员面前签字。

收银员还应提醒客人在离开酒店前将房间钥匙交还前台。

When checking out at the end of his stay, the guest should settle his bill. As most hotel bills are computerized, the procedure should be accomplished very quickly and smoothly. The guest usually has paid a reservation deposit. If he has, the cashier should take the amount of his deposit out of the bill. If the guest settles his account in traveler's check, make sure that he signs in front of the cashier. The cashier should remind the guest to return his room key to the reception desk before he leaves the hotel.

退房手续的流程包括：

The procedure of check-out includes：

●确认离店日期和时间。

Confirm the departure date and time.

●检查离店日期前使用的客房服务和额外服务。

Check the room service and extra services used prior to the departure date.

●给客人出示账单，并做相应的解释。

Show and explain the bill for guests.

●询问支付方式。

Ask about the way of payment.

词库 Word Bank

支付方式 Payment methods			
汉语 Chinese	英语 English	汉语 Chinese	英语 English
信用卡 xìn yòng kǎ	credit card	支票 zhī piào	check
借记卡 jiè jì kǎ	debit card	维萨卡 wéi sà kǎ	Visa
万事达卡 wàn shì dá kǎ	Master Card	美国运通卡 měi guó yùn tōng kǎ	American Express
大来卡 dà lái kǎ	Diners Club	中国银联 zhōng guó yín lián	China UnionPay
旅行支票 lǚ xíng zhī piào	traveler's check	现金 xiàn jīn	cash
微信支付 wēi xìn zhī fù	WeChat Pay	支付宝 zhī fù bǎo	Alipay
常用词汇 Common vocabulary			
汉语 Chinese	英语 English	汉语 Chinese	英语 English
收据 shōu jù	receipt	发票 fā piào	invoice
密码 mì mǎ	PIN number	刷卡 shuā kǎ	swipe

续表

押金 yā jīn	deposit	服务费 fú wù fèi	service charge
账单 zhàng dān	bill	签单 qiān dān	sign the bill
结账 jié zhàng	pay the bill	退房 tuì fáng	check out

常用句型 Useful Expressions

提醒 Remind

1. 恐怕要请您在 12 点以前腾出房间了。I'm afraid you'll have to vacate your room by 12.

2. 王先生，您今天可以结账吗？Are you checking out today, Mr. Wang?

3. 您现在要退房吗？Would you like to vacate your room now?

4. 您的账单合计 886 美元。Your bill totals ＄886.

5. 总计是 628 美元。That makes a total of ＄628.

6. 共计 628 美元。That comes to ＄628 altogether.

7. 这是您的账单，请您核对一下好吗？Here is your bill. Would you please check it?

8. 那笔钱是您从房间冰箱里取用饮料的费用。That charge is for drinks taken from the room mini-bar.

9. 您的国际长途电话费用包括在这个账单里。Your international long-distance call fee is included in the bill.

10. 这个账单包括服务费。The service charge is included in this bill.

11. 那您曾使用过酒店设施吗？Have you used any hotel facilities?

12. 您准备怎样付账？How would you like to settle your bill?

13. 您准备以何种方式付账？In what form will your payment be made?

14. 您准备用现金还是信用卡付款？Are you going to pay in cash or by credit card?

15. 我们接受下列信用卡……We accept the following credit cards …

16. 对不起，我们不收个人支票。I'm sorry, we don't accept personal checks.

17. 先生，请问您想怎样付账？How would you like to pay your bill, sir?

18. 您准备将这笔费用记到您酒店的总账上吗？Would you like to put this fee on your hotel bill?

19. 请您在这儿签上您的姓名和房号。Please sign your name and room number here.

20. 我需要您的签名和房号。I need your signature and room number, please.

21. 请把您的房号也告诉我好吗？May I also have your room number, please?

22. 先生，所有的账单都需要另加 15% 的服务费。All the bills are subject to an extra 15% service charge, sir.

23. 对不起，我们这里不能签单，请付现款。Sorry, you can't sign the bill here. Cash

49

only, please.

24. 谢谢，我们这里不收小费。Thank you. We don't accept tips.

25. 对不起，我们昨天忘了跟您结账，您现在付钱可以吗？Sorry, we forgot to settle your bill yesterday. Would you please pay it now?

26. 谢谢，这是找您的钱。Thank you, and here's your change.

27. 当然可以，扫码付款吧。Sure, please scan the QR code and pay for it.

28. 请出示您的二维码。Please show your QR code.

29. 先生，请问您愿意签单吗？Would you like to sign the bill, sir?

客户请求 Customer Request

1. 我可以结账吗？Can I have my bill, please?

2. 这是做什么的？What's this for?

3. 你们收旅行支票吗？Do you accept traveler's check?

4. 你好，我是3406房间的李先生。我准备明天一早离开这里，所以我想今晚下楼结账。Hello, this is Mr. Li in Room 3406. I'll be leaving early tomorrow morning. So I'd like to go down sometime tonight to settle my bill.

5. 我没带现金，我可以用微信支付吗？I have no cash on me. May I pay by WeChat?

6. 我能提前退房吗？Can I check out ahead of time?

7. 你们接受微信支付，还是支付宝支付？Do you accept WeChat Pay or Alipay?

情景对话 Situational Dialogues

对话1 Dialogue 1 退房 Checking Out

场景：客人打算结账离店，他来到收款处。

Scene：A guest comes to the cashier's desk to check out of his room.

G：Guest（客人）　　C：Cashier（收银员）

C：早上好，先生。有什么能为您效劳的吗？Good morning, sir. How may I help you?

G：我要结账退房。I'd like to check out and settle the bills.

C：好的，先生。请告诉一下您的房号好吗？OK, sir. May I have your room number?

G：706房。Room 706.

C：好的，王先生。请退还您的房卡。您取用过小冰箱内的东西吗？OK, Mr. Wang. Please return your room card. Did you have anything from your mini-bar?

G：没有，我从未用过小冰箱。No, nothing from the mini-bar.

C：那您曾使用过酒店设施吗？Have you used any facilities?

G：没有。No.

C：王先生，这是您的账单，请您确认一下是否有误。Here is your bill. Please check it, Mr. Wang.

G：没什么问题，谢谢！Everything seems fine. Thank you！

C：请问您想怎样付账？How would you like to pay your bill?

G：信用卡。By credit card.

C：好的。请您在账单和信用卡收据上签字。OK. Please sign the bill and the credit card receipt.

G：好的，给。Certainly. Here you are.

C：谢谢，王先生。请您保管好您的这一联账单和信用卡收据。您需要我们帮您拿行李吗？Thank you, Mr. Wang. Please keep this copy of your bill and your credit card receipt. Do you need any help with your luggage?

G：不用了，谢谢。再见！No, thank you. Goodbye！

C：谢谢您，欢迎再次光临！Thank you. See you next time.

对话2 Dialogue 2 结账 Paying the Bill

场景：王先生在花园酒店住了五个晚上。今天准备离开，现在他去前台办理退房手续。

Scene：Mr. Wang has stayed at Garden Hotel for five nights. Today he is going to leave, and now he is coming to the front desk to check out.

C：Cashier（收银员） G：Guest（客人）

C：早上好。您有什么需要效劳的？Good morning. May I help you?

G：现在结账。请给我出一下账单好吗？I'm checking out now. Can I have my bill, please?

C：好的。先生，请问您的名字和房间号是什么？Sure. May I have your name and room number, sir?

G：王林，1106室。这是我的钥匙卡。Wang Lin, Room 1106. Here is my key card.

C：稍等一下，王先生。您五天前3月3日下午办理了入住手续，这是您的账单，含税总共2490元。请检查一下。One minute, Mr. Wang. You checked in five days ago on the afternoon of March 3rd and here is your bill. It's 2,490 yuan all together, tax included. Please check it.

G：能详细解释一下吗？Can you explain it in detail?

C：是的，当然。账单包括您五晚的房间租金、在餐厅的两顿晚餐以及洗衣费。Yes, of course. The bill includes your room rental for five nights, two dinners in the restaurant and the laundry charge.

G：好的。我可以用旅行支票付款吗？OK. Can I pay with traveler's check?

C：当然。请给我您的护照好吗？Sure. Can I have your passport, please?

G：给你。Here you are.

C：谢谢。王先生，您对在这里的住宿感到满意吗？Thanks. Are you satisfied with your stay here, Mr. Wang?

G：非常好。房间很舒适，服务也很好。顺便问一下，能提前把我的行李送到机场吗？Very good. The room is cozy and the service is good. By the way, could you deliver my luggage to the airport in advance?

C：当然。行李一定会安排好的，王先生。您坐哪班飞机？Sure. Your luggage will definitely be arranged for you, Mr. Wang. Which flight do you take?

G：CA 2230。我的行李应在4点前送到那里。CA 2230. And my luggage should be delivered there by 4 o'clock.

C：明白了，王先生。祝您旅途愉快。Got it, Mr. Wang. I hope you'll have a pleasant trip.

对话3 Dialogue 3 现金结账 Check-out in Cash

场景：一位客人今天离店，上午他打算提前去前台用现金结账。

Scene：A guest is leaving today, and this morning he plans to go to the front desk in advance to settle the bill in cash.

C：Cashier（收银员）　　G：Guest（客人）

C：早上好！先生。需要我帮忙吗？Good morning, sir. May I help you?

G：早上好，今天我要离开。我现在想把在酒店的账单付了可以吗？Good morning, I'm leaving today. May I settle my hotel bill now?

C：请告诉我您的名字和房间号。Your name and your room number, please.

G：王林，1206室。Wang Lin in Room 1206.

C：那您使用过房间里付费项目吗？Have you used any of the paid items in the room?

G：没有。No.

C：请稍等一下。我准备下您的账单……对不起，让您久等了。这是您的账单，共计人民币890元，包括10%的服务费。请您核查一下。Just a moment, please. I'm preparing your bill... Sorry to have kept you waiting. Here is your bill, RMB 890 in all, including a 10% service charge. Please check it.

G：对的。That's right.

C：您已支付1000元押金，对吗？You have paid a deposit of RMB 1,000, haven't you?

G：是的，这是收据。Yes. Here is the receipt.

C：谢谢您，这是发票和零钱，请检查。Thank you. Here is the invoice and your change. Have a check, please.

G：相当不错，谢谢你。It's quite all right. Thank you.

C：不用谢。You're welcome.

补充阅读 Supplement Reading

国际惯例——12点退房

中午12点结账退房是酒店行业内通用的国际惯例。超过中午12点退房，就要按第二天计费或加收房费，为此很多消费者感到不满。因为如果住宿不满24小时也要中午12点退房，并且按一天收费，这对消费者来说显然不公平。而且午餐时间一般是11点半到12点半，退房时间正好卡在这个时间段内，这让很多客人不得不拎着行李就餐。

在美国，位于纽约时代广场附近的威斯汀酒店、威灵顿酒店，以及巴克莱洲际酒店，其入住时间均为下午3点，而退房时间无一例外均为中午12点。中间的空档期则是打扫、整理房间的时间，如果12点不退房，一般要另交半天房费。

在英国伦敦，惯例是下午2点入住，中午12点退房，入住时间略微提前，但退房时间依然是12点。位于伦敦的肯辛顿广场假日酒店和索菲特圣詹姆士酒店如果12点不退房，则要适当收费；伦敦斯马特卡姆登旅馆的规定是，延迟退房需多交10英镑，大约相当于半天房费。

International Practice—Check-out at 12 O'clock

Checking out at 12 noon is a common international practice in the hotel industry. If guests check out after 12 noon, they will be charged the next day or an additional room fee. Many consumers are dissatisfied with this. Because if the accommodation is less than 24 hours, it is also necessary to check out at 12 noon and charge a daily fee, which is obviously unfair to consumers. Moreover, lunchtime is usually from 11:30 to 12:30, and the check-out time unfortunately coincides with this period, forcing many guests to carry their luggage to dine.

In the United States, the Westin Hotel, Wellington Hotel, and Barclays Intercontinental Hotel located at Times Square in New York City all have check-in times of 3 p.m. and check-out times of 12 noon without exception. The middle period is the time for cleaning and organizing the room. If you don't check out at 12 o'clock, you usually have to pay an additional half day's room fee.

In London, the usual practice is to check in at 2 p.m. and check out at 12. The check-in time is slightly earlier, but the check-out time is still at 12 noon. If guests do not check out by 12 o'clock at the Kensington Square Holiday Inn and Sofitel St. James Hotel in London, they will be charged appropriately. The policy of the Smart Camden Hotel in London is to pay an additional £10 for delayed check-out, which is approximately equivalent to half a day's room rate.

练一练 Activities

一、请写出汉语

receipt　　　　　swipe　　　　　invoice　　　　　bill

check out　　　　service charge　　PIN number　　　pay the bill

二、请将下列句子翻译成汉语

1. Good morning, front office cashier's desk, can I help you?

2. Are you checking out today, Miss Evans?

3. Would you like to vacate the room now, sir?

4. Did you take any drinks from the mini-bar this morning, sir?

5. Here is your bill, and please check it.

6. Would you like to check and see if your bill is correct?

7. Is your luggage down yet, sir? If not, I will send a bellman to help with your luggage.

8. I'll draw up your bill for you.

9. Have you used any hotel service facilities this morning or had breakfast at the hotel coffee shop?

10. Thank you for waiting, and the hotel including service charge for the three days is $470.

三、翻译下列句子

1. 恐怕要请您在12点以前腾出房间了。

2. 那笔钱是您从房间冰箱里取用饮料的费用。

3. 您准备以何种方式付账？

4. 我可以结账吗？

5. 我能提前退房吗？

Unit 8　处理投诉 Dealing with Complaint

导言 Preview

作为酒店员工，你处理问题的方式可以帮助顾客建立信任，让他们感受到你关心他们以及他们提出的问题。有时候事情会出错，顾客可能会感到不满。无论你或你的同事是否有错，你都要主动为顾客提供帮助。当你真诚地道歉并跟进顾客的问题时，能够改变一个糟糕的体验，并赢得一个忠诚的未来客户！毕竟，你的工作就是提供最好的服务。以下方式可以帮助酒店职员处理投诉。

  As a hotel clerk, how you handle a problem can help guests develop trust and make them feel that you care about them and their problems. Sometimes things go wrong and guests will be unhappy. Whether or not you or your colleague is at fault, you should offer to help the guest. When you provide a genuine apology and sincerely follow up with the guest, you can turn a bad experience around and win a loyal future customer! After all, it is your job to give the best service. The following ways can help the clerk in the hotel to deal with complaints.

倾听： • 注意顾客反映问题的内容和情绪 • 保持眼神交流 • 使用适当的身体语言、词语和语气 • 当顾客在发言时不要打断 • 提出明确的问讯 LISTEN： • Take notice of the content of the issue and emotion of the guest • Make eye contact • Use appropriate body language, words and tone • Never interrupt when said by the guest • Ask clarifying questions	道歉： • 使用"我"作为主语的表述 • 使用适当的身体语言、词语和语气 • 不要责怪别人 • 不要说"对不起，但是……" APOLOGIZE： • Use "I" statements • Use appropriate body language, words and tone • Never blame someone else • Never say, "I'm sorry, but…"
回应： • 对问题负责 • 确定解决问题的行动方案 • 在适当情况下向顾客提供选择 • 确认解决方案能满足顾客的要求 RESPOND： • Take ownership of the problem • Determine what actions you could take to resolve the problem • Offer the guest options when appropriate • Confirm that the solution will satisfy the guest	随访： • 跟进顾客的问题 • 跟进与问题相关的所有员工或部门 • 在酒店的追踪系统中记录问题 FOLLOW UP： • Follow up with the guest • Follow up with all associates or departments involved • Record the problem in property tracking system

词库 Word Bank

道歉常用口语 Common apologies			
汉语 Chinese	英语 English	汉语 Chinese	英语 English
对不起 duì bù qǐ	sorry	道歉 dào qiàn	apologize
抱歉 bào qiàn	I'm sorry	遗憾 yí hàn	regret
打扰了 dǎ rǎo le	excuse me	请原谅 qǐng yuán liàng	pardon
给您添麻烦了 gěi nín tiān má fan le	sorry to have incommoded you	不好意思 bù hǎo yì si	sorry
常用词汇 Common vocabulary			
汉语 Chinese	英语 English	汉语 Chinese	英语 English
不满意的 bù mǎn yì de	unsatisfied	异味 yì wèi	peculiar smell
难以置信的 nán yǐ zhì xìn de	unbelievable	用完了 yòng wán le	run out
丢 diū	miss	理解 lǐ jiě	understand
误会 wù huì	misunderstand	拒绝 jù jué	refuse
不合理的 bù hé lǐ de	unreasonable	允许 yǔn xǔ	admit

常用句型 Useful Expressions

投诉 Complaints

1. 卧室的电灯开关坏了。The switch on the lamp in my bedroom is broken.

2. 房间有异味，而且太吵了。The room smells bad, and it is too noisy.

3. 窗帘上满是灰尘。The window curtain is full of dust.

4. 您的服务令人难以置信。Your service is unbelievable.

5. 浴室里没有毛巾/洗漱用品/卫生纸。There are/is no towels/toiletries/toilet paper in the bathroom.

6. 我的项链/手表/钱包不见了。My necklace/watch/wallet is missing.

7. 房间太热/太冷了。My room is too hot/cold.

8. 空调声音太大。The air conditioner is too loud.

9. 这件毛衣洗坏了。This sweater is ruined.

10. 厕所堵住了。The toilet is stopped/clogged up.

11. 我对你们的酒店服务很不满意。I'm very unhappy with your hotel service.

道歉 Make an Apology

1. 听到这个消息我非常抱歉。I'm terribly sorry to hear that.

2. 我会马上处理的。I'll attend to/take care of this right away.

3. 我马上调查此事。I'll look into this matter at once.

4. 我马上派一个女服务员来。I'll send a chambermaid immediately.

5. 我们可能会忽略一些要点。We might overlook some points.

6. 对于给您带来的不便，我们深表歉意。We do apologize for the inconvenience.

解释 Give an Explanation

1. 前一位客人退房晚了，您要求立即入住，所以女服务员没有时间及时打扫房间。The previous guest checked out late and you demanded immediate access to your room. So the chambermaid didn't have time to clean the room.

2. 您把"DND"标志放在把手上，所以女服务员没有打扫房间。You put the "DND" sign on the knob, so the chambermaid didn't clean the room.

3. 我相信服务员不是故意无礼的。也许他没有听明白您的意思。I'm sure the waiter didn't mean to be rude. Perhaps he didn't understand you correctly.

4. 对不起，先生，一定有误会。I'm sorry, sir, but there must be some misunderstanding.

采取措施 Take Measures

1. 我们的经理不在。我帮您找我们的大堂副理，好吗？Our manager is not in the hotel. Shall I get our assistant manager for you?

2. 如果您准备好行李，我们就把您换到另一个房间。If you get your luggage ready, we will move you to another room.

3. 我会派一个行李生帮您搬行李。I will send a porter to help you with the luggage.

4. 为了表达我们对给您带来麻烦的歉意，我们给您 10% 的折扣。To express our regret for all the trouble, we offer you a 10% discount.

5. 请允许我派一个女服务员到您的房间帮您再找一遍。Please allow me to send a chambermaid to your room to help you look for it again.

6. 帮您报警好吗？Shall I call the police for you?

7. 我会和我们的经理谈谈这件事。I will speak to our manager about it.

8. 我们能为您做的实在太有限了。This is really the least we can do for you.

9. 我们将尽力解决这个问题。We'll try our best to solve the problem.

10. 很抱歉听到这个消息。对于给您带来的不便，我们深表歉意。我会立即把淋浴器修好，浴缸清洗干净，地板擦干，并为您的房间准备好卫生间用品。I'm sorry to hear that. We do apologize for the inconvenience. I'll have the shower fixed, the tub cleaned, the floor dried and toilet items sent to your room immediately.

拒绝不合理的要求 Decline an Unreasonable Demand

1. 对不起，但这超出了我的能力范围。I am sorry, but it is beyond my power to do this.

2. 我们很抱歉地通知您，我们不能按照您的要求去做。We are sorry to inform you that we cannot do what you ask for.

3. 事实上，我们对未能处理您的请求深感遗憾。Indeed, we deeply regret not being able to handle your request.

4. 我希望我能帮助您，但我做不到。I wish I could help you, but I couldn't.

5. 我必须拒绝您的要求，因为这违反了我们酒店的规定。I must refuse to meet your request, as it is against our hotel's regulation.

6. 我必须拒绝您的要求，因为满足或执行您的要求会损害我们酒店的声誉。I must refuse your wish, as complying or carrying it out will give harm to our hotel's reputation.

7. 我们将对您的所作所为提出申诉。We shall file a complaint against what you have done.

8. 我们遗憾地声明，您的行为将损害我们两国人民之间的友好关系。We regretfully state that your behavior will cause harm to the friendly relations between our two people.

9. 这是不可能的，因为这个国家的外汇管理条例不允许您这样做。It cannot be done, as the Regulations on Foreign Exchange Administration of this country will not allow you to do so.

10. 您应该尊重我们的海关规定。You should respect our customs regulations.

11. 您的所作所为违反了安全规定。What you have done is contrary to the safety regulations.

12. 我国法律不允许您这样做。The law of our country does not allow you to do so.

情景对话 Situational Dialogues

对话1 Dialogue 1 房间投诉 Complaint about the Room

场景：孙莉在前台上班，一位客人打来电话，对自己的房间不满意。

Scene: Sun Li is working at the front desk. A guest calls and he is dissatisfied with his room.

S：Sun Li（孙莉）　　G：Guest（客人）

S：早上好，前台，请问有什么可以帮您的？Good morning. Front office. Can I help you?

G：我是1602的王林。我刚刚入住，但对房间不满意。This is Wang Lin, Room 1602. I've just checked in and I'm dissatisfied with my room.

S：请问房间有什么问题？May I know what is wrong?

G：房间有味儿而且床上有头发！我没想到你们酒店会发生这样的事情。The room

is smelly and there is someone's hair on my bed! I didn't expect such things would happen in your hotel.

S：很抱歉，王先生。我马上派人去您房间。她会带去一台空气净化器，并重新打扫床铺。对于给您带来的不便，我们深表歉意。I'm sorry, Mr. Wang. I'll send someone to your room at once. She will bring an air fresher and make up the bed again for you. We do apologize for the inconvenience.

G：我想至少你应该给我换一下房间。I think at least you should change my room.

S：好的，王先生。我想我们可以帮您换房间。我会派一位礼宾员几分钟后带您去一个新房间。Yes, Mr. Wang. I think we can change a room for you. I will send a concierge to take you to a new room in a few minutes.

G：非常感谢。那我在房间等着。Thank you. I am waiting!

S：不客气，王先生。我叫孙莉，如果有什么事情，请您随时打电话给我。You're welcome, Mr. Wang. My name is Sun Li, and if there is anything else I can do for you, please don't hesitate to call me.

对话 2 Dialogue 2 行李寄送服务投诉 Complaint about the Luggage Sending Service

场景：唐先生给礼宾部打电话。

Scene：Mr. Tang calls the concierge.

T：Tang（唐）　C：Concierge（礼宾员）

C：下午好，我是礼宾部的马宁。有什么可以帮您的吗？Good afternoon, concierge, Ma Ning speaking. May I help you?

T：我在房间内已经等了将近半个小时，为什么行李还没有送上来？是不是出什么问题了？I have been waiting in my room for almost half an hour. Why hasn't my luggage been sent up yet? Is there a problem?

C：对不起，先生。请告诉我您的姓名和房号，好吗？I'm sorry, sir. May I have your name and room number, please?

T：我是唐平，住906号房。Tang Ping, Room 906.

C：对不起，因为您属于旅行团，贵团的人数很多，所以我们只能一层楼一层楼地送行李。您可以告诉我您的行李有些什么特征吗？I'm sorry, because you are in a tour group and your group is big, we need to send the luggage floor by floor. Would you please give me some features of your luggage?

T：一个蓝色的大箱子。A big blue suitcase.

C：您的箱子上是否附有名牌？如果有，我们会立刻找到它，然后马上为您送来。Is your name tag attached to it? If so, we will find it immediately and deliver it to you right now.

T：是的。我需要件衣服，请尽快送过来！Yes, it is. I need my clothes. Please

deliver it as soon as possible!

对话 3 Dialogue 3 收费投诉 Complaint about the Charge

场景：王先生正在办理退房，但出了点问题。

Scene：Mr. Wang is checking out, but there is a problem.

C：Cashier（收银员） W：Mr. Wang（王先生） DM：Duty Manager（大堂副理）

C：对不起，王先生。请问您见过浴室内的浴袍吗？Excuse me, Mr. Wang, but have you seen a bathrobe in the bathroom?

W：抱歉，我不记得了。Sorry, I can't remember.

C：客房服务员进入房间查房后，没找到浴袍。王先生，很抱歉地告诉您，我们必须收您160元人民币的浴袍费用。Our room attendant entered your room to check, and she could not find your bathrobe. Mr. Wang, I'm sorry to tell you that we need to charge you RMB 160 for a bathrobe.

W：不行！我没拿你们的浴袍，你们为什么要收我钱？难道你们认为我偷了浴袍吗？我可以给你看我的包！No way! I didn't take your bathrobe. Why will you charge me? Do you think I stole your bathrobe? I can show you my bag!

C：请冷静一下，王先生。我打电话给大堂副理来处理这件事情。Please calm down, Mr. Wang. I'll call our duty manager to handle this.

DM：早上好，王先生。我是大堂副理。很高兴见到您。Good morning, Mr. Wang. I'm the duty manager. Nice to meet you.

W：你好。Yeah.

DM：您是否记得自己把浴袍放在哪儿了？或者会不会在去游泳时把它留在了游泳池？Do you remember where you put a bathrobe or if you brought it to the swimming pool when you went swimming?

W：我已经告诉过你们的员工，我没有拿浴袍，也不记得把它放在哪儿了。I already told your clerk I didn't take it and I don't know where I put it.

DM：好，没问题。我们始终相信我们的客人，但也希望您能理解，我们的工作是要对客房内的所有物品负责。OK, no problem. We always trust our guests, but please understand it's our job to account for all items in the room.

W：那么，我最后一共要付多少钱呢？So how much should I pay for my final bill?

DM：我们会打印出来给您看。别担心，王先生，我们不收这项费用。We will print it and show you. Please don't worry, Mr. Wang. We will not charge you this fee.

W：那太好了。谢谢你。That's very kind. Thank you.

DM：不客气。You are welcome.

补充阅读 Supplement Reading

顾客的投诉是顾客对酒店提供的设施、设备及员工的服务等各方面表示不满而提出的批评或申诉。其表现途径有：电话、书面、面对面。酒店对顾客投诉管理的目的在于减少顾客的投诉，将因顾客投诉而造成的危害降到最低限度，最终使其对投诉的处理感到满意，甚至通过投诉管理提高顾客对酒店的忠诚度。

酒店要做好顾客投诉管理，可以考虑以下几点：

1. 积极倾听：当顾客投诉时，要耐心倾听他们的问题和不满，并给予认真回应，体现出对顾客的尊重和关注，让顾客感到被重视。

2. 道歉并解决问题：对于顾客的投诉，酒店应及时道歉，并寻找解决问题的方案，努力解决顾客的不满，并给予合理的补偿，以重建顾客的信任。

3. 培训员工：酒店应对员工进行培训，提高他们解决投诉的能力。员工应具备耐心、友好和解决问题的能力，对投诉进行妥善处理。

4. 建立反馈渠道：酒店应建立顾客反馈渠道，让顾客能够方便地表达意见和投诉。并及时回复顾客的反馈，向顾客展示酒店对他们的关注和重视。

5. 持续改进：酒店要不断改进自身的服务质量，从源头上减少顾客的投诉，通过持续的反馈和改进措施，不断提升顾客的满意度。

Customer complaints are criticisms, or appeals made by customers expressing dissatisfaction with various aspects of the hotel's facilities, equipment, services provided by staff members, etc. They can be expressed through phone calls, written communication, or face-to-face interaction. The purpose of hotel customer complaint management is to reduce customer complaints, minimize the harm caused by customer complaints, and ultimately ensure that customers are satisfied with the handling of their complaints, and even increase customer loyalty through complaint management.

To effectively manage customer complaints, hotels can consider the following:

1. To listen actively. When customers complain, patiently listen to their problems and grievances, and respond seriously. Show respect and concern for the customers, making them feel valued.

2. To apologize and resolve the problem. In response to customer complaints, the hotel should apologize promptly and seek solutions to resolve the problem. Efforts should be made to address customer dissatisfaction and provide reasonable compensation to rebuild customer trust.

3. To train employees. The hotel should provide training to employees to enhance their ability to handle complaints. Employees should have patience, friendliness, and problem-solving skills to handle complaints properly.

4. Establish feedback channels. The hotel should to establish customer feedback channels to allow customers to express their opinions and complaints conveniently. Timely responses to customer feedback demonstrate the hotel's concern and attention to customers.

5. To improve continuously. The hotel should continuously improve the quality of its services to minimize customer complaints at the source. Through continuous feedback and improvement measures, customer satisfaction can be constantly enhanced.

练一练 Activities

一、请写出汉语

sorry   pardon   sorry to have incommoded you
excuse me   regret   apologize

二、请将下列句子翻译成汉语

1. What's the problem, sir? Can I be of assistance?

2. This is quite unusual. I will look into the matter.

3. I will get you another one.

4. Shall I have the dish cooked again?

5. I will take to the chef and see what he can do.

6. I'm terribly sorry. I can give you something else if you'd like. That will be on the house, of course.

7. I'm sorry, sir. Please excuse her. We are very busy today.

8. I'm sorry to hear it. Please be assured that we will look into the matter. Our chef is very particular.

9. My wife's freezing, waiter.

10. Perhaps you'd like to sit over there in the corner. There's less wind.

三、翻译下列句子

1. 如果您准备好行李，我们会把您换到另一个房间。

2. 很抱歉听到这个消息。对于给您带来的不便，我们深表歉意。我会立即把淋浴器修好，浴缸清洗干净，地板擦干，并为您的房间准备好卫生间用品。

3. 我们很抱歉地通知您，我们不能按照您的要求去做。

4. 您应该尊重我们的海关规定。

5. 您的所作所为违反了安全规定。

Chapter 2 客房服务 Housekeeping Service

客房部作为酒店运营中的一个重要部门,其主要的工作任务是为宾客提供一个舒适、安静、优雅、安全的住宿环境,并针对宾客的习惯和特点提供细致、便捷、周到、热诚的服务。

As an important department in the operation of the hotel, the main task of the housekeeping department is to provide guests with a comfortable, quiet, elegant and safe accommodation environment, and to provide meticulous, convenient, thoughtful and warm service to guests according to their habits and characteristics.

本章主要学习酒店服务员与客人在客房服务中的对话,包括迎接客人、打扫房间、介绍房间配置、叫醒服务和洗衣服务。同时,了解基本的客房管理知识,比如客房的清洁、保养与服务。

This chapter focuses on the dialogue between hotel attendants and guests in the housekeeping service, including greeting guests, cleaning the room, introducing the room configuration, wake-up service and laundry service. At the same time, understand the basic knowledge of room management, such as room cleaning, maintenance and service.

客房部行政架构图
(Administrative Structure Diagram of Housekeeping Department)

客房部经理 (Housekeeping manager)
- 洗衣房主管 (Laundry supervisor)
  - 洗衣房 (Laundry) → 洗衣房员工 (Laundry staff)
  - 布草制服 (Linen uniform) → 布草 (Linen)
- 客服中心 (Customer service center) → 客房中心 (Room center)
- 楼层主管 (Floor supervisor) → 楼层领班 (Floor foreman) → 楼层 (Floor)
- 公区主管 (District superintendent) → 公区领班 (District foreman) → 公区员工 (Public employee)

Unit 1　清洁服务 Cleaning Service

导言 Preview

　　清洁卫生服务与管理工作的质量直接影响着酒店的形象、环境，甚至经济效益。酒店客房清洁整理操作流程和标准客房的清洁程度是客人入住酒店最关心的问题之一，同时也是客人选择酒店的标准之一。

　　The quality of cleaning service and management directly affects the image, environment and even economic benefits of the hotel. The operation process of cleaning guest rooms and the cleanliness of standard guest rooms are not only one of the most important concerned issues for guests to check in at the hotel, but also one of the criteria for guests to choose a hotel.

词库 Word Bank

常用词汇 Common vocabulary			
汉语 Chinese	英语 English	汉语 Chinese	英语 English
开关 kāi guān	switch	水龙头 shuǐ lóng tóu	faucet
干洗 gān xǐ	dry-clean	空调器 kōng tiáo qì	air conditioner
国际直拨 guó jì zhí bō	international direct dialing (IDD)	浴缸 yù gāng	bathtub
毛巾 máo jīn	towel	洗衣 xǐ yī	laundry
国内直拨 guó nèi zhí bō	domestic direct dialing (DDD)	衣架 yī jià	hanger
毛巾架 máo jīn jià	towel rail	快洗服务 kuài xǐ fú wù	express laundry service
衣橱 yī chú	wardrobe	浴室 yù shì	bathroom
面盆 miàn pén	wash basin	熨烫 yùn tàng	iron
床垫 chuáng diàn	mattress	壁橱 bì chú	closet

常用句型 Useful Expressions

1. 进入客房。Enter the guest room.
2. 清理垃圾。Dispose of the rubbish.
3. 更换床单。Change the bed linen.
4. 整理床铺。Make up the bed.
5. 清理房间。Clean the room.

6. 补充客用品。Replenish guest supplies.

7. 清洁浴室。Clean the bathroom.

8. 卧室地板吸尘。Vacuum the sleeping room floor.

9. 登记并离开。Fill in the form and leave.

10. 客房服务，我可以进来吗？Housekeeping, may I come in?

11. 对不起，打扰您了，先生。I'm sorry to disturb you, sir.

12. 先生，我们可以现在打扫您的房间吗？May we clean your room now, sir?

13. 哦，我现在正忙着呢。Well, I'm a bit tied up at the moment.

14. 您希望我们什么时候再来？What time would you like us to come back?

15. 先生，我过会儿再来好吗？Shall I come back later, sir?

16. 我们马上就来打扫您的房间。We will come and clean your room immediately.

17. 您的房间过半小时就会打扫干净。Your room will be ready in half an hour.

18. 恐怕中午12点到下午2点期间我们不能打扫房间，我们在下午2点至3点之间打扫您的房间行吗？I'm afraid no cleaning can be done between 12 noon and 2 p.m. May we come between 2 p.m and 3 p.m?

19. 已经快到中午了，我的房间还没打扫。It's almost noon, and my room hasn't been made up yet.

20. 如果您需要什么，就告诉我们，只要能做到，我们都会尽力为您效劳。Just let us know what you need, and if we can, we will oblige.

21. 开夜床服务，我可以进来吗？晚上好，先生。Turn-down service, may I come in? Good evening, sir.

22. 如果您需要在房间内休息，请在门上挂上"请勿打扰"牌，服务员就不会再敲门了。Please put out a "Do Not Disturb" sign on the door if you need to rest in the room, and the housekeeper won't knock on the door again.

23. 对不起，先生，我可以继续清扫您的房间吗？Excuse me, sir, shall I continue cleaning your room?

24. 我很累了，还需要多长时间你才能结束？I'm very tired, and how long will it take you to finish?

25. 你能否过会再来？我下午5点要出去。Would you please come back later? I will go out at 5 p.m.

26. 我可以进房间为您开夜床吗？May I come in for turn-down service?

27. 噢，晚饭前我们几个人要在房间喝几杯，你等会儿再来好吗？Oh, we are expecting a few people for drinks in the room before going to dinner. Could you come back later?

28. 当然可以，如您认为方便，我半小时后再来，可以吗？Certainly, would it be

convenient if I return in half an hour?

29. 打扰一下，都快下午了，为什么我的房间还没有打扫？Excuse me, it's almost afternoon, but my room hasn't been made up yet, why?

30. 对不起，我结束这间房后立即为您打扫。I'm sorry. I'm going to clean your room as soon as I have finished this one.

31. 以后每天能不能早点儿打扫我的房间？Can you clean up my room earlier every day?

32. 当然可以，先生，明天我将早点儿为您打扫房间。Certainly, sir. I will clean up your room earlier tomorrow.

情景对话 Situational Dialogues

对话1 Dialogue 1 客房服务（1）Housekeeping Service（1）

场景：客房服务员夜间打扫房间。

Scene: The housekeeper cleans the room at night.

H：Housekeeper（客房服务员）　　G：Guest（顾客）

H：客房服务，我可以进来吗？Housekeeping, may I come in?

G：请进。Come in, please.

H：晚上好，夫人。我现在可以打扫您的房间吗？Good evening, madam. May I do your room now?

G：当然。你能先整理一下浴室吗？我刚刚洗浴过，里面很乱。Sure. Could you tidy up the bathroom first? I've just taken a bath, and it's quite a mess.

H：当然可以，夫人。我还能为您做些什么吗？Certainly, madam. Is there anything else I can do for you?

G：哦，是的。我在哪里可以借吹风机？Oh, yes. Where can I borrow a hairdryer?

H：我马上派人拿来。I'll send someone to bring it up right away.

G：谢谢你！你帮了我很多忙。Thank you! You've been very helpful.

H：不客气。晚安，夫人。祝你做个好梦。You're welcome. Good night, madam. Have a nice dream.

对话2 Dialogue 2 客房服务（2）Housekeeping Service（2）

场景：客房服务员清晨打扫房间。

Scene: The housekeeper cleans the room early in the morning.

H：Housekeeper（客房服务员）　　G：Guest（顾客）

H：客房服务。我可以进来吗？Housekeeping. May I come in?

G：请进来。Yes, please.

H：先生，您要我什么时候给您打扫房间？When would you like me to do your room, sir?

G：如果你愿意，现在就可以做。你来的时候我正准备下楼吃早饭，但在你开始之前，你能帮我做件事吗？You can do it now if you like. I was just about to go down for my breakfast when you came, but before you start, would you do me a favor?

H：可以，什么事呢？Yes, what is it?

G：我想请你去给我拿瓶热水来。早饭后我需要一些热水把药喝了。I would like you to get me a flask of hot water. I need some hot water to wash down medicine after breakfast.

H：很抱歉，您的水瓶空了。我马上去给您再拿一瓶满的来。I'm sorry that your flask is empty. I'll go and get you another full flask at once.

G：谢谢。Thank you.

对话3 Dialogue 3 客房服务（3）Housekeeping Service（3）

场景：客房服务员打扫房间。

Scene: The housekeeper cleans the room.

H：Housekeeper（客房服务员）　G：Guest（顾客）

G：打扰一下，可以请你打扫一下我的房间吗？Excuse me, could you please clean my room?

H：当然，我会立刻处理的。Of course, I'll take care of it right away.

G：谢谢，我很感激。Thank you, I appreciate it.

H：不客气。有什么特别需要我关注的地方吗？You're welcome. Is there anything specific you'd like me to focus on?

G：请你清洁一下浴室并换掉毛巾，好吗？Could you please clean the bathroom and replace the towels?

H：当然，我会彻底清洁浴室并提供新的毛巾。Certainly, I'll clean the bathroom thoroughly and provide fresh towels.

G：太好了，谢谢你的帮助。That's great, and thank you for your help.

H：不客气。我很愿意帮助您。You're welcome. It's my pleasure to assist you.

G：还有一件事，你能倒一下垃圾桶吗？One more thing, could you also empty the trash bin?

H：当然，我会确保倒掉垃圾桶。Of course, I'll make sure to empty the trash bin as well.

G：那太好了，再次感谢您的帮助。That would be great. Thank you again for your assistance.

H：不客气。我负责确保您满意。You're welcome. It's my job to ensure your satisfaction.

补充阅读 Supplement Reading

能不能先帮我们打扫？

住在1208套房的张先生，是一位杭州商人。今天早上9点钟，他要在客房接待一位来自国外的朋友，谈些生意上的事情。但早晨起床后，他发现房间很脏乱，急需整理。他正想开门去叫服务员来清扫，却发现了在走廊的另一头工作的服务员，他赶紧向服务员说明了请求，但服务员听完后，面露难色地望着他，"张先生，很抱歉，我们的主管告诉过我们，清扫房间一定得按照顺序，得从1201房开始打扫，到您的08房间，我估计得10点多了。"张先生看看面露难色的服务员，"能不能变换下顺序呢？""为保证工作的效率，给客人提供更好的质量，我们公司规定一定要按照规范来操作，否则得扣钱。"看看一脸无辜的服务员，张先生苦笑着摇摇头走开了。

问题：

1. 客房服务员根据酒店的要求，有不妥吗？如有，哪里不妥？
2. 如何看待酒店的规定与客人的要求相冲突？

解答：

1. 在员工培训方面，管理者单方面强调规则和程序的执行，而没有告诉他们服务中要讲求灵活性。虽然所有规范和程序都是确保服务质量的基础，但制定这些规范和程序的唯一依据应该是考虑客人的立场。在正常情况下，盲目强调程序可以确保大多数客人满意。然而，有些客人的特殊需求并不在规定条款范围内，甚至这些需求可能与酒店服务程序相矛盾。只要这些特殊需求是合理的，酒店就应该尽量予以满足。

2. 服务员在工作中一定要灵活机智地处理每件事情，绝不能因僵化教条造成不良后果，这样会减少酒店潜在客源。

Can You Help Us Clean Up First?

Mr. Zhang, who lived in Suite 1208, is a Hangzhou businessman. At 9 o'clock today, he would receive a friend from abroad in the guest room to talk about some business matters. But when he got up in the morning, he found his room messy and in desperate need of tidying up. He just wanted to open the door to call the attendant to clean, but found the attendant working at the other end of the corridor. He hurriedly explained the request to the attendant. After hearing that, the attendant looked at him with a troubled expression, "Mr. Zhang, I am sorry. Our supervisor told us that the room must be cleaned in accordance with the order. From Room 1201 to your Room 08, I reckon it'll be after ten o'clock." Mr. Zhang noticed the troubled expression on the attendant's face, "Can you change the order?" "In order to ensure the efficiency of our work and provide better quality to our customers, our company stipulates that we must operate according to the regulations; otherwise we have to be deducted money." Looking at an innocent expression on the attendant's face, Mr. Zhang shook his head and walked away with a wry smile.

Questions:

1. Is there anything wrong with the room attendant according to the hotel's requirements? If so, what is wrong?

2. How to view the hotel regulations conflict with the requirements of guests?

Answers:

1. In terms of staff training, managers have a one-sided emphasis on implementing the rules and procedures, without informing them of the flexibility required in service. While all norms and procedures are fundamental to ensuring quality, the only basis for developing these norms and procedures should be to consider the guest's position. Blindly emphasizing procedures can ensure satisfaction for most guests under normal circumstances. However, there are special needs of guests that fall outside the scope of the provisions. These needs may even contradict hotel service procedures. As long as those special needs are reasonable, the hotel should meet them as much as possible.

2. The waiters in the work must be flexible and resourceful to deal with everything, and must not be paralyzed to cause bad consequences, which may reduce the hotel's potential customer sources.

练一练 Activities

一、朗读下列词汇

开关　毛巾架　水龙头　浴缸

熨洗　空调器　床垫　浴室

二、角色扮演，两人一组，完成顾客要求服务员打扫房间的对话

Unit 2　常规服务 Regular Service

导言 Preview

"客人就是上帝。"使客人满意是酒店的唯一宗旨。酒店的顾客各不相同，但他们对客房产品有共性的需求，比如说要求客房干净卫生。这就要求客房提供一些常规性的服务来满足住店客人的共性需求。

"The guest is God." Making the guest satisfied is the sole purpose of the hotel. Hotel customers are different, but they have common needs for guest room products, such as requiring clean rooms. This requires the room to provide some regular services to meet the common needs of guests.

词库 Word Bank

常用词汇 Common vocabulary			
汉语 Chinese	英语 English	汉语 Chinese	英语 English
客房服务 kè fáng fú wù	housekeeping service	客房服务员 kè fáng fú wù yuán	housekeeper
客房小酒吧服务 kè fáng xiǎo jiǔ bā fú wù	room mini-bar service	比例 bǐ lì	proportion
客房送餐服务 kè fáng sòng cān fú wù	room service	维修 wéi xiū	maintenance
夜床服务 yè chuáng fú wù	turn-down service	万能钥匙 wàn néng yào shi	master key
送洗客衣服务 sòng xǐ kè yī fú wù	laundry service	个人身份 gè rén shēn fèn	personal identification
会议服务 huì yì fú wù	conference service	请勿打扰 qǐng wù dǎ rǎo	Do Not Disturb
访客接待服务 fǎng kè jiē dài fú wù	visitor reception service	消费 xiāo fèi	consumption
擦鞋服务 cā xié fú wù	shoe shining service	消耗品 xiāo hào pǐn	expendables
客房部 kè fáng bù	Housekeeping Department	热情好客 rè qíng hào kè	hospitality

常用句型 Useful Expressions

进房前 Before Entering the Room

1. 客房服务，我可以进来吗？Housekeeping service. May I come in?

2. 抱歉打扰您，我现在可以清理房间吗？I'm sorry to disturb you. May I clean your room now?

3. 哦，我现在有点事情。Well, I'm a bit tied up now.

4. 我正在打电话。I'm on the phone.

5. 先生，要我等会儿再来吗？Shall I be back later, sir?

6. 你等会儿再来好吗？Can you be back later?

7. 您希望我什么时候再来？What time would you like me to be back?

8. 您什么时间更合适呢？What time would be better for you?

9. 您什么时间方便呢？What time would be convenient for you?

10. 晚饭后的时间比较好。Some time after supper would be fine.

11. 请再等30分钟好吗？Could you wait another 30 minutes, please?

12. 当您需要清理房间时可以给前台打电话。You can call the front desk when you want your room done.

13. 我能进房检查一下服务员清理房间的情况吗？May I come in to check the housekeeper's work?

进房后 After Entering the Room

1. 我可以为您的房间吸尘吗？May I vacuum your room now?

2. 我帮您整理一下书桌好吗？May I tidy up your desk?

3. 为了清洁书桌，我可以移动您桌子上的物品吗？May I move the things on your desk so that I can dust it?

4. 好的，请吧！Sure, go ahead!

5. 就让它们放在那儿吧。Just leave the things as they are, please.

6. 我宁愿您别动这些东西。I prefer you don't move these things.

情景对话 Situational Dialogues

对话1 Dialogue 1 房间介绍 Room Introduction

场景：一名顾客想预订海景房。

Scene：A customer wants to reserve a room with an ocean view.

H：Housekeeper（客房服务员）　　G：Guest（顾客）

H：您的房间正好面对大海，非常美丽。我希望您会喜欢。Your room is facing the sea. It's very beautiful. I hope you will like it.

G：是的，非常喜欢。这个房间看上去很不错。Yes, I will. The room looks very nice.

H：怀特先生，这是灯具开关、衣柜和小冰柜。Mr. White, there is the light switch, the wardrobe, and the mini-bar here.

G：太棒了！Wonderful!

H：这是总开关。这是温度控制器。您可以按照您的喜好进行调整。床头柜上的控制板控制着房间里的各种电器装置。另外说一下，浴室里有两个插座，一个是110伏的，另一个是220伏的。这里的电压比美国的高。Here is the master switch. This is the temperature control. You may adjust it as you like. And the panel on the nightstand controls the different devices in the room. By the way, there are two sockets in the bathroom, for 110V and 220V respectively. The voltage here is much higher than that in the U.S.A.

G：噢，我能用电动剃须刀了，经过跨洋飞行以后，我很想洗个澡来恢复一下精神。如果有事情打电话到外边，我该怎么拨号呢？Oh, I can use my electric shaver. And I feel like taking a bath to fresh up after the international flight. And how can I make an outside call?

H：如果您想打出去，要先拨"0"号键。写字台上有一个电话簿，可供您参考。If you want to make an outside call, please dial "0" first. There is a telephone directory on the writing desk for your reference.

G：那电视呢？What about the TV?

H：这是遥控器。一共有16个频道，包括三个英语频道和一个法语频道。这是节目单。在我离开之前您还有什么需要帮忙的吗？This is the remote control. There are sixteen channels in total, including three English channels and a French channel. Here is a program list. Well, is there anything I can do before I leave the room?

G：你使我有宾至如归的感觉。顺便问一句，这儿的自来水能喝吗？You've made me feel very welcome. By the way, is the tap water drinkable?

H：怀特先生，请不要喝自来水，除非水是烧开的。浴室有两瓶饮用水，都是免费的。如果您需要其他任何东西，请拨"8"号键。我们随时会为您服务。Oh, Mr. White, please don't drink the tap water unless it is boiled. And there are two bottles of drinking water in the bathroom, free of charge. If you need anything else, please dial 8. We're always at your service.

G：谢谢。Thank you very much.

H：预祝您在我们这里度过愉快的时光。I hope you will enjoy your stay with us.

对话2 Dialogue 2 夜床服务（1）Turn-down Service（1）

场景：一名顾客咨询夜床服务。

Scene：A customer asks about turn-down service.

H：Housekeeper（客房服务员）　　G：Guest（顾客）

H：晚上好，女士和先生。我现在能够为你们做开夜床服务吗？Good evening, madam and sir. May I do the turn-down service for you now?

G：噢，谢谢。不过我们有些朋友要来。我们准备举行一个小聚会，您能够三个小时以后再来吗？Oh, thank you. But we are having some friends here. We're going to have a small party here in the room. Could you come back in three hours?

H：好的，女士。我会让上通宵班的同事知道的。他们到时候会来。Certainly,

madam. I'll let the overnight staff members know. They will come then.

G：好。哦，我们的朋友可能要晚到了，你能够帮我收拾一下洗浴间吗？我刚刚洗澡了，浴室显得有点乱。另外，请帮我拿一瓶纯净水过来。That's fine. Well, our friends seem to be a little late. Would you tidy up the bathroom? I've just taken a bath and it is a bit of a mess now. Besides, please bring me a bottle of just purified water.

H：好的，我立即拿洁净毛巾和饮用水过来。Yes, I'll bring in some fresh towels together with the drinking water.

G：好的。OK.

H：我能够为您开灯吗？May I turn on the lights for you?

G：好的。我需要写字及阅读。Yes, please. I'd like to do some writing and reading.

H：好的，先生。还有什么能够帮到您吗？Yes, sir. Is there anything I can do for you?

G：没有了。你确实是一个好女孩，很感谢你。No more. You're a smart girl indeed. Thank you very much.

H：我将一直为你们服务。再见，女士和先生，祝你们有个很愉快的夜晚。I'm always at your service. Goodbye, madam and sir, and wish you a very pleasant night.

对话3 Dialogue 3 夜床服务（2）Turn-down Service（2）

场景：如何做夜床服务

Scene：How to make turn-down service

H：Housekeeper（客房服务员）　　G：Guest（顾客）

（敲门 Knocking on the door）

H：客房服务。我可以进来吗？Housekeeping. May I come in?

G：进来。Come in.

H：晚上好。我现在可以为您做夜床服务吗？Good evening. May I do the turn-down service for you now?

G：你说的"夜床服务"是什么意思？What do you mean by "turn-down service"?

H：对于"夜床服务"，我会打开特定的灯，拉上窗帘，整理您的床，清空垃圾箱……For "turn-down service", I'll switch on certain lights, draw the curtains, make up your bed, empty the waste bin…

G：现在不行。我们要和朋友们在这里举行联欢会。你能晚点儿来吗？Not now, please. We are going to have a get-together with our friends here. Could you come later?

H：当然，夫人。要不要我把窗帘放下来？Certainly, madam. Would you like me to put down the curtains for you?

G：好的。这样好多了。Yes, please. That's much better.

补充阅读 Supplement Reading

客房清洁工作由客房女服务员承担。她们的工作包括铺床、擦家具、清除地板和地毯上的灰尘、打扫浴室、更换浴巾以及提供酒店所规定应有的和客人所需求的一些物品。有些饭店，服务员还为客人提供洗衣服务。在高档的酒店中，还会提供开夜床服务，也给客人营造一种温馨的感觉。

The actual work of cleaning for the guestrooms is performed by chambermaids. Their duties include making beds, dusting furniture, sweeping or cleaning floors and carpets, washing bathrooms, replacing towels, and supplying the rooms with the items that are specified by management or custom. In some hotels, the chambermaids offer the laundry and valet service. In the luxury hotels, there is a nightly "turn-down service", in which the bed covers are turned down to make the look more inviting.

练一练 Activities

一、将下列词汇匹配

（1）客房服务　　　　　　　（A）Laundry service
（2）客房小酒吧服务　　　　（B）Housekeeping service
（3）客房送餐服务　　　　　（C）Do Not Disturb
（4）送洗客衣服务　　　　　（D）Conference service
（5）会议服务　　　　　　　（E）Room mini-bar service
（6）请勿打扰　　　　　　　（F）Room service

二、请将下列句子翻译成汉语

1. I'm sorry to disturb you. May I clean your room now?
2. Could you wait another 30 minutes, please?
3. Just leave the things as they are, please.
4. The room looks very nice.
5. By the way, is the tap water drinkable?

Unit 3　洗衣服务 Laundry Service

导言 Preview

随着酒店业的发展，酒店洗衣服务也逐渐细分化，形成了外包洗衣服务和自助式洗衣服务。外包洗衣服务形式已经被大多数酒店所采纳。

With the development of the hotel industry, the hotel laundry service is gradually segmented and divided into outsourced laundry service and self-service laundry service. The form of outsourced laundry service has been adopted by most hotels.

词库 Word Bank

常用词汇 Common vocabulary			
汉语 Chinese	英语 English	汉语 Chinese	英语 English
布草 bù cǎo 布草房 bù cǎo fáng	linen linen room	较小的 jiào xiǎo de 次要的 cì yào de	minor
储藏室 chǔ cáng shì 库房 kù fáng	storeroom	观念 guān niàn 概念 gài niàn	concept
重叠 chóng dié	overlap	女裁缝 nǚ cái feng 做针线工的 zuò zhēn xiàn gōng de	seamstress
可洗的 kě xǐ de 耐洗的 nài xǐ de	washable	分发 fēn fā 分配 fēn pèi	distribute
相当地 xiāng dāng de	considerably	窗帘 chuāng lián	curtain
制服 zhì fú	uniform	洗涤 xǐ dí 洗烫 xǐ tàng	launder
补给 bǔ jǐ 供给 gōng jǐ	supply	循环 xún huán 流通 liú tōng	circulation

常用句型 Useful Expressions

洗衣服务说明 Laundry Service Instructions

1. 您能不能派人到2587房取我的送洗衣物呢？Can you send someone to Room 2587 to pick up my laundry?

2. 我想知道你们洗衣服务一般要多久时间。I'd like to know how long your laundry service usually takes.

3. 现在恐怕已经过了今天的洗衣时间。I'm afraid it is too late for today's laundry time.

4. 收费是怎样的呢？How about the rates?

5. 洗衣单和洗衣袋在写字台右边的第一个抽屉里。The laundry forms and bags are in the first drawer on the right side of the writing desk.

6. 我来收取您的衣服。I come to collect your laundry.

7. 您要什么时候取回送洗的衣服？When would you like your laundry back?

8. 女士，请在送洗衣服清单上签字。Please sign on the laundry list, madam.

9. 您送洗的衣服在傍晚6时可取。Your laundry will be ready by 6 p.m.

收取送洗衣物 Collect Laundry

1. 请填写洗衣单。Please fill in the laundry form.

2. 我们会在明天中午以前送回您的房间。We will deliver it to your room by tomorrow noon.

3. 我们有两小时的快速服务。We have a two-hour quick service.

4. 快速服务要外加50%的费用。There is an extra charge of 50% for quick service.

5. 我们可以在4小时内送回，但要收50%的费用。We can deliver it within 4 hours at a 50% extra charge.

送洗衣物与洗衣单不符 Laundry Do Not Tally with the Laundry List

1. 您要送洗的衣服有点小问题。There is a small problem with your laundry.

2. 洗衣袋里的衣物与洗衣单上登记的不符。The items in your bag don't match up with the items on the laundry list.

3. 您的洗衣袋里应有3件T恤，但是这里只有2件。There should be three T-shirts in your bag, but here are only two.

4. 您的洗衣袋里有一件文胸，但是洗衣单上没有标出来。There is a bra in your bag, but that isn't marked on the form.

5. 少了一只袜子。One sock is missing.

送洗服务投诉 Laundry Service Complaints

1. 我送洗的衣物在哪里？Where is my laundry?

2. 我还没有收到我送洗的衣物。I haven't received my laundry yet.

3. 我们马上去查看这件事。We'll check it right now.

4. 我检查了一下送回的衣物，发现一件衬衫不见了。I checked my returned laundry, and found a shirt was missing.

5. 您能描述一下它是什么样的吗？Could you describe it?

情景对话 Situational Dialogues

对话1 Dialogue 1 送洗服务（1）Laundry Service (1)

场景：客房服务人员上门提供送洗服务。

Scene：The housekeeper provides on-site laundry service.

H：Housekeeper（客房服务员）   G：Guest（顾客）

H：客房服务。我可以收您的送洗衣物了吗？Housekeeping. May I collect your laundry?

G：可以，在洗衣袋里。Yes, it is in the laundry bag.

H：谢谢您，女士。洗衣单放在洗衣袋里了吗？Thank you, madam. Is the laundry form in the bag?

G：是的。对了，干洗需要多长时间？Yes, by the way, how long does it take for dry-cleaning?

H：干洗一般需要两天。It usually takes two days.

G：天哪，我们明天就要走了。Oh, dear. We're leaving tomorrow.

H：如果您急着要，我们有两小时的快速服务，不过要外加50%的费用。If you are in a hurry, we have a two-hour quick service with an extra charge of 50%.

G：唉，也只好这样啦。Well, if that's the case.

对话 2 Dialogue 2 送洗服务（2） Laundry Service (2)

场景：客房服务人员上门提供送洗服务。

Scene: The housekeeper provides on-site laundry service.

H：Housekeeper（客房服务员）   G：Guest（顾客）

H：打搅一下。请问您有需要洗的衣服吗？洗衣工将在这儿为您服务。Excuse me. Have you any laundry? The laundry man is here to serve you.

G：哦，现在没有，多谢。No, not now, thank you.

H：当您需要的时候请将衣物留在洗衣袋中，洗衣工会在每天早上过来收取。If you have any, please just leave it in the laundry bag. The laundry man comes over to collect it every morning.

G：谢谢。Thank you.

H：当您衣服需要湿洗、干洗或熨烫服务时，请随时通知我们或是填写洗衣单，并告诉我们您需要取回衣物时间。Please feel free to tell us or notify in the list when you need your clothes to be laundered, dry-cleaned or pressed and also what time you want to get them back.

G：好的，如果衣物损坏怎样处理呢？我想知道贵酒店是否有相关政策去处理。I see. What if there is any laundry damage? I wonder if your hotel has a policy on dealing with it.

H：在这种情况下，酒店当然需要赔偿，赔偿金额不超出洗衣费用十倍。In such a case, the hotel should certainly pay for it. The indemnity shall not exceed ten times the cost of the laundry.

G：这么听起来是比较合理，当然我期望是不会有任何损坏。That sounds quite reasonable. I hope there's no damage at all.

H：不用担心，先生。洗衣部门有着很丰富经验。Don't worry, sir. The laundry department has wide experience in their work.

G：好的。感谢您带来的信息。All right. Thank you for your information.

H：不客气。Not at all.

对话3 Dialogue 3 送洗服务（3）Laundry Service (3)

场景：客房服务人员上门提供送洗服务。

Scene：The housekeeper provides on-site laundry service.

L：Laundry Attendant（洗衣房服务员）　G：Guest（客人）

L：客房服务，我可以进来吗？Housekeeping, may I come in?

G：请进。Come in, please.

L：早上好，夫人。我是洗衣房服务员。您今天有要洗的衣服吗？Good morning, madam. I'm the laundry attendant. Do you have any laundry today?

G：是的，给你。Yes, here you are.

L：一件衬衫、一件连衣裙和两双袜子。对吗？One shirt, one dress and two pairs of socks. Is that right?

G：是的，没错。Yes, that's right.

L：请问要怎么洗？How do you want them cleaned, please?

G：我已经在洗衣单上做了记号。I've marked it down on the laundry list.

L：谢谢您，夫人。您希望什么时候取回？Thank you, madam. When do you want them back?

G：通常需要多长时间？How long does it usually take?

L：一般服务大约需要12个小时。The regular service takes about 12 hours.

G：这很好。谢谢你！That's fine. Thank you.

补充阅读 Supplement Reading

酒店洗衣房经营之道

经济发展带动酒店业发展，而作为酒店服务支柱之一的洗涤业务也相应发展起来。目前，酒店洗涤业务主要分为客衣洗涤、客房布草洗涤、餐饮台布洗涤和工衣洗涤，它们的特点相差较大，因此洗涤方法也完全不同。客衣洗涤是指入住酒店的客人日常所需洗涤的自有衣物，其特点是织物种类较多，且多为高档织物；织物污渍也呈现多样性，譬如酒渍、果汁、血渍等；总洗涤量不稳定，客人取衣时间要求短，衣物熨烫效果必须好。客房布草洗涤是指为客房服务所提供的毛巾、床单、被套等客房配套布草洗涤，其特点是污染程度较轻，以白料为主，总洗涤量随入住率的变化而变化，有较明显的季节性。餐饮台布洗涤是指配套餐厅的台布以及其他设施的特殊布草洗涤,其特点是污染程度高,布草主要以化纤类为主。工衣洗涤是指酒店工作人员的制服等的洗涤,这部分织物特点与客衣洗涤较为类似,但洗涤量较为稳定。

Hotel Laundry Management

Economic development has driven the development of the hotel industry, and laundry as one of the pillars of hotel service has also developed accordingly. At present, the hotel laundry business is mainly divided into guest clothes washing, room linen washing, dining table cloth washing and work clothes washing. Their characteristics are quite different, so the washing methods are completely different. Guest clothes washing refers to the daily need of hotel guests to wash their own clothes, which is characterized by a wide variety of fabrics, and most of them are high-grade fabrics; fabric stains also show diversity, such as wine, juice, blood and so on; the total amount of washing is not stable, and the guest needs a short time to take clothes, and the ironing effect must be good. Room linen washing refers to towels, sheets, quilt sets and other room linen washing provided for housekeeping service, which is characterized by a light pollution degree, mainly white materials. The total amount of washing changes with the occupancy rate, and there is a more obvious seasonal variation. Dining table cloth washing refers to the tablecloth of the supporting restaurant and other facilities of special linen washing, which is characterized by a high degree of pollution, with linen mainly based on chemical fiber. Work clothes washing refers to the washing of the uniforms of hotel staff members, etc., and the characteristics of this part of the fabrics are similar to those of customer clothes washing, but the amount of washing is more stable.

练一练 Activities

一、将下列词汇匹配

(1) 储藏室　　　　(A) uniform
(2) 洗涤　　　　　(B) storeroom
(3) 分发　　　　　(C) overlap
(4) 重叠　　　　　(D) launder
(5) 窗帘　　　　　(E) curtain
(6) 制服　　　　　(F) distribute

二、根据语意排列句子顺序

　　A. 您好,我是洗衣房服务员。
　　B. 可是,我明天上午要参加会议,可以加快清洗吗?

C. 我们也可以在4小时内送回，但要额外收50%的费用。

D. 你好，我有几件衣服需要清洗。

E. 我们会在明天中午以前送回您的房间。

F. 好的，请您把需要清洗的衣服放在房间的洗衣袋里，稍后有人收取。

G. 什么时候可以送回？

H. 那好吧，我选择加急服务。

Unit 4 维修服务 Maintenance Service

导言 Preview

随着现代科技的不断进步和发展，其最新成果也不断应用于酒店的设备之中。酒店的设备设施向着追求舒适和豪华及设备的复杂化、多样化发展。酒店的经营对设备的依赖程度也越来越高。一个明智的酒店总经理除了抓好酒店的经营，必定要亲自过问设备的完好情况。酒店工程设备的管理与维修在酒店中占了重要位置。

With the continuous progress and development of modern science and technology, its latest achievements are also constantly applied to the hotel equipment. The hotel equipment and facilities are oriented toward the pursuit of comfort and luxury, and complex and diversified development of equipment. The hotel's operation is more and more dependent on equipment. A wise hotel general manager in addition to the management of the hotel, must personally ask about the good condition of the equipment. The management and maintenance of hotel engineering equipment plays an important role in the hotel.

词库 Word Bank

常用词汇 Common vocabulary			
汉语 Chinese	英语 English	汉语 Chinese	英语 English
用水冲洗 yòng shuǐ chōng xǐ	flush	电工 diàn gōng 电学家 diàn xué jiā	electrician
塞住了 sāi zhù le	clogged	维修 wéi xiū 保养 bǎo yǎng	maintenance
滴下 dī xià	drip	设备工具 shè bèi gōng jù	facility
摇摆不定的 yáo bǎi bú dìng de	wobbly	效率 xiào lù	efficiency

常用句型 Useful Expressions

1. 我房间里的抽水马桶好像出了点毛病。There seems to be something wrong with the toilet in my room.

2. 我们会马上派人来修。We'll send someone to repair it immediately.

3. 哪儿坏啦？What's the trouble?

4. 抽水马桶不放水了。The toilet doesn't flush.

5. 让我看看。噢，堵住了。Let me see. Oh, it's clogged.

6. 水龙头一整夜滴水。The water tap has been dripping all night long.

7. 有个零件要换了。我片刻就来。Some part needs to be replaced. I will be back soon.

8. 啊，电视机好像有些毛病。Ah, I'm afraid there's something wrong with the TV.

9. 图像不稳定。The picture is wobbly.

10. 很遗憾，我可以看看吗？I'm sorry. May I have a look at it?

11. 我去请维修部的电工来。I'll send for an electrician from the maintenance department.

12. 我们能找人修理。We can have it repaired.

13. 请稍等几分钟。Please wait just a few minutes.

14. 电视机有毛病了。The TV set is not working well.

15. 怎么了，有什么需要维修吗？What is the trouble? Anything needs repairing?

16. 我来修理。I will fix it for you.

17. 我马上去做。I will do it right away.

18. 我马上给您拿来。I will bring it right away.

19. 我会亲自解决这件事的。I will take care of it personally.

20. 我们会派人去修。We will send someone up to repair it.

21. 我们马上给您换一个。We will bring the replacement immediately.

22. 很难再找到和这个一样的了。It is hard to get a similar one.

23. 对不起，我们今天修不了。I am sorry, and we can't fix it today.

24. 给您换个房间好吗？卫生间今天修不好了。Would you mind changing a room? The toilet is hard to repair today.

25. 我叫一个修理工来。Let me call a repairman to do it.

26. 马桶堵住了。The toilet is stopped up.

27. 由于水管维修，上午9点至下午4点没有冷水供应。Since the water pipes are being repaired, cold water is not available from 9 a.m. to 4 p.m.

28. 很抱歉给您带来不便,真心希望您住店愉快。Sorry for the inconvenience. We do hope you enjoy your stay here.

29. 喷头坏了。There is something wrong with the shower.

30. 马桶没有水,请修理一下好吗? There is no water in the water closet. Would you please have it repaired?

31. 请稍等,我马上通知工程部来人修理。Wait a moment, please. I will inform the engineering department to send someone to repair it.

32. 先生,马桶不能冲了,我去找人来修理。Sir, the flush isn't working. I will send someone to fix it.

33. 水龙头漏水,吵得我无法入睡。I can't fall asleep because the tap is dripping.

情景对话 Situational Dialogues

对话 1 Dialogue 1 维修服务（1）Maintenance Service (1)

场景：客房服务人员上门提供维修服务。

Scene：The housekeeper provides on-site maintenance service.

H：Housekeeper（客房服务员）　　G：Guest（顾客）

H：客房服务。我能帮您吗? Housekeeping. Can I help you?

G：是的,厕所好像出了点问题。Yes, there seems to be something wrong with the toilet.

H：我们马上派人去修。请问您的房间号是多少? We'll send someone to repair it immediately. What's your room number, please?

G：1287。1287.

H：我可以进来吗? May I come in?

G：进来吧。Come in.

H：出什么事了? What's the trouble?

G：马桶不冲水了。The toilet doesn't flush.

H：让我看看。哦,堵塞了,现在没事了。您可以试试。Let me see. Oh, it's clogged…It's all right now. You may try it.

G：是的,现在可以用了。谢谢你! Yes, it's working now. Thank you!

H：不客气。还有别的事吗? You're welcome. Anything else?

G：水龙头一整夜都在滴水。我几乎睡不着。The water tap has been dripping all night long. I can hardly sleep.

H：非常抱歉,先生,有个零件需要更换。我很快就回来。I'm very sorry, sir. Some part needs to be replaced. I will be back soon.

Chapter 2 客房服务 Housekeeping Service

对话 2 Dialogue 2 维修服务（2） Maintenance Service（2）

场景：客房服务人员上门提供维修服务。

Scene：The housekeeper provides on-site maintenance service.

H：Housekeeper（客房服务员）　　G：Guest（顾客）　　E：Electrician（电工）

G：我把自己锁在房间外面了。我可以借一把备用钥匙吗？I've locked myself out of the room. May I borrow a spare key?

H：别担心，贝尔先生。我来给您开门。Don't worry, Mr. Bell. I'll open the door for you.（她用一把备用钥匙打开了门。She opens the door with a spare key.）

G：非常感谢。有时我很健忘。Thank you very much. Sometimes I'm quite absent-minded.

H：没关系，贝尔先生。我还能为您做些什么？It doesn't matter, Mr. Bell. What else can I do for you?

G：啊，恐怕电视有点问题。画面不稳定。Ah, I'm afraid there's something wrong with the TV. The picture is flickering.

H：我很抱歉。我可以看一下吗？I'm sorry. May I have a look at it?

G：在这里。Here it is.

H：（她试图修理，但没有成功。）我去请维修部的电工来。我们可以找人把它修好。请稍等几分钟，贝尔先生。（她离开了房间。十分钟后，有人敲门。）(She tries to fix it, but in vain.) I'll send for an electrician from the maintenance department. We can have it repaired. Please wait just a few minutes, Mr. Bell. (She leaves the room. Ten minutes later, there is a knock on the door.)

E：我可以进来吗？May I come in?

G：（他打开门。）你好！(He opens the door.) How do you do?

E：您好！这台电视机坏了。是这样吗，贝尔先生？How do you do? The TV set is not working well. Is that right, Mr. Bell?

G：是的。Yes, it is.

E：让我看看。（他修理完毕并检查了房间里的其他电气设备。）贝尔先生，现在一切正常了。Let me have a look. (He finishes the repairing and checks other electric facilities in the room.) Mr. Bell, everything is OK now.

G：效率真快！非常感谢。（他拿出一些钱。）这是给你的。What efficiency! Thanks a lot. (He takes out some fee.) This is for you.

E：哦，不。我们不收小费，不过还是谢谢您。希望您在我们酒店过得愉快，贝尔先生。Oh, no. We won't accept tips, but thank you, anyway. We wish you a nice stay with us, Mr. Bell.

对话3 Dialogue 3 维修服务（3） Maintenance Service (3)

场景：客房服务人员上门提供维修服务。

Scene：The housekeeper provides on-site maintenance service.

G：Mr. Geller（盖勒先生）　　A：Attendant（服务员）

G：是客服部吗？Is this the customer service department?

A：是的，先生。请问您有什么需求吗？Yes, sir. What can I do for you?

G：我房间的空调一直发出很大的声响，让我没法休息。The air conditioner in my room keeps making such a loud noise that I can't rest.

A：稍等一下，您是305号房的盖勒先生，对吗？Just a moment, you are Mr. Geller in Room 305, right?

G：是的。Yes, I am.

A：请问除了有噪音，空调的制冷效果有问题吗？Is there any problem with the cooling effect of the air conditioner besides the noise?

G：现在是没有问题的，不过一直在往下滴水。The cooling effect is fine, but it's dripping water all the time.

A：很抱歉给您造成这种困扰，但是现在酒店的维修服务很忙，维修人员可能不能立即为您服务，不过我们会尽快为您安排。We are so sorry for this trouble, but now the maintenance service is busy. The maintenance staff may not be able to serve you immediately, but we will arrange for you as soon as possible.

G：什么？我已经没有睡好午觉了，我需要你们立即找人来修理。What? I haven't had a good nap, and I need you to get someone to fix it right away.

A：盖勒先生，实在抱歉，我们已经通知了维修部，他们会尽快安排的。如果您不想待在房间里，不如到我们的桑拿房做水疗，正好可以缓解疲劳，维修好后，我们会直接通知您。I'm sorry, Mr. Geller. We have informed the maintenance department that they will arrange it as soon as possible. If you don't want to stay in the room, you can go to the sauna room for SPA, which will relieve the fatigue, and we'll let you know when it's done.

G：那行吧，也只能这样了。All right, that's it.

补充阅读 Supplement Reading

工匠精神

工匠是指擅长做某事或制作某物的人。从广义上说，工匠精神指的是努力为客户提供优质产品和优质服务的精神。

工匠精神是提高员工参与度的重要理念。如果你能专注于你所做的工作，你会更快乐，并为出色地完成工作而感到自豪。如果没有工匠般的品质，在如今快节奏的社会中，人们很容易从一个任务快速地转移到下一个任务，而不能把任何事情做得出色。

　　酒店员工如果能注重培养自己的工匠精神，便可以为客人创造各种价值，从而帮助酒店实现可持续发展。

Craftsman Spirit

　　A craftsman is a person who is skilled in doing or making something. The craftsman spirit, in a broader sense, refers to the desire to offer high-quality products and outstanding services to customers.

　　The craftsman spirit is an important concept for improving employee engagement. If you are engaged and focused on the job you are doing, you will be happier and take pride in completing it excellently. Without craftsman-like qualities, in today's fast-paced society, people tend to quickly switch from one task to the next without excelling at anything.

　　If hotel employees can focus on cultivating their craftsman spirit, they can create various values for guests, thus helping the hotel achieve sustainable development.

练一练 Activities

一、朗读下列词汇

　　用水冲洗　　滴下　　　　维修
　　电工　　　　设备工具　　塞住了

二、翻译下列句子

　　1. 水龙头一整夜都在滴水。我几乎睡不着。
　　2. 电视机有毛病了。
　　3. 您换个房间好吗？卫生间今天修不好了。
　　4. 马桶堵住了。
　　5. 我把自己锁在房间外面了。我可以借一把备用钥匙吗？
　　6. 效率真快！非常感谢。

Unit 5　其他客房服务 Other Housekeeping Services

导言 Preview

　　除了常规服务，大型酒店还会根据客人的不同需求提供各种各样的服务，如按需购物、婴儿看护等。许多服务也可以通过电话获得。

Besides regular services, large hotels often provide miscellaneous services according to guests' different requirements, for instance, buying things on request, babysitting, etc. Many services can also be obtained by phone.

婴儿看护就是暂时照顾孩子。一些酒店自己培训有经验的保姆，而另一些酒店则从育儿中介机构雇用保姆。保姆应该是可靠的、有耐心的、负责任的、喜欢孩子的。

Babysitting is temporarily caring for a child. Some hotels train experienced babysitters themselves, while others hire babysitters from nanny agencies. A babysitter should be reliable, patient, responsible and fond of children.

客房服务或"客房内用餐"是一项酒店服务，客人可以选择菜单上的食物，由工作人员送到他们的房间消费。《商务词典》将其简单地定义为"在酒店房间里为客人提供的食物和饮料"。在非高端酒店提供客房服务是很少见的。

Room service or "in-room dining" is a hotel service enabling guests to choose menu items for delivery to their hotel rooms for consumption there, served by staff. *Business Dictionary* defines it simply as "food and beverages served to a guest in his or her hotel room". It is uncommon for room service to be offered in hotels that are not high-end.

叫醒服务几乎相当于叫早服务。叫醒服务的工作原理是为服务设置一个期望的时间来打电话叫醒某人。

Wake-up service is almost equivalent to a morning call service. Wake-up calls work by setting up a desired time for the service to call in order to wake someone.

词库 Word Bank

常用词汇 Common vocabulary			
汉语 Chinese	英语 English	汉语 Chinese	英语 English
多种多样的 duō zhǒng duō yàng de 多方面的 duō fāng miàn de 混杂的 hùn zá de	miscellaneous	客房送餐服务员 kè fáng sòng cān fú wù yuán	room service waiter
托婴服务 tuō yīng fú wù	babysitting service	电话分机 diàn huà fēn jī	extension
婴儿看护 yīng ér kān hù	babysitting	罐装的 guàn zhuāng de	canned
叫醒服务 jiào xǐng fú wù	wake-up service	冷冻的 lěng dòng de	frozen

续 表

客房用餐服务 kè fáng yòng cān fú wù	room service	递送 dì sòng	deliver
接线员 jiē xiàn yuán	operator	门把手菜单 mén bǎ shou cài dān	doorknob menu

常用句型 Useful Expressions

添加物品 Add Items

1. 我的厕纸用完了。I'm out of toilet paper.

2. 我能多要一个枕头/茶包/浴巾/……吗？Can I have an extra pillow/teabag/bath towel/…?

3. 能给我送个吹风机/变压器/婴儿床/英文报纸/……吗？Can you bring me a(an) hairdryer/transformer/cot/English newspaper/…?

4. 马上去办，先生/女士。Right away, sir/madam.

5. 好的，先生/女士。Certainly, sir/madam.

6. 我立刻就送到您的房间去。I'll send it to your room at once.

7. 恐怕另外一位客人正在使用。我会尽快送到您的房间去。I'm afraid another guest is using it. I'll bring it to your room as soon as it's available.

客房设备需要维修 Room Equipment Needs Repairing

1. 我的卫生间里有一股特别难闻的气味。There's a terrible smell in my bathroom.

2. 我的抽水马桶堵住了。My toilet is clogged/blocked up.

3. 我的抽水马桶往外溢水。My toilet overflowed.

4. 我的浴盆/天花板漏水。My bathtub/ceiling is leaking.

5. 我的空调/电冰箱/暖气/电视机/……坏了。My air conditioner/refrigerator/heating system/TV/… isn't working.

6. 我的一个抽屉卡住了，打不开。One of my drawers is stuck. I can't get it open.

7. 我的窗帘卡住了，拉不开/关不上。My curtains are stuck. I can't open/close them.

8. 很抱歉听到这样的事。I'm sorry to hear that.

9. 我马上叫工程部派人来维修。I'll ask the maintenance department to send someone to fix it at once.

10. 我马上派人给您修理。I'll have someone to fix it for you right away.

11. 修理需要时间。恐怕您得换个房间了。It takes time to repair. I'm afraid you have to change to another room.

12. 我们在 15 楼给您安排了另外一个房间，行李员会帮您拿行李过去。We have

87

arranged another room on the 15th floor for you; a bellman will help you with your baggage.

13. 我们很抱歉给您带来不便。We do apologize for the inconvenience.

贵重物品保管服务 Valuables Safekeeping Service

1. 我想使用保险箱。I'd like to use a safety deposit box.

2. 请您填写这张表格，好吗？Could you fill out the form, please?

3. 您的保险箱号数是605。这是您的钥匙。Your box number is 605. Here is the key.

4. 请您小心保管钥匙好吗？我们没有备用钥匙。Could you keep this key carefully, please? We have no spare key.

5. 如果您需要使用里面的物品，请亲自来取。只有在确认您的签名之后，我们才会打开保险箱。If you would like to use the contents, please come here in person. Only after confirming your signature, will we open the safety deposit box.

小冰箱的使用和添加 Mini-bar Usage and Addition

1. 我想多放些雪碧和可乐在我的小冰箱里。I'd like to have more Sprites and Cokes in my mini-bar.

2. 我能要几瓶健怡可乐吗？Can I have some diet cokes?

3. 你们有橙汁汽水/冰茶/柠檬水/……吗？Do you have any orange soda/iced tea/lemonade/… available?

4. 可以在小冰箱里面多放一点果汁吗？Can I have some more juice in the mini-bar?

5. 您喜欢哪样果汁呢？Which kind of juice would you prefer?

6. 您喜欢哪种牌子的呢？Which brand would you prefer?

7. 我马上去帮您拿。I'll get them for you right away.

递送物品与帮客人邮寄物品 Deliver Items and Help Customers Mail Items

1. 百货公司送来一箱东西给您。The department store has delivered a box for you.

2. 这是您的信件/传真/包裹。Here is a letter/fax/parcel for you.

3. 请您在这儿签个名好吗？Could you sign here, please?

4. 帮我寄这几张明信片好吗？要多少钱？Would you have these postcards sent? How much will that be?

5. 很抱歉，我现在不知道。我们稍后告诉您，好吗？Sorry, I don't know at the moment. We'll let you know later. Will that be fine?

6. 没关系，就加在我的账上吧。Never mind. Just add it to my bill.

托儿服务 Babysitting Service

1. 我和我丈夫今晚要出去，你能帮我照看一下我们的宝贝吗？My husband and I want to go out this evening. Can you look after the baby for us?

2. 恐怕不行。这是违反我们酒店规定的。I'm afraid I can't do that. It's against our hotel's regulations.

3. 服务员是不允许在上班时间照看小孩的。The attendants are not allowed to look after children while they're on duty.

4. 我可以向您推荐我们部门的托儿服务吗？May I recommend the babysitting service of our department to you?

5. 托儿中心有一些经验丰富的保姆。There are some experienced babysitters in the babysitting center.

6. 托儿服务每小时收费20元，最低按4小时计费。The babysitting service charge is 20 yuan per hour, with a minimum charge of 4 hours.

7. 托儿中心是由客房部管理的。请拨电话6，他们会告诉您有关资料，并且派人送来确认单的。The babysitting center is run by the housekeeping department. Please dial telephone number "6", and they will tell you the terms and send up a confirmation form.

无法提供客人所要求的服务 Unable to Provide Guests with Required Services

1. 恐怕客房部不卖饮料。我把您的电话转给客房送餐服务部好吗？I'm afraid we don't sell drinks in the housekeeping department. Shall I transfer your call to the room service department?

2. 您可以试试10楼电梯间的自动售货机。You may try the vending-machine in the elevator hall on the 10th floor.

3. 我们不提供擦鞋服务。不过，您可以在床头柜里找到擦鞋纸。I'm afraid we don't offer any shoe shining service, but you may find the shoeshine paper in the nightstand.

情景对话 Situational Dialogues

对话1 Dialogue 1 外币兑换服务 Currency Exchange Service

场景：在服务台兑换外币。

Scene: Exchange foreign currency at the information desk.

H：Housekeeper（客房服务员） G：Guest（顾客）

H：早上好，需要我帮忙吗？Good morning, can I help you?

G：是的，我想把部分美元换成人民币。Yes. I want to change some US dollars into RMB.

H：多少呢？How much is that?

G：一百美元。100 US dollars.

H：我们按照今天的汇率兑换外币……100美元折合人民币797元。We change

foreign currencies according to today's exchange rate…100 US dollars is equivalent to RMB 797.

G：好的，我要兑换。OK, I'll take it.

H：请填写兑换水单、您的护照号码和总金额，并签署姓名。Please fill in the exchange memo, your passport number and the total sum, and sign your name.

G：在这里，是吧？Here it is, right?

H：是的。Yes.

G：你有什么面额的？What denominations do you have?

H：有100元纸币、50元纸币、20元纸币、10元纸币、5元纸币和1元硬币。There are 100-yuan notes, 50-yuan notes, 20-yuan notes, 10-yuan notes, 5-yuan notes and 1-yuan coin.

G：给我90元纸币、7元硬币，其他的都要100元纸币。Give me 90 yuan notes, 7 yuan coins, and the rest in 100-yuan notes.

H：当然可以。这是797元人民币。请检查，保管好兑换单。Certainly. This is RMB 797. Check it, please, and keep the memo.

G：好的。谢谢你的帮助。OK. Thank you for your help.

对话2 Dialogue 2 客房服务 Housekeeping Service

场景：一名客人需要客房服务。

Scene：A guest needs housekeeping service.

H：Housekeeper（客房服务员）   G：Guest（顾客）

H：客房服务。能够进来吗？Housekeeping. May I come in?

G：请进。Yes, please.

H：您要我什么时间来给您打扫房间呢，女士？When would you like me to do your room, madam?

G：假如你愿意，现在就能够打扫。我正想下去吃早饭，你就进来了。在打扫前，能不能先帮个忙？You can do it now if you like. I was just about to go down for my breakfast when you came. But before you start, would you do something for me?

H：好的，什么事？Yes, what is it?

G：我想请你给我拿一瓶开水来，早饭后我需要热水喝药。I would like you to go and get me a flask of hot water. I need some hot water to wash down medicine after breakfast.

H：很抱歉，您的水瓶空了。我立即去给您拿一瓶满的来。I'm sorry that your flask is empty. I'll go and get you another full one at once.

G：谢谢。Thank you.

对话3 Dialogue 3 洗衣服务 Laundry Service

场景：特殊衣物的洗衣要求

Scene：Special laundry requirements

H：Housekeeper（客房服务员）　　G：Guest（顾客）

H：您需要帮忙吗？Can I help you?

G：我有些衣服需要洗。I have some laundry to be done.

H：好的，先生。请您填写一下要洗的衣服好吗？Certainly, sir. Could you fill out the laundry form?

G：我能用一下你的笔吗？May I use your pen?

H：当然，给您。Sure. Here you are.

G：谢谢，这些衬衫是不需要浆的。Thanks. I don't want these shirts starched.

H：不浆，我了解，先生。No starch. I know, sir.

G：什么时候能洗好？When will they be ready?

H：明天晚上六点左右我会给您送过去。I will deliver them tomorrow evening around 6.

G：好的，谢谢。Fine, thanks a lot.

补充阅读 Supplement Reading

根据《商务词典》，客房服务被定义为在酒店房间里为客人提供的食物和饮料。总的来说，酒店的客房服务部是在你要求时把食物和其他物品送到你房间的部门。他们对食物和服务收费，送餐的人希望得到小费。客房送餐服务是指在酒店或预订住宿场所（如汽车旅馆或服务式公寓）为客人提供食物或饮料的服务。在全套房酒店，它通常被称为"套房内服务"。

在任何规模的机构中，通常都有一个专门的客房服务部门，由餐饮经理负责。客房服务部必须与厨房、前厅部和客房部紧密合作，以确保服务标准满足或超过客人的期望。人们对酒店的评价，和对其他事物的评价一样，往往是根据其提供的客房服务的标准。五星级酒店如果不是全天候提供客房服务，那至少也要提供18个小时，而且服务必须在任何时候都是友好、快速和高效的。

According to the *Business Dictionary*, room service is defined as the service of food and beverages brought to a guest in his or her hotel room. Overall, the room service department in a hotel is the department that brings food and other items to your room when you request them. They charge for the food and the service, and the person making the delivery expects a tip. Room service is the service of providing food or beverages to guests in hotels or booked accommodations, such as motels or serviced apartments. In all-suite hotels it is often referred to as "in-suite service".

In establishments of any size, there is usually a specialist room service department responsible to the food and beverage manager. The room service department must work closely with the kitchen, the front office and the housekeeping department to make sure that the standard of service satisfies, or exceeds guests' expectations. Hotels are often judged, as much as anything else, by the standard of the room service they provide. A five-star hotel will be expected to provide room service for at least 18 hours of the day, if not all hours of the day and night, and that service must at all times be friendly, quick and efficient.

练一练 Activities

一、连线题

(1) 早餐　　　　　　　　　(A) babysitting service
(2) 婴儿看护　　　　　　　(B) babysitting
(3) 托婴服务　　　　　　　(C) wake-up service
(4) 门把手菜单　　　　　　(D) room service
(5) 叫醒服务　　　　　　　(E) breakfast
(6) 客房送餐服务员　　　　(F) doorknob menu
(7) 客房用餐服务　　　　　(G) room service waiter

二、翻译下列句子

1. 我的厕纸用完了。
2. 我的抽水马桶往外溢水。
3. 我想使用保险箱。
4. 你们有橙汁汽水吗？
5. 没关系，就加在我的账上吧。
6. 托儿中心有一些经验丰富的保姆。

Unit 6　紧急事件 Emergency

导言 Preview

紧急情况是指需要立即采取行动进行处理的严重或危险的事件或情况。不管在酒店里还是酒店外，客人都可能偶尔突发疾病或受到意外袭击，或者他们可能会遇到一些紧急问题。提供及时帮助对酒店员工来说是必不可少的。毫无疑问，正确、迅速地处理紧急情况可以在关键时刻挽救人们的生命。

紧急服务	电话号码
紧急报警	110
火警	119
生病急救	120
交通事故	122

Emergency means a serious or dangerous event or situation which needs immediate action to deal with. Occasionally guests may be hit by sudden illness or accidents in or out of a hotel, or they may come across some urgent problems. To offer immediate help is essential for hotel staff. There is no doubt that to deal with emergency in a correct and quick way can save people's lives at a critical moment.

Emergency Service	Telephone Number
Police	110
Fire	119
Ambulance	120
Traffic Accident	122

词库 Word Bank

常用词汇 Common vocabulary			
汉语 Chinese	英语 English	汉语 Chinese	英语 English
紧急情况 jǐn jí qíng kuàng 突发事件 tū fā shì jiàn	emergency	营救 yíng jiù 援救 yuán jiù	rescue
应急预案 yìng jí yù àn	emergency preplan	接近 jiē jìn 途径 tú jìng 方法 fāng fǎ	approach
突然的 tū rán de 意外的 yì wài de	sudden	珠宝 zhū bǎo 珠宝类 zhū bǎo lèi	jewelry
疾病 jí bìng	illness	疏散 shū sàn 撤出 chè chū 排泄 pái xiè	evacuate
紧急的 jǐn jí de	urgent	生病的 shēng bìng de	sick
恐慌 kǒng huāng	panic	胃疼 wèi téng	stomachache
蹲伏 dūn fú 低头 dī tóu 屈膝 qū xī	crouch	缺乏 quē fá 缺少 quē shǎo	be out of

93

常用句型 Useful Expressions

意外事故 Accidents

1. 请注意！酒店发生火警。请立即离开房间，从安全门撤离。谢谢您的配合。Attention, please! There is a fire emergency in the hotel. Please leave your room immediately and exit through the emergency exit door. Thank you for your cooperation.

2. 女士们、先生们，请注意！酒店发生了一场小火灾，但火势已经得到控制。请各位保持冷静。为了您的安全起见，请随我由紧急出口到大堂。请勿携带任何行李，也不要使用电梯。多谢您的配合。Ladies and gentlemen, attention please! There is a small fire in the hotel but it is already under control, so please remain calm. For your safety, please follow me to the lobby by the emergency exit. Please leave your luggage behind and don't use the elevator. Thank you for your cooperation.

3. 我妻子在浴室摔倒了。她没法站起来。My wife has slipped in the bathroom. She can't stand up.

4. 我丈夫晕倒了。My husband has fainted.

5. 我的鼻子/脸/腿/手/……在流血。My nose/face/leg/hand/… is bleeding.

6. 我头痛/胃痛/牙痛得厉害。I have a terrible headache/stomachache/toothache.

7. 那里很痛。It's painful.

8. 那里受伤了！That hurts!

9. 请别动！您的肋骨可能骨折了。Please don't move! Your rib might be broken.

10. 我立刻去叫人来帮忙。请别动他。I'll get help immediately. Please don't move him.

11. 我去叫医生/救护车。I'll call the doctor/ambulance.

12. 很快就会有人来帮忙了，女士。Help is on the way, madam.

13. 一切都会好起来的。Everything will be alright.

14. 别担心，有我呢。Don't worry. Leave it to me.

15. 您是否需要一些阿司匹林/止痛药/绷带/胶布/药棉？Do you need some aspirin/painkillers/bandages/plasters/absorbent cotton?

16. 您现在感觉好些了吗？Are you feeling better now?

客人遗失物品 Guest Lost Items

1. 我的包被偷了，护照还在里面呢！My bag was stolen, and my passport was in it.

2. 我对此深表遗憾，先生。I'm sorry to hear that, sir.

3. 您最后一次见到它是在什么时候、什么地方呢？Would you tell us when and

where you last saw it?

4. 您能不能描述一下它是什么样子呢？Could you describe it, please?

5. 先生，我帮您报警，好吗？Shall I call the police for you, sir?

6. 你们能做的就只有这些吗？Is that all you can do?

7. 我要见你们经理，我要求马上见他。Get me your manager. I want to speak to him right now.

8. 很抱歉，我们已经提醒过您要小心您的贵重物品了，先生。如果您允许的话，我去为您叫值班经理来。Sorry. I'm afraid we had warned you to mind your valuables, sir. And if you permit, I'll find our duty manager for you.

突发事件 Emergencies

1. 我想和你们经理谈一件紧急的事。I want to talk to your manager about an urgent matter.

2. 他碰到紧急事件时总是保持镇定。He always keeps/stays calm in an emergency.

3. 有一个小时空闲处理紧急事件。There is an hour available for emergency cases.

4. 防止和预防紧急事件方案 Program for Emergency Prevention and Preparedness

5. 高速公路紧急事件与安全系统研究 Study on Superhighway Emergency and Security System

6. 在处理紧急事件时，速度是非常重要的。Speed is of the essence in dealing with an emergency.

7. 蹲下来，尽量不要吸入烟雾。Crouch down and try not to breathe in the smoke.

8. 紧急事件使他的潜能发挥了出来。The emergency brought out his hidden abilities.

9. 有紧急事件发生，所以我们把你的计划暂时搁置。Something urgent has occurred, so we put your project on the back burner temporarily.

10. 它在全世界范围内提供紧急事件应对的培训。It provides emergency preparedness training around the world.

11. 世界卫生组织于1993年公开宣布肺结核紧急事件。The World Health Organization declared TB a public health emergency in 1993.

情景对话 Situational Dialogues

对话1 Dialogue 1 紧急求助 Emergency Help

场景：在酒店紧急求助

Scene：Emergency help at the hotel

S：Staff（员工）　　G：Guest（旅客）

G：我肚子痛得厉害，可能是我吃了太多的海鲜食品。I have a bad stomachache. Maybe I had too much seafood.

S：要不要为您叫一个医生？Shall I call a doctor for you?

G：好的，请快点叫医生来。Yes, please do it and make it quick.

S：对了，先生，请问您的房间号码是多少？By the way, sir, may I have your room number, please?

G：1569 房间。Room 1569.

S：我明白了，先生，在医生到来前，有什么我可以为您做的吗？I see, sir. Before the doctor arrives, is there anything I can do for you?

G：没有，谢谢。No, thanks.

对话2 Dialogue 2 急诊室 Emergency Room

场景：顾客看病。

Scene：A guest is seeing a doctor.

D：Doctor（医生）　G：Guest（顾客）

D：您能告诉我哪儿痛吗？Can you tell me where it hurts?

G：我很高兴他们给你打电话。感觉就像我的胃出了毛病！I am so glad they called you. It feels like something is really wrong with my stomach!

D：我按这里时疼吗？Does it hurt when I press here?

G：主要是我的右边疼得厉害。就是这里！It's mostly on my right side. Right here!

D：您有这种感觉有一段时间了吗？Have you been feeling this way for a while?

G：昨晚晚饭后我开始觉得有点恶心，但是今早开始疼得厉害了！I felt kind of sick last night after dinner, but this morning the pain got really bad!

D：最近是不是吃了什么不常吃的东西？Have you eaten anything unusual lately?

G：没有，我不记得。No, not that I remember.

D：现在我们要带您到急诊室。We are going to take you to the emergency room right now.

G：当我知道是什么问题时，我会感觉好点。谢谢你！I will feel better if I know what the problem is. Thank you.

对话3 Dialogue 3 火灾急救逃生 Emergency Fire Escape

场景：大楼着火逃生方式

Scene：Building fire escape

S：Staff（员工）　G：Guest（旅客）

G：发生了什么？What's happening?

S：大楼着火了。你们需要立即撤离。There is a fire in your building. You need to evacuate immediately.

G：什么？着火吗？我的天啊！我该怎么办呢？请让我出去！What? A fire? Oh, my God! What shall I do? Please get me out of here!

S：别慌！我们会帮您安全离开这栋楼。Don't panic! We'll help you get out of the building safely.

G：我闻到烟味了！I can smell smoke!

S：请按照我的指示去做。用湿毛巾捂住口鼻。安静地走到最近的紧急出口。现在去拿湿毛巾来。Please follow my instructions. Use a wet towel to cover your mouth and nose. Walk quietly to the nearest emergency exit. Now go to get the wet towel.

G：好的。OK.

S：跟我来。Come with me.

G：先生，我得回去拿我的首饰盒。Sir, I need to go back to get my jewelry box.

S：不要带您的私人物品。我们得马上离开这栋楼！Don't take your personal belongings. We need to get out of the building now!

G：天啊！我看到火焰了！Gosh! I can see the flames!

S：蹲下来，尽量不要吸入烟雾。Crouch down and try not to breathe in the smoke.

补充阅读 Supplement Reading

急 救

如果你看见有人晕倒，而你又了解一些急救措施，那很可能会挽救一条生命。通常人们什么都不做，因为他们认为自己的做法可能会害死病人。但是学习些简单的急救措施，你就可以救死扶伤了。

首先，你需要触摸他们的颈动脉，确定是否有脉搏，并大声呼喊来确定他们是无意识了，还是睡着了或者喝醉了。如果没有回应的话，你需要确定他们是死了还是仅仅晕过去了，虽然有时很难分辨清楚。

如果没有明显的脉搏和心脏跳动，那就是没有生命迹象了。此时要立刻叫救护车，并开始心脏复苏以保持血液在大脑和心脏之间流通。把一只手放在他们的前额，慢慢地把头向后倾，同时抬高下颚以确保呼吸顺畅。把手交叉相扣，按住胸腔中心部分上上下下不停地按，直到救护车到达。保持一分钟一百次的频率。你这样做不会伤害到他们，但却能挽救一条生命。

Emergency

If you see someone faint and you know a few things about first aid, it's likely to save a life. Often people don't do anything because they think what they're doing might kill the patient. But by learning a few simple first aid measures, you can save lives.

First, you need to touch their carotid artery to determine if there is a pulse, and shout loudly to see if they are unconscious, asleep, or drunk. If there's no response, you need to determine if they're dead or just passed out, though sometimes it's hard to tell.

If there's no obvious pulse and no beating heart, there's no sign of life. Call an ambulance immediately and start cardiopulmonary resuscitation to keep blood flowing between the brain and heart. Place a hand on their forehead and slowly tilt their head back while raising their lower jaw to ensure smooth breathing. Interlock your hands, and press the center of their chest up and down until the ambulance arrives. Keep it at a rate of 100 beats a minute. You won't hurt them, but you could save a life.

练一练 Activities

一、紧急电话拨号填空题

紧急情况	电话号码
火警	
生病急救	
交通事故	
紧急报警	

二、翻译下列句子

1. 我妻子在浴室摔倒了。她没法站起来。
2. 我头痛得厉害。
3. 您现在感觉好些了吗？
4. 在医生到来前，有什么我可以为您做的吗？
5. 我按这里时疼吗？
6. 别慌！我们会帮您安全离开这栋楼。

Chapter 3 餐饮服务 Food & Beverage Service

餐饮部是酒店非常重要的收入来源。越来越多的酒店经营者认识到，餐饮服务是酒店经营的一个重要因素。在许多大型酒店，餐饮服务带来的收入超过了客房租金。酒店有各种提供餐点和服务的区域，如餐厅、酒吧、自助餐厅、咖啡厅以及客房服务、酒廊服务和宴会服务。

The food and beverage department is a very important revenue source for a hotel. More and more hoteliers come to realize that food and beverage service is a major factor in hotel operation. In many large hotels, it brings in more income than room rentals. There are a number of different areas offering a variety of meals and services within a hotel, such as restaurants, bars, cafeterias and coffee shops as well as room service, lounge service and banquet service.

酒店餐饮部主要负责制定和执行餐饮策略和菜单、食材采购和库存管理、餐厅及其设施的运营管理，以及宴会和会议等特殊场合的餐饮安排。酒店餐饮部是酒店经营的核心之一，它不仅提供了美食和饮品，还为客人提供了舒适和愉快的用餐体验，同时为酒店的价值和声誉做出了重要贡献。

The food and beverage department is primarily responsible for formulating and implementing catering strategies and menus, food procurement and inventory management, operation and management of restaurants and their facilities, and catering arrangements for special occasions such as banquets and conferences. The hotel food and beverage department is one of the core components of hotel operations, providing not only delicious food and beverages but also a comfortable and enjoyable dining experience for guests. It also contributes to the value enhancement and reputation of the hotel.

餐饮部 Food &Beverage Department
- 中餐服务 Chinese Food Service
- 西餐服务 Western Food Service
- 宴会服务 Banquet Service
- 自助餐 Buffet
- 酒吧服务 Bar Service

Unit 1　订餐和领位 Reservations and Seating Guests

导言 Preview

餐厅预订包括电话预订和现场预订。

Restaurant reservations include phone reservations and in-person reservations.

电话预订时，要做到以下几点：①电话铃响三声之内接听电话，用热情礼貌的语言向客人表示欢迎。②仔细倾听客人讲话，详细询问客人预订的具体信息，比如人数、就餐时间、餐标、宾客姓名、联系电话，记录时内容要准确，详细注明客人的要求。③向客人复述记录下的预订内容，以获客人确认。④礼貌道别，待客人挂断电话后方可挂电话。

For phone reservations, the following points should be taken into consideration: ①Answer the phone within three rings and warmly welcome the guest with polite language. ②Carefully listen to the guest's speech, and ask detailed questions about the reservation, such as the number of people, dining time, menu options, guest's name, and contact information. It is important to accurately record the information and note the guest's specific requirements. ③Repeat the recorded reservation details to the guest to ensure confirmation. ④Politely say goodbye and hang up the phone after the guest has ended the call.

如果是现场预订，要做到看到宾客来时，欢迎并请宾客入座。然后询问宾客姓名，以姓名称呼宾客。耐心向客人询问预订的人数、就餐时间、偏好、联系电话，进行详细记录。尽量满足宾客要求，向宾客介绍餐厅的特色。把记录内容向客人复述，以获取客人确认。道别时要向客人表示感谢，并送行。

For in-person reservations, when a guest arrives, welcome him or her to have a seat. Then, ask for the guest's name and address him or her by the surname. Patiently inquire about the number of people, dining time, preferences, and contact information, and make detailed notes. Try to accommodate the guest's requests, and introduce the restaurant's specialties. Repeat the reservation details to the guest for confirmation. When bidding farewell, express gratitude to the guest and see him or her off.

餐厅领位步骤
Procedures of Seating Guests

问候客人 Greet guests
↓
问客人信息 Ask guests about their information
↓
- 已预订 Guests who have booked → 确认信息（姓名、电话、房号）Confirm the information(name/phone number/room number) → 领位 Lead guests to the booked table
- 未预订 Guests who have not booked
  - 安排餐桌 Arrange the table → 领位 Direct guests to their seats
  - 无空桌安排等候区 Arrange a waiting area if there is no table available → 尽快安排 Seat guests as soon as the table is available

↓
递菜单 Present the menu to guests

词库 Word Bank

餐厅类型 Type of restaurant			
汉语 Chinese	英语 English	汉语 Chinese	英语 English
中餐厅 zhōng cān tīng	Chinese Food Restaurant	西餐厅 xī cān tīng	Western Food Restaurant
自助餐 zì zhù cān	buffet	大堂吧 dà táng bā	lobby bar
行政酒廊 xíng zhèng jiǔ láng	executive lounge	宴会厅 yàn huì tīng	banquet hall
酒吧 jiǔ bā	bar	快餐 kuài cān	fast food
咖啡厅 kā fēi tīng	coffee shop		
常用词汇 Common vocabulary			
汉语 Chinese	英语 English	汉语 Chinese	英语 English
确认 què rèn	confirm	标准 biāo zhǔn	standard
以……名义 yǐ……míng yì	under the name of	活动 huó dòng	event
传统的 chuán tǒng de	traditional	领位 lǐng wèi	seat
迎候 yíng hòu	greeting	预订 yù dìng	reserve
空桌 kòng zhuō	table available	吃饭 chī fàn	dine

常用句型 Useful Expressions

常见服务用语 Common Service Phrases

1. 您好,花园餐厅,我可以帮您吗？Hello, Garden Restaurant, may I help you?

2. 我们中餐厅在早上6点30分开门,晚上11点关门。Our Chinese restaurant opens at 6:30 a.m. and closes at 11 p.m.

3. 你们一共几个人？How many people are there in your party?

4. 请问您的姓名和电话是什么？May I have your name and telephone number, please?

5. 我们下午5:30开门,接受点菜最后的时间是晚上9:30。We open at 5:30 p.m., and we take last orders at 9:30 p.m.

6. 先生,请问您想什么时候用餐？What time would you like your table, sir?

7. 好的,先生,我将为您预订晚8点的两人餐桌,请问您的姓名和房号是什么？Fine, I'll reserve a table for two at 8 p.m., sir. May I have your name and room number, please?

8. 您为谁预订？Who's the reservation for?

9. 我们期待您尽早光临。We look forward to having you with us soon.

10. 对不起,我们餐厅预订已满。I'm sorry. The restaurant's reservation is full.

11. 我们晚餐的开餐时间是下午5点到晚11点。We are open from 5:00 p.m. until 11:00 p.m. for dinner.

12. 我们咖啡厅24小时营业。We open 24 hours in the coffee shop.

13. 对不起,今晚6点餐厅的预订已满了,不过我们可以在晚7:30给您安排一张餐桌,您是否愿意等到那时？I'm sorry. There aren't any tables left for 6:00 p.m., but we can give you a table at 7:30 p.m. Would you like to wait till then?

14. 我们已经接到了许多预订,尽管我不能向您保证什么,但请相信我会尽力帮您,戴维斯先生,希望您能理解。We have already received many bookings and though I cannot guarantee anything, please be assured that I'll try my best, Mr. Davis. I hope you'll understand.

15. 您喜欢什么菜？What kind of dishes do you like?

16. 您打算每个人的用餐标准是多少？How much would you like to pay for dining budget each person?

17. 我们餐厅有每人50元、80元、100元的标准,不含酒水,您想订哪种？There are dining standards of 50 yuan, 80 yuan, 100 yuan per person, excluding drinks. Which one would you prefer?

宾客订餐 Guest Reservation for Dining

1. 我今晚要请几个朋友吃饭，如何订餐？I'm going to invite some friends to dinner tonight, and how should I make a reservation?

2. 我想预订今晚的座位。I'd like to make a reservation for tonight.

3. 马先生，今晚7点30分，一张三个人的桌位。A table for three this evening at 7:30 for Mr. Ma.

4. 我想订一张四人桌，12月23日，也就是下星期三。I would like to book a table for four for next Wednesday, December 23rd.

5. 请以王林先生的名义订餐。Please book it under the name of Mr. Wang Lin.

6. 我想预订一个桌位用餐。I'd like to reserve a table for dinner.

7. 有没有可能订靠近窗子的桌位？Is there any chance of getting a table by the window?

8. 我们想要坐在非吸烟区。We'd like to sit in the nonsmoking area.

9. 我们想要吸烟区的桌位。We'd like a table in the smoking area.

10. 如果可能的话，我想要安静的角落。I'd like a quiet corner, if possible.

11. 这里都有哪几种价格？What are the prices here?

12. 我想预订一张五人桌。I'd like to reserve a table for five, please.

迎接已预订的客人 Receive the Guest with a Reservation

1. 请问您有预订吗？Do you have a reservation?

2. 请问您贵姓？May I have your name, please?

3. 我们正恭候您的光临。We are expecting you.

4. 恐怕您预订的餐位还没有准备好。I'm afraid the table you reserved is not ready yet.

5. 因为您没有按照预订的时间来，所以我们将座位给另一位客人了。I'm afraid that we let another guest sit at your table since you did not arrive at the reserved time.

6. 您介意等会儿，或者去另外一桌吗？Would you mind waiting a moment or would you prefer another table?

迎接未预订的客人 Receive the Guest without a Reservation

1. 我们很快就会安排您入座。We can seat you very soon.

2. 可能需要10分钟才有空位。It may take about 10 minutes before a table is available.

3. 您再等5分钟好吗？Could you wait for another 5 minutes, please?

4. 请您排队等空位好吗？Could you wait in line until a table is available, please?

5. 很抱歉让您久等了。I'm sorry to have kept you waiting.

6. 这张餐台已经预订了7点的时间段。This table is reserved for 7 p.m.

引领入座 Seat Guests

1. 一共几位呢？How many persons, please?

2. 您喜欢坐在哪里？Where would you prefer to sit?

3. 我来为您领位。I'll show you to your table.

4. 这张桌可以吗？Is this table fine? / How about this table?

5. 服务员很快会来为您点菜。A waiter/waitress will come soon to take your order.

6. 您有餐券/早餐券吗？Do you have a meal/breakfast voucher?

7. 请跟我来，先生/女士。Please follow me, sir/madam.

8. 请这边走，先生/女士。This way please, sir/madam.

9. 请留意脚下，先生/女士。Please mind your steps, sir/madam.

10. 对不起，先生/女士。我们现在没有空餐桌，请您在酒吧（大堂）稍等一下，好吗？一有空桌，我们会立即通知您。I am sorry, sir/madam. We do not have a free table now. Would you like to wait for a moment in the bar(lounge)? We will inform you immediately when a table is available.

11. 请问您对这张餐桌满意吗，先生/女士？Is this table fine with you, sir/madam?

12. 这是菜单，先生/女士。Here is the menu for you, sir/madam.

13. 如果您在用餐时有什么问题，请告诉我。If you have any questions during your meal, please call me.

14. 对不起，先生/女士，您介意随我去另一张餐桌吗？I am sorry, sir/madam. Would you care to follow me to another table?

15. 您是愿意靠窗坐呢，还是靠门坐？Which would you prefer, by the window or near the door?

16. 对不起，先生/女士，所有靠窗的餐桌都满了。I am sorry, sir/madam. All the tables by the window are occupied.

餐桌安排 Arrange a Table

1. 恐怕没办法让你们坐同一桌。I'm afraid we can't seat you at the same table.

2. 你们是否介意分开坐？Would you mind sitting separately?

3. 要不要给您的孩子拿一张高椅呢？Would you like a high chair for your child?

4. 恐怕那张桌子已经有人预订了。I'm afraid that table is reserved.

5. 您介意和别人同桌吗？Would you mind sharing a table?

6. 别的客人想跟您共享这张桌子。Some other guests wish to join this table.

7. 您介意移过去一点儿吗？Would you mind moving over a little?

8. 另外一位客人想坐在柜台边。您可以挪过去一点儿吗？Another guest wishes to sit at the counter. Could you move over a little bit, please?

9. 抱歉，先生，我可以从这儿过去吗？Excuse me, sir, but may I pass?

10. 您可以把椅子拉近桌子一些吗？Could you move your chair closer to the table,

please?

情景对话 Situational Dialogues

对话1 Dialogue 1 个人预订 Individual Reservation

场景：王先生想预订中餐厅的餐位。

Scene：Mr. Wang wants to reserve a table at a Chinese restaurant.

G：Guest（客人）　　C：Clerk（餐厅工作人员）

G：嗨，我想预订今晚在你们中餐厅的位置。Hi, I'd like to make a reservation at your Chinese restaurant for tonight.

C：当然，您几位？Of course, how many people are there in your party?

G：我们有四个人。There will be four of us.

C：好的。您想什么时候来？Great. What time would you like to come?

G：大约晚上7点，可以吗？Around 7 p.m., is that OK?

C：好的，可以。请问您的名字是什么？Yes, that's fine. May I have your name, please?

G：我叫王林。It's Wang Lin.

C：谢谢您，王先生。您的预订已确认。我们期待今晚见到您！Thank you, Mr. Wang. Your reservation is confirmed. We look forward to seeing you tonight!

G：谢谢。再见！Thank you. See you later!

对话2 Dialogue 2 团队预订 Group Reservation

场景：导游想为旅游团队预订餐位。

Scene：The tour guide wants to reserve a table for the tour group.

T：Tour Guide（导游）　　C：Clerk（餐厅工作人员）

C：您好，花园餐厅，我可以帮您吗？Hello, Garden Restaurant, may I help you?

T：我想预订今晚的餐位。I'd like to make a reservation for tonight.

C：好的。您团队有多少人？OK. How many people are there in your tour group?

T：我们有25个人。We have 25 people.

C：好的。您计划什么时候用餐？Alright. When do you plan to have the meal?

T：我们打算晚上7点用餐，有包间可以预订吗？We plan to have the meal at 7 p.m. Do you have private rooms available for reservation?

C：抱歉，今晚没有包间了。我们能为您预留一张大桌子。请问您的名字是什么？I'm sorry. There are no private rooms available tonight. We can reserve a large table for you. May I have your name, please?

105

T：我叫李明。My name is Li Ming.

C：谢谢您，李明先生。您的预订已确认。请问您有任何特殊饮食要求吗？Thank you, Mr. Li Ming. Your reservation is confirmed. Do you have any special dietary requirements?

T：是的，我们有几位素食者和一些对海鲜过敏的人。Yes, we have a few vegetarians and some people who are allergic to seafood.

C：我们会为他们准备合适的餐点。谢谢您的告知。We will prepare suitable meals for them. Thank you for letting us know.

T：非常感谢！我们期待今晚的用餐。Thank you very much! We are looking forward to tonight's meal.

C：再次感谢您的预订。Thank you again for your reservation.

对话3 Dialogue 3 接待预订客人 Receiving the Guest with a Reservation

场景：王先生已经预订了餐位。现在和他的朋友到达餐厅。

Scene：Mr. Wang has reserved the table. Now he and his friend arrive at the restaurant.

W：Waiter（服务员）　G：Guest（宾客）

W：先生、女士，晚上好。欢迎来到花园餐厅，有什么可以帮您的吗？Good evening, madam and sir. Welcome to the Garden Restaurant. May I help you?

G：是的。Yes, please.

W：请问您有预订吗？Did you make a reservation?

G：是的，我昨天下午以王林先生的名义预订了一张桌。Yes, I reserved a table yesterday afternoon, in the name of Mr. Wang Lin.

W：请稍候，我查一下我们的预订记录。哦，是的，王先生，我们恭候您的光临。我们给您留了一张靠窗的桌子，请这边走。这张桌子可以吗？Just a moment, please. I'll have a look at our reservation book. Oh, yes, Mr. Wang. We're expecting you. We have a window seat reserved for you. This way please. Will this table be fine?

G：可以。That's OK.

W：请坐。这是菜单。我一会儿为您点菜。Please take a seat. Here is the menu. I'll take your order a moment later.

G：好的，谢谢。All right. Thank you.

W：不用谢。能为您服务是我们的荣幸。You are welcome. It's our pleasure to serve you.

对话4 Dialogue 4 接待未预订客人 Receiving the Guest without a Reservation

场景：王林夫妇去餐厅用餐，但未提前预订。餐厅服务人员接待了他们并带他们去一张空座。

Scene：Mr. Wang Lin and his wife go to the restaurant to have dinner. But they have no reservation. The waiter receives them and leads them to a table that is available.

W：Waiter（服务员）　　G：Guest（宾客）

W：您好，欢迎来到我们的餐厅！请问您是否预约了用餐？Hello, welcome to our restaurant! Did you make a reservation for dining?

G：抱歉，我们没有预约。No. I'm afraid we haven't.

W：没关系，先生。是两位吗？Never mind, sir. A table for two?

G：是的。Yes.

W：非常抱歉，今天我们的预约桌已经全部预订完毕。不过，我们还有一些非预约区域的座位，我会尽量安排给您。请稍等片刻，让我去找一个适合您的位置。I'm sorry, but all our reserved tables have been booked for today. However, we still have some seats available in the non-reserved section, and I will try to accommodate you. Please wait a moment while I find a suitable spot for you.

G：谢谢。我希望能找到一个空桌子用餐。Thank you. I hope to find an available table for dining.

W：非常抱歉让您久等了。现在我们有一张位于角落的桌子，是非预约区域的最后一张桌子。您愿意坐那里吗？I'm so sorry to keep you waiting. We have a table in the corner available, and it's the last table in the non-reserved section. Would you like to sit there?

G：好吧，既然没有其他选择，我可以接受。Alright, since there are no other options, I can accept that.

W：非常感谢您的理解。请这边走。Thank you very much for your understanding. This way, please.

G：好的，谢谢。OK, thanks.

W：先来点喝的怎么样？Would you like to have a drink first?

G：好的，先来两杯啤酒吧。Yes. We'll have two beers.

W：当然可以，先生。Certainly, sir.

G：请拿菜单给我们，可以吗？Can we have the menu, please?

W：菜单在这里，先生。我稍后再来取您的点菜单。Here's the menu, sir. I'll be back to take your order in a minute.

补充阅读 Supplement Reading

膳食金字塔常被用作我们日常饮食的指南，让我们了解每天应食用多少种不同的营养食物以保持健康的生活方式。

107

膳食金字塔分为五层。第一层是五谷类；第二层是蔬果类；第三层是畜禽肉蛋类；第四层是坚果及蛋白质类；第五层，也就是最上面的一层是油盐糖类。当然食物金字塔只是一个饮食的参考标准，在日常生活中可以根据自己的独特需求和饮食功能做修改。总之，我们一定要做到均衡饮食。

The food pyramid is often used as a guideline for us to see how many servings of each food should be eaten each day in order to maintain a healthy lifestyle.

The food pyramid is divided into five layers. The first layer is grains; the second layer is fruits and vegetables; the third layer is meat and eggs; the fourth layer is nuts and protein-rich foods; and the fifth layer, which is the topmost one, is oil, salt, and sugar. Of course, the food pyramid is only a referencing standard. You can modify it for yourself in your daily life, depending on your own singular needs and dietary functions. In short, we must have a balanced diet.

练一练 Activities

一、连线题

（1）中餐厅　　　　　　　　（A）buffet

（2）西餐厅　　　　　　　　（B）lobby bar

（3）快餐厅　　　　　　　　（C）Western Food Restaurant

（4）宴会厅　　　　　　　　（D）Chinese Food Restaurant

（5）自助餐　　　　　　　　（E）coffee shop

（6）咖啡厅　　　　　　　　（F）banquet hall

（7）大堂吧　　　　　　　　（G）fast food restaurant

二、排列下列对话的顺序

（A）请问您的名字是什么？

（B）我们有25个人。

（C）好的。您计划什么时候用餐？

（D）是的，我们有几位素食者和一些对海鲜过敏的人。

（E）我们打算晚上7点用餐，有包间可以预订吗？

（F）好的。您团队有多少人？

（G）我们会为他们准备合适的餐点。谢谢您的告知。

（H）我们也是！再次感谢您的预订。

（I）谢谢您，李明先生。您的预订已确认。请问您有任何特殊饮食要求吗？

（J）我想预订今天的晚餐。

（K）您好，花园餐厅，我可以帮您吗？

（L）非常感谢！我们期待今晚的用餐。

（M）我叫李明。

（N）抱歉，今晚没有包间了。我们能为您预留一张大桌子。

Unit 2　点菜 Taking Order

导言 Preview

点菜服务流程与规范 Process and Standards of Taking Order

流程 Process	规范 Standards
递上菜单 Hand over the Menu to Guests	●客人入座后，服务员询问客人需要的茶水类型；After guests are seated, the waiter asks them what kind of tea they would like to order; ●按"女士优先，先宾后主"的原则从右边为客人斟上茶水；Pour the tea for guests from the right side according to the principle of "ladies first, guests first, then hosts"; ●用双手从客人右侧将菜单送至客人手中。Deliver the menu with both hands from the right side of guests.
推荐 & 介绍酒店菜品 Recommend & Introduce Dishes	●在客人翻看菜单时，应及时向客人简单介绍菜单上的菜，回答客人的询问；When guests are looking through the menu, the waiter should briefly introduce the dishes on the menu to them in time and answer their inquiries; ●介绍厨师长今日特别推荐的菜品、其他的特色菜、畅销菜和高档菜等菜品；Introduce the dishes that the head-chef especially recommends today, other specialties, best sellers and upscale dishes, etc.; ●介绍其样式、味道、温度和特点。Introduce their style, flavor, temperature and characteristics.
接受点菜 Take Order	●在点菜单上记下日期、台号、就餐人数等；Write down the date, table number, and the number of people who dine and so on on the menu; ●客人点菜时，准确地记录菜名；When guests order, the waiter records the names of dishes accurately; ●对于特殊菜品，应介绍其特殊之处，并问清客人所需火候、配料及调料等；For special dishes, the waiter should introduce their special features and ask guests about the required heat, ingredients and seasonings; ●客人有特殊要求，应在点菜单上清楚注明，并告知传菜服务员。Special requirements from guests should be clearly indicated in the order, and the service staff should be informed.

续 表

流程 Process	规范 Standards
复述点菜内容 Repeat the Content of the Dishes	●点菜完毕后，服务员应清楚地重复一遍所点菜品内容，并请客人确认；After ordering, the waiter should clearly repeat the content of the dishes ordered and ask guests to confirm it; ●点菜单的右上角写明当时的时间；Write down the time in the upper right corner of the menu; ●收回菜单并向客人致谢，说明大致的等候时间。Take back the menu and thank guests, indicating the approximate waiting time.
分送点菜单 Send the Menu Respectively	●将点菜单分别送给收银处、厨房、传菜员和值台服务员处。Send the menu to the cashier's desk, kitchen, dish bearer, and table attendant respectively.

词库 Word Bank

餐具类型 Type of tableware			
汉语 Chinese	英语 English	汉语 Chinese	英语 English
筷子 kuài zi	chopsticks	碗 wǎn	bowl
刀 dāo	knife	叉 chā	fork
勺子 sháo zi	spoon	杯子 bēi zi	cup
酒杯 jiǔ bēi	wine cup	盘子 pán zi	plate
常用词汇 Common vocabulary			
汉语 Chinese	英语 English	汉语 Chinese	英语 English
服务员 fú wù yuán	waiter/waitress	菜单 cài dān	menu
点菜 diǎn cài	take order	早餐 zǎo cān	breakfast
晚餐 wǎn cān	dinner	午餐 wǔ cān	lunch
推荐 tuī jiàn	recommend	特色菜 tè sè cài	specialty
套餐 tào cān	table d'hôte	零点 líng diǎn	à la carte
自助 zì zhù	buffet	过敏 guò mǐn de	allergic

常用句型 Useful Expressions

询问是否可以开始点菜 Ask if Guests Want to Start Ordering

1. 这是我们的菜单，先生。我们的服务员等会会过来给您点菜。Here is the menu, sir. The waiter will be here to take your order.

2. 请慢慢选择，我一会儿来为您点菜。Please take your time. I'll be back to take your

order.

3. 打扰一下，先生。请问现在可以给您点菜了吗？Excuse me, sir. May I take your order now?

4. 您准备好点菜了吗，先生？Are you ready to order, sir?

5. 请问您是准备好点菜了还是需要再等一会儿呢？Are you ready to order or you need another minute?

询问 & 提供细节 Ask for Details & Give Details

1. 您选择套餐还是点餐呢？Would you like to have table d'hôte, or à la carte?

2. 我们有自助式和点菜式，您喜欢哪一种？We have both buffet-style and à la carte dishes, and which would you prefer?

3. 为什么不尝一下我们的自助晚餐呢？Why not try our buffet dinner?

4. 您的牛排要几分熟呢？How would you like your steak done?

5. 您点的煎蛋是不是单面煎？Would you like your fried eggs sunny-side up?

6. 请问您的牛排上面浇什么汁呢？Which sauce would you like for the steak?

7. 请问您有什么忌口的吗？Is there anything you can't eat?

8. 先生，请问您对某些食物过敏吗？Are you allergic to any particular food, sir?

9. 它能帮您开胃。It will stimulate the appetite.

10. 您对饮食有什么特别要求吗？Do you have any special dietary requirements?

11. 请在汤里加点胡椒粉。Please add some pepper to the soup.

12. 晚饭我想吃点清淡的/香脆的/酸的/甜的。I'd like something light/crisp/sour/sweet for dinner.

13. 我们有特殊食谱，可以满足不同的饮食需要。We offer special menus for different diets.

14. 我们有很多素菜可供您选择。We have a wide range of vegetarian dishes for your choice.

15. 您更喜欢哪种口味，甜的还是辣的？Which flavor would you prefer, sweet or hot?

16. 也许苏菜会合您的口味。Maybe Jiangsu Cuisine will suit you.

17. 请问您是要大份的还是小份的？Would you like large or small portions?

18. 您希望记在您酒店的账单上吗？Would you like to put it on your hotel bill?

情景对话 Situational Dialogues

对话1 Dialogue 1 中式点餐服务 Taking Chinese Food Orders

场景：几位外国女士想品尝中国菜。服务员正在为她们点餐。

Scene: Some foreign ladies want to taste Chinese dishes. A waiter serves them.

W: Waiter（服务员）　　G: Guest（客人）

W: 晚上好，女士们，请问你们有预订吗？Good evening, ladies. Do you have a reservation?

G: 有，我是H夫人。Yes, I'm Mrs. H.

W: 这边请，H夫人。这是你们的座位，这里可以吗？This way, please, Mrs. H. Here is your table. Is this all right?

G: 谢谢，非常好。Thank you. It's nice, indeed.

W: 不客气，这是菜单。（过了一会儿）你们准备好点菜了吗，女士们？My pleasure. Here's the menu. (After a while) Are you ready to order now, ladies?

G: 是的。我们想点一些中国菜，但我们对中国菜不熟悉。Yes. We would like to order some Chinese food, but we are not familiar with Chinese cuisine.

W: 一般来说，粤菜清淡；川菜麻辣；鲁菜咸脆；而上海菜浓油赤酱。您更喜欢哪种口味？Generally speaking, Cantonese Cuisine is light; Sichuan Cuisine is spicy and hot; Shandong Cuisine is salty and crispy; and Shanghai dishes are rich in oil and soy sauce. Which flavor would you prefer?

G: 我们晚餐想吃点儿辣的，你有什么建议？Well, we'd like something spicy for dinner. What do you recommend?

W: 如果您想吃辣的，川菜是相当美味的。我们餐厅的川菜就很有名。我推荐麻婆豆腐和宫保鸡丁。它们是众所周知的美食。Sichuan food is quite delicious if you really want something hot. And our restaurant is famous for Sichuan food. I recommend Mapo Tofu and Kung Pao Chicken. They're well-known delicacies.

G: 听起来不错，谢谢。我们全要了。It sounds very nice, thank you. We'll take them both.

W: 糖醋脆皮鱼怎么样？这是我们的特色菜。很多客人都是慕名而来。How about Sweet and Sour Crispy Fish? It is our specialty. Many guests come here to try that.

G: 好的，我们也要了。有蔬菜吗？OK. We'll get that as well. Are there any vegetables?

W: 现在正是芦笋上市的季节。要尝尝吗？Asparagus is in season now. Would you like to have a try?

G: 好的，你有什么汤推荐？Sure. What soup do you recommend?

W: 我推荐主厨特制的酸辣汤。I suggest the chef's speciality: Sour and Spicy Soup.

G: 我们要这个。We'll have that.

W: 还需要什么吗，女士？Anything else, madam?

G：不用了，谢谢。No, thanks.

W：要我给各位拿刀叉吗？Shall I bring you some knives and forks?

G：不用了，谢谢。筷子就行了。No, thanks. The chopsticks will do.

W：我可以重复您点的菜吗？宫保鸡丁、麻婆豆腐、糖醋脆皮鱼、清炒芦笋、酸辣汤。是这样吗？May I repeat your order? Kung Pao Chicken, Mapo Tofu, Sweet and Sour Crispy Fish, Stir-fried Asparagus and Sour and Spicy Soup. Is that right?

G：是的，谢谢。Yes, thank you.

W：不客气。我马上回来。You are welcome. I'll be right back.

对话2 Dialogue 2 西餐点餐服务 Taking Western Food Orders

场景：琼斯一家人今晚想吃西餐。他们来到一家餐馆吃西餐，但他们没有提前预订。

Scene：The Jones want to have Western food this evening. They come to a restaurant to have a Western dinner. But they have no reservation.

H：Hostess（领位员）　　G：Guest（客人）　　W：Waiter（服务员）

H：晚上好。欢迎光临我们的餐厅。您预订了吗？Good evening. Welcome to our restaurant. Have you made a reservation?

G：没有。No, we haven't.

H：您是三位吗？Three people?

G：是的。Right.

H：这边请。这张桌子怎么样？This way, please. How is this table?

G：可以。It's fine.

H：好的。请坐。Excellent. Take your seat, please.

W：晚上好！请问您是准备好点菜了还是需要再等一会儿呢？Good evening. Are you ready to order or you need another minute?

G：有什么特色菜吗？Do you have any specialties?

W：是的，您可以尝尝我们的开胃菜烟熏三文鱼，它非常美味。Yes, you can try our appetizer, smoked salmon. It's very delicious.

G：开胃菜烟熏三文鱼。For an appetizer, smoked salmon.

W：您想点沙拉吗？您想要哪种配料？Do you want to order salad? Which dressing would you like?

G：我想要三份大份的水果沙拉，配醋油沙司调味汁。I'd like three large fruit salads with balsamic and vinaigrette dressing.

W：您点什么汤？What soup would you like?

G：法式鱼汤。Fish soup, in the French style.

W：主菜呢？And for the main course?

G：两份T骨牛排和一份臀部牛排。Two T-bone steaks and a rump steak.

W：牛排要怎么做呢？How would you like your steak done?

G：三分熟。Medium-rare.

W：您想要配什么酱汁？What kind of sauce do you want?

G：黑胡椒蘑菇奶油酱。Black pepper and mushroom cream sauce.

W：需要点儿蔬菜吗？Would you like some vegetables?

G：是的。来份咖喱蔬菜。Yes. The curried vegetables, please.

W：来点儿甜点吗？Anything for dessert?

G：每人一份香草冰激凌。Vanilla ice cream for all.

W：还需要点儿别的吗？Anything else?

G：不，我想这些够了。No, I'm afraid that's all.

对话3 Dialogue 3 儿童餐 About Kids' Meal

场景：一对夫妇为他们的女儿点餐，但是他们对菜单有些疑问。

Scene：A couple wants to order for their daughter, but they have questions about the menu.

C：Couple（夫妇）　W：Waitress（女服务员）

W：您好！需要我帮您看看菜单吗？Hi! Can I help you with the menu?

C：是的，你们有儿童套餐吗？Yes, do you have a kids' meal?

W：当然有。我们的儿童套餐有鸡肉条、炸鱼薯条和小汉堡。Of course. For our kids' meal, we have chicken fingers, fish and chips, and mini burgers.

C：好多油炸食品啊。分量有多大？That's a lot of deep-fried food. How big are the portions?

W：都是儿童分量的。They're all kid-sized.

C：好的，汉堡套餐有什么？OK. What does the burger come with?

W：还配有果汁和甜点。It also comes with juice and dessert.

C：太好了。能不能不要生菜？我女儿很挑食。Great. Can you skip the lettuce? My daughter is a picky eater.

W：没问题。我马上给您送过来。No problem. I'll be right back with your order.

对话4 Dialogue 4 点酒水 Taking a Wine Order

场景：服务员正在为一对夫妇点酒水。

Scene：A waiter is taking and serving a wine order for a couple.

W：Waiter（服务员）　G：Guest（客人）

W：晚上好，唐先生、唐太太，二位想好了要点什么酒吗？Good evening, Mr. and

Mrs. Tang. Have you decided which wine you would like?

　　G1：我想要歌海娜配我点的牛排。I think this Grenache would go with the steak that I ordered.

　　W：可以的，但梅洛酒配菲力牛排可能更好。It would, but maybe the Merlot wines would go better with the Filet.

　　G1：太棒了，那我们就要这个了。Great! We will go with that one then.

　　W：您想为开胃菜配一些白葡萄酒吗？Do you want to order a white wine with your starter as well?

　　G2：不用了，刚才点的红酒就行了。No, thank you, just the red.

　　W：好的，这是2000年的波尔多葡萄酒（把酒瓶拿给唐先生看）。Certainly. Here is the Chateau Bordeaux 2000 (Show the wine bottle to Mr. Tang.)

　　G1：啊，好酒！打开让我尝尝。Ah, a good vintage! Go ahead and open it so I can taste it.

　　W：请品尝，先生。Please taste the wine, sir.

　　G1：嗯，闻起来很香，口感也不错！Yes, a nice bouquet when I smell it, and it tastes lovely.

　　W：夫人，我可以为您斟酒了吗？Would you like me to pour the wine now, madam?

　　G2：谢谢，但我想等到我的菜上来再倒吧。Thank you, but I think I'll wait until my main course is served.

　　W：好的，那您呢，先生？Very good. How about you, sir?

　　G1：不不，我不想等，把酒倒上吧！No, I don't want to wait. Pour away!

　　W：好的，愿意效劳！Very good, sir. My pleasure!

补充阅读 Supplement Reading

　　随着线上到线下（O2O）服务的深入发展，餐饮服务与互联网的联系越来越紧密。2021年，中国使用网上点餐服务的人数达到创纪录的5.44亿。在餐馆和街头小贩那里，消费者可以通过扫描二维码轻松付款，而不用再支付现金。用餐者在用餐或排队等位时，可以通过餐厅应用小程序阅读菜单并点餐。送餐服务蓬勃发展不仅是因为互联网的快速发展和数字技术的广泛运用，还有物流成本低以及人们对在家做饭的兴趣下降的原因。除了消费者行为的变化，越来越多的餐饮供应商利用基于大数据的智能管理系统，帮助他们更好地了解消费者的喜好，并做出相应的改变。

　　With the deep development of online-to-offline services, the connection between catering services and the Internet is becoming increasingly closer. In 2021, the number of people using online food ordering services in China reached a record of 544 million. At restaurants and street vendors, consumers can easily make payments by scanning QR codes without the need for cash.

When dining in or waiting in line, customers can read menus and place orders through restaurant application mini-programs. The booming delivery service industry is not only due to the rapid development of the Internet and the widespread use of digital technology, but also because of the low logistics costs and a decrease in people's interest in cooking at home. In addition to changes in consumer behavior, an increasing number of catering suppliers are utilizing big data-based intelligent management systems to better understand consumer preferences and make corresponding changes.

练一练 Activities

一、连线题

(1) 筷子　　　　　　(A) wine cup

(2) 勺子　　　　　　(B) recommend

(3) 碗　　　　　　　(C) specialty

(4) 酒杯　　　　　　(D) chopsticks

(5) 特色菜　　　　　(E) allergic

(6) 过敏　　　　　　(F) bowl

(7) 推荐　　　　　　(G) spoon

二、翻译下列句子

1. 我们有自助式和点菜式，您喜欢哪一种？
2. 请在汤里加点胡椒粉。
3. 请慢慢选择，我一会儿来为您点菜。
4. 您准备好点菜了吗，先生？
5. 您的牛排要几分熟呢？
6. 我们有很多素菜可供您选择。
7. 先生，请问您对某些食物过敏吗？

Unit 3　中餐服务 Chinese Food Service

导言 Preview

中餐服务全流程 The Whole Process of Chinese Food Service

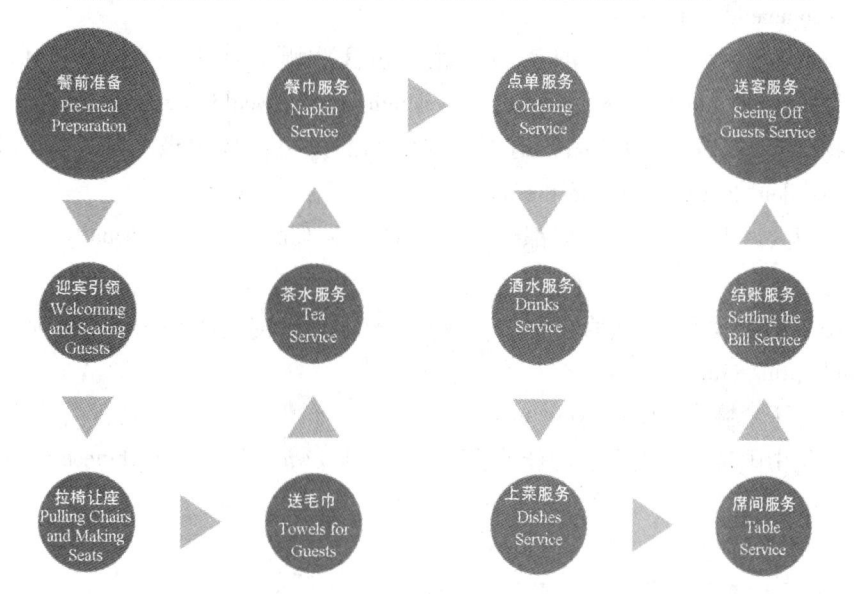

餐前准备 Pre-meal Preparation → 餐巾服务 Napkin Service → 点单服务 Ordering Service → 送客服务 Seeing Off Guests Service

↓ ↑ ↑ ↑

迎宾引领 Welcoming and Seating Guests → 茶水服务 Tea Service → 酒水服务 Drinks Service → 结账服务 Settling the Bill Service

↓ ↑ ↑ ↑

拉椅让座 Pulling Chairs and Making Seats → 送毛巾 Towels for Guests → 上菜服务 Dishes Service → 席间服务 Table Service

词库 Word Bank

烹饪方法 Way of cooking			
汉语 Chinese	英语 English	汉语 Chinese	英语 English
炒 chǎo	stir-fry	烤 kǎo	bake
炸 zhá	fry	炖 dùn	stew
煮 zhǔ	boil	熏 xūn	smoke
拌 bàn	mix	蒸 zhēng	steam
常用词汇 Common vocabulary			
汉语 Chinese	英语 English	汉语 Chinese	英语 English
中国菜 zhōng guó cài	Chinese dishes	辣的 là de	spicy
广东的 guǎng dōng de	Cantonese	佳肴 jiā yáo	delicacy
菜系 cài xì	cuisine	茶 chá	tea
应季 yìng jì	in season	过季 guò jì	out of season
面条 miàn tiáo	noodle	传统的 chuán tǒng de	traditional

常用句型 Useful Expressions

1. 能为我们介绍一下这道菜吗？Could you tell me about this dish?

2. 这是我们第一次来中国，你可以给我们推荐一些中国菜吗？This is our first trip to China. Will you recommend us some Chinese dishes?

3. 我不了解中餐，您能给我推荐一下吗？I don't know much about Chinese food, so can you recommend something?

4. 我们有粤菜、川菜、沪菜和京菜，您喜欢哪一种呢？We serve Cantonese, Sichuan, Shanghai and Beijing Cuisines, and which cuisine would you prefer?

5. 我们不喜欢吃辛辣食品，请不要在我们的菜里面放辣椒。We don't like spicy food. Please don't put any chili in the meal.

6. 中国人过生日的时候一般都吃什么？What do Chinese people usually have on their birthdays?

7. 您要的蟹是清蒸还是姜葱炒？Would you like your crabs steamed or fried with ginger and spring onion?

8. 祝您用餐愉快！Enjoy your meal!

9. 它是中国菜里一道有名的佳肴。It's a well-known delicacy in Chinese Cuisine.

10. 这道菜色、香、味俱全。It looks good, smells good and tastes good.

11. 这个已经过季了。It's out of season.

12. 这是一道应季菜。It's a dish in season.

13. 做好这道菜大约需要20分钟。It takes about 20 minutes to prepare the dish.

14. 川菜中最有名、最受欢迎的菜是什么？What is the most famous and popular dish in Sichuan Cuisine?

15. 我喜欢麻婆豆腐，它是最有名的川菜之一。I like Mapo Tofu. It is one of the most famous dishes in Sichuan Cuisine.

16. 它是用什么做的？What is it made of?

17. 这么多已经够了。These are enough.

18. 我不习惯用筷子，这里有刀叉吗？I am not used to chopsticks. Do you have knives and forks here?

19. 您觉得今天的菜怎么样？What do you think of the food today?

20. 这是我吃过的最好吃（难吃/奇特/辣）的麻婆豆腐。It is the most delicious (unpalatable/fantastic/spicy) Mapo Tofu that I've ever had.

情景对话 Situational Dialogues

对话1 Dialogue 1 介绍中式早餐 Introducing Chinese Breakfast

场景：在一个提供中式自助早餐的中餐厅里，唐先生端着盘子走在摆满美食的餐桌前。

Scene：In a Chinese restaurant offering a Chinese-style buffet breakfast, Mr. Tang is walking around a dining table laden with a variety of delicious food, holding a plate.

T：Mr. Tang（唐先生）　W：Waiter（服务员）

T：你们这里提供中式自助早餐吗？Do you serve buffet for Chinese breakfast here?

W：是的，先生。有什么需要帮助的吗？Certainly, sir. What can I do for you?

T：我对中式早点不是太了解，能帮我介绍一下吗？I'm not very familiar with Chinese breakfast. Can you introduce it to me?

W：好的。所有的早点都摆在这里。这是鲜奶，那是豆浆。OK. They are all here on the stand. This is fresh milk and that is soybean milk.

T：我想来杯茶。I'd like a cup of tea.

W：好的，这个茶壶装的是红茶，那个茶壶装的是菊花茶。Well, this tea pot is for black tea and that for Chrysanthemum tea.

T：哦，我明白了。菊花茶是花草茶，对吗？Oh, I see. Chrysanthemum tea is herbal tea, isn't it?

W：是的。这边是几种点心。这是红豆包，那是虾丁、笋丁和蘑菇丁包。Yes, it is. And here are several kinds of dim sum. These are steamed bread stuffed with red bean puree, and those are with diced shrimps, bamboo shoots and mushroom.

T：太好了！我两样都要。那这是什么？Great! I'll have both. And what is that?

W：是白菜猪肉馅的炸春卷。It is fried spring rolls stuffed with shredded cabbage and pork.

T：好极了！Terrific!

W：此外，我们还有两种面条。一种是不同卤的汤面，另一种是炒面。Besides, we have two kinds of noodles. One is noodle soup with different dressings and the other is stir-fried noodles.

T：好的。那是麦片吗？I see. Is that cereal?

W：不是，先生。那是中式白粥。您可以配上咸菜。还有皮蛋瘦肉粥。I'm afraid not, sir. That's Chinese plain porridge. You may enjoy it with pickles. Also available is porridge with minced pork and preserved egg.

T：太好了！我什么都要尝尝。Wonderful! I'll taste some of everything here.

W：请慢用！Enjoy your meal!

对话2 Dialogue 2 介绍北京烤鸭 Introducing Beijing Roast Duck

场景：一个外国人走进一家烤鸭店，想品尝一下北京烤鸭。

Scene：A foreigner walks into a roast duck restaurant to try some Beijing Roast Duck.

G：Guest（客人）　　W：Waiter（服务员）

W：欢迎光临我们的餐厅！您好，我是负责您的服务员。您是否对我们的招牌菜——北京烤鸭有所了解呢？Welcome to our restaurant! Hello, I am your waiter. Are you familiar with our signature dish—Beijing Roast Duck?

G：嗯，我听说过北京烤鸭，但是对这道菜的制作和特点还不太清楚。Well, I have heard of Beijing Roast Duck, but I'm not quite familiar with its preparation and characteristics.

W：没问题，我可以为您介绍一下。北京烤鸭是北京传统的名菜之一，以其皮薄肉嫩、色泽红亮而闻名。烤鸭需要经过特别的烹饪过程，先用特制的调料腌制，再放入炉子里慢慢烘烤。No problem, I can introduce it to you. Beijing Roast Duck is one of the traditional and renowned dishes in Beijing, known for its thin and tender skin and bright color. The duck undergoes a special cooking process, first marinated with special seasonings and then slowly roasted in the oven.

G：听起来很有特色。那应该怎么吃呢？That sounds intriguing. How should I eat it?

W：通常，我们会将烤鸭皮切成薄片，配上葱段、黄瓜片和甜面酱，然后将这些材料包在薄饼里，卷起来食用。这样可以最大限度地保持烤鸭的原汁原味和口感。当然，您也可以根据自己的喜好尝试其他食用方式。Usually, we slice the roasted duck skin into thin pieces and serve it with scallions, cucumber slices, and sweet bean sauce. Then they can be wrapped in thin pancakes and enjoyed. You can fully savor the original flavor and texture of the roast duck in this method. Of course, you can also try other ways of eating it according to your preference.

G：听起来很美味！我一定要尝尝北京烤鸭。还有其他推荐的菜品吗？It sounds delicious! I definitely want to try Beijing Roast Duck. Are there any other recommended dishes?

W：除了北京烤鸭，我们还有许多其他美味的传统菜品，如京酱肉丝等。如果您对其他菜品有兴趣，我可以给您一些建议。Besides Beijing Roast Duck, we also have many other delicious traditional dishes, such as Beijing-style Shredded Pork in Sauce, and more. If you are interested in other dishes, I can give you some recommendations.

G：太好了，我想试试这些传统菜品。麻烦您给我推荐几道吧。That's great, and I'd like to try these traditional dishes. Could you please recommend a few?

W：当然，我会为您推荐一些我们的招牌菜和当地特色菜品。请稍等片刻，我将为您准备菜单。Absolutely, I will recommend some of our signature dishes and local specialties for you. Please wait a moment, and I will prepare the menu for you.

对话3 Dialogue 3 评论食物 Commenting on the Food

场景：一位客人点完餐后不一会儿，菜就上齐了。服务人员想知道菜的味道怎么样，是否吃得习惯，于是上前询问。

Scene: A few moments after a guest orders, all the dishes are ready. The waiter wants to know how the guest thinks of the dishes and whether he is used to eating them or not, so the waiter steps forward to ask him.

G：Guest（客人）　　W：Waiter（服务员）

W：您好，菜的味道怎么样？吃得惯吗？Hello, how do the dishes taste? Do you like them?

G：烤鸭很好吃。京酱肉丝也不错，但是那个麻婆豆腐太辣了。Beijing Roast Duck is very delicious. The Shredded Pork in Beijing Sauce is also good, but that Mapo Tofu is too hot.

W：中国菜的味道有很多讲究，有鲜咸、酸甜、清淡、麻辣等。Chinese Cuisine is very particular in its taste, including fresh and salty, sour and sweet, light, hot and spicy, and so on.

G：鲜咸、酸甜、清淡都还不错，麻辣就不是很习惯。Fresh and salty, sour and sweet, and light are all OK for me, but I am not used to the hot and spicy.

W：中国菜系很多，最著名的有四大菜系，每种菜系口味都不同。There are many Chinese Cuisines, and the most famous ones are the four major cuisines, each with different flavors.

G：这么多种，能帮我简单介绍一下吗？There are so many different kinds, and can you give me a brief introduction?

W：川菜以麻辣为特点，善于使用大量的辣椒和花椒。粤菜追求原汁原味，以清淡爽口而闻名。鲁菜强调火候掌握的精准度，烹调方法多样。苏菜口味清淡微甜，强调烹调技巧，善于变换菜品的形状和摆盘。Sichuan Cuisine is characterized by spiciness and is good at using a lot of chili peppers and peppercorns. Cantonese Cuisine pursues original flavor and is famous for its lightness and freshness. Shandong Cuisine emphasizes the precision of fire mastery and has a variety of cooking methods. Jiangsu Cuisine has a light and slightly sweet taste, which emphasizes cooking skills, and is good at changing the shape and presentation of dishes.

G：听起来不错，那我都要尝尝。Sounds good. I would like to taste them all.

补充阅读 Supplement Reading

中餐种类繁多，俗话说：南甜，北咸，东辣，西酸。菜的风格和味道也根据地域和文化背景的不同而不同，这也造就了中餐在材料、菜品、吃法、烹饪技术等方面的无与伦比的多样性，进而形成了不同菜系，其中最主要的有四大菜系，包括鲁菜、苏菜、粤菜、川菜。

　　鲁菜具有悠久的历史。其在北方很受欢迎，曾经是御膳的支柱。由济南菜系和胶东菜系组成，讲究调味醇正，口味偏咸鲜，以其鲜、嫩、香、脆而闻名，善用葱蒜调味和清汤浓汤增鲜。烹调技法以爆、扒为主。

　　粤菜源自中国最南部的省份广东省。由于广东是著名的侨乡，因而广东菜是国外最广泛的中国地方菜系，味道清、淡、脆、鲜，为西方人所熟知。它的基础烹饪方法多种多样，其中蒸和炒最常用于保存天然风味。粤菜厨师也注重菜肴的艺术感。

　　苏菜，又叫淮扬菜，以水产作为主要原料，注重原料的鲜味，善于使用雕刻技术。淮扬菜的特色是淡、鲜、甜、雅。江苏菜系以其精选的原料、精细的准备、不辣不温的口感而出名，是中国菜系中完美的平衡者。

　　川菜是世界上最著名的中国菜系之一。四川菜系以其口感麻辣和菜品多样而闻名，川菜调味多用辣椒、花椒、胡椒和鲜姜、豆瓣酱，不同配比形成各种口味，具有"一菜一味""百菜百格"的特殊风味。如果没有品尝过川菜，这将是中国之行的一大遗憾。

　　Chinese Cuisine is diverse. As the saying goes, sweet in the south, salty in the north, spicy in the east and sour in the west. The style and taste of the dishes also vary from different regions and cultural backgrounds, which results in the unparalleled diversity of Chinese Cuisine in terms of ingredients, dishes, eating methods, and cooking techniques, thus forming different culinary schools. It is widely agreed that Chinese food can be divided into four basic groups: Shandong Cuisine, Jiangsu Cuisine, Cantonese Cuisine, and Sichuan Cuisine.

　　Shandong Cuisine, with its long history, is very popular in the north and was a main part of the royal cuisine. It is composed of two styles: Jinan Cuisine and Jiaodong Cuisine. Shandong Cuisine, pure and salty, is characterized by aroma, freshness, crispness and tenderness. Shallot and garlic are frequently used as seasonings. And it is also good at using the "clear soup" and "milky soup" to make food taste better. Common cooking techniques are "bao" and "pa".

　　Cantonese Cuisine originates from Guangdong Province, the southernmost province of China. As Guangdong is a famous hometown of overseas Chinese, Cantonese Cuisine is the most widely represented Chinese local cuisine abroad. Tasting light, crisp and fresh, it is familiar to Westerners. Lots of cooking techniques are used, especially stir-frying and steaming, which help to preserve the ingredient's natural flavors. Chefs of Cantonese Cuisine also pay more attention to the artistic presentation.

　　Jiangsu Cuisine, also called Huaiyang Cuisine, uses aquatic products as the main ingredient, with a focus on the freshness of the raw materials. The carving techniques are delicate. The flavor of Huaiyang Cuisine is light, fresh, sweet and elegant. Jiangsu Cuisine is famous for its selected raw materials, fine preparation and mild taste. It is the perfect balance in Chinese Cuisine.

Sichuan Cuisine is one of the most famous Chinese Cuisines in the world. It is renowned for its diverse dishes and spicy taste. Sichuan Cuisine is mainly seasoned with chilies, Sichuan peppercorns, fresh ginger and bean paste to create an astonishing variety of flavors with different proportions. Each dish has its own style; a hundred dishes have a hundred different flavors. It will be a regrettable omission from a trip to China for those who do not savor Sichuan Cuisine.

练一练 Activities

一、用汉语写出下图的菜名

A.

B.

C.

D.

二、连线题

（1）炒　　　　　（A）boil

（2）煮　　　　　（B）fry

（3）烤　　　　　（C）stir-fry

（4）蒸　　　　　（D）bake

（5）拌　　　　　（E）stew

（6）熏　　　　　（F）steam

（7）炸　　　　　（G）mix

（8）炖　　　　　（H）smoke

三、翻译下列句子

1. 它是中国菜里一道有名的佳肴。

2. 做好这道菜大约需要 20 分钟。
3. 川菜中最有名、最受欢迎的菜是什么？
4. 我不习惯用筷子，这里有刀叉吗？
5. 这是我们第一次来中国，你可以给我们推荐一些中国菜吗？
6. 祝您用餐愉快！
7. 您觉得今天的菜怎么样？

Unit 4　西餐服务 Western Food Service

导言 Preview

正式的西餐有六或七道菜，七道菜时上菜的顺序为：头盘（开胃菜）→ 汤 → 副菜 → 主菜 → 蔬菜（沙拉）→ 甜点 → 热饮。

Formal Western Cuisine has six or seven courses, and the order of serving the seven courses is as follows：starter（appetizer）→ soup → side dishes → main course → vegetables（salad）→ dessert → hot drinks.

头盘即开胃菜，目的是刺激味蕾，增加食欲。开胃菜通常是由蔬菜、水果、海鲜、肉食所组成的拼盘。

The starter is the appetizer. The purpose is to stimulate the taste buds and increase the appetite. Appetizers are usually a platter of vegetables, fruits, seafood, and meat.

西餐中汤也是起开胃作用的。西餐中的汤有冷汤、清汤、奶油汤、蔬菜汤四大类。

The soups in Western Cuisine also serve as appetizers. There are four major types of soups in Western Cuisine：cold soups, clear soups, cream soups, and vegetable soups.

副菜是开胃类菜品和主菜之间的过渡，除了在一些比较正式的场合，一般是可以选择的。副菜通常是海鲜和鸡肉。

Side dishes are the transition between appetizers and main dishes, and are generally optional except for more formal occasions. Side dishes in Western Cuisine are usually seafood and chicken.

主菜是西餐的门面。西餐中的主菜多是精美的肉菜，代表着该餐的水平与档次。西餐中的主菜有冷菜和热菜之分，一般以热菜为主。

The main course is the facade of Western Cuisine. The main course in Western Cuisine, mostly fine meat dishes, represents the level and grade of the meal. The main course in Western Cuisine is divided into cold dishes and hot dishes, generally hot dishes.

蔬菜类菜肴在西餐中被称为沙拉，通常是在主菜之后上桌，有时也会与主菜一起上桌。

Vegetable dishes, also known as salads in Western Cuisine, are usually served after the main course, or sometimes together with the main course.

用餐尾声的甜点被当作宴请宾客的最高礼遇。常见的甜点有：布丁、冰激凌、水果等。

The dessert at the end of the meal is treated as the highest courtesy to guests. Common desserts include: pudding, ice cream, and fruit, etc.

热饮通常被视为一次用餐结束的标志，在一些非正式场合，热饮常被包含在甜品里。

Hot drinks are often seen as a sign of the end of a meal, and are often included in desserts in informal settings.

词库 Word Bank

西餐 Western Cuisine			
汉语 Chinese	英语 English	汉语 Chinese	英语 English
头盘 tóu pán	starter	主菜 zhǔ cài	main course
开胃菜 kāi wèi cài	appetizer	汤 tāng	soup
沙拉 shā lā	salad	甜点 tián diǎn	dessert
热饮 rè yǐn	hot drinks	配菜 pèi cài	side dish
常用词汇 Common vocabulary			
汉语 Chinese	英语 English	汉语 Chinese	英语 English
份额 fèn é	portion	调味汁 tiáo wèi zhī	sauce
调料 tiáo liào	condiment	烤土豆 kǎo tǔ dòu	baked potatoes
土豆泥 tǔ dòu ní	mashed potatoes	煮土豆 zhǔ tǔ dòu	boiled potatoes
煎土豆 jiān tǔ dòu	fried potatoes	炸薯条 zhá tǔ dòu tiáo	French fries
一分熟的 yì fēn shú de	rare	五分熟的 wǔ fēn shú de	medium
全熟的 quán shú de	well-done	牛排 niú pái	steak

常用句型 Useful Expressions

1. 这是今天大厨的推荐菜。This is our chef's recommendation.

2. 今天的特色菜是什么？What's today's special?

3. 您想要三分、五分还是全熟的牛排？How would you like the beefsteak done, medium-rare, medium or well-done?

4. 您想要单面煎蛋还是双面煎蛋？How would you like the fried egg to be done, one side or two sides?

5. T骨牛排不错，你可以试一下这个主菜！T-bone steak is good, and you can try this main course!

6. 先生、女士，你们的牛排已经好了，请慢用！Your steak is ready, sir and madam. Please enjoy your meal!

7. 您想先来一份开胃菜吗？Do you want to have an appetizer first?

8. 还需要什么其他的东西吗？Is there anything else you would like?

9. 鸡蛋是要炒的、煎的、水波蛋，还是全熟煮鸡蛋？How would you like the eggs to be cooked, scrambled, fried, poached or boiled?

10. 你好！这里是送餐部。请问有什么能为您效劳的吗？Hello! Room Service. How can I help you?

11. 您要看一下甜点单吗？Would you like to see the dessert menu?

12. 晚上好，王先生、王太太，可以为您二位上菜了吗？Good evening, Mr. and Mrs. Wang. May I serve your dinner now?

情景对话 Situational Dialogues

对话1 Dialogue 1 开胃菜和主菜 Starter and Main Course

场景：服务员孙莉正在为一对夫妻点餐。

Scene：Waitress Sun Li is taking an order for a couple.

S：Sun Li（孙莉）　　W1：Mr. Wang（王先生）　　W2：Mrs. Wang（王太太）

S：王太太、王先生，晚上好！您二位要点餐吗？Good evening, Mr. and Mrs. Wang! Are you ready to order?

W1：是的。今天的主菜配蔬菜和土豆吗？Yes. Do the main courses come with vegetables and potatoes?

S：没有，但您可以从菜单的这一部分中挑选。No, they don't, but you can order them from this section of the menu.

W1：哦，我现在看到了。Ah, yes. I see that now.

S：王太太，头盘点什么？Mrs. Wang, what would you like to start with?

W2：我想先来一份鹅肝酱。I would like foie gras for a starter.

S：好的，然后呢？Very good, and to follow?

W2：再来一份牛排。The steak, please.

S：您想要三分、五分还是全熟的牛排？How would you like the beefsteak done, medium-rare, medium or well-done?

W2：我要五分熟的。Medium.

S：王先生，您要点什么？Mr. Wang, what would you like to order?

W1：开胃菜我要焗蜗牛，主菜要挪威烤鲑鱼。Baked snail for the appetizer and Norwegian grilled salmon for the main course.

S：好的，先生。土豆还要吗？Certainly, sir. Would you like potatoes as well?

W1：不要，我要一份意大利酱沙拉。No, I'd like a salad with Italian dressing.

S：好的，先生。您要些蔬菜吗？OK, sir. Would you like to order any vegetables?

W1：是的，我想来点儿煎芦笋。Yes, please. Some fried asparagus.

S：好的，先生。我重复一下您二位点的菜。您点了鹅肝酱和焗蜗牛作为开胃菜，然后是五分熟的牛排和挪威烤鲑鱼各一份，还有意大利酱沙拉配芦笋，对吗？OK, sir. Let me repeat your order. You would like the foie gras and baked snail to start, followed by the steak cooked medium, and Norwegian grilled salmon. Also, a salad with Italian dressing and a side order of asparagus. Is that correct?

W1：是的，谢谢。Yes, that's it. Thank you.

S：不客气。还需要别的吗？You are welcome. Anything else?

W1：不需要了，谢谢。No, thanks.

S：祝您用餐愉快！Enjoy your meal!

对话 2 Dialogue 2 甜点 The Dessert Course

场景：孙莉正在为王先生和王太太提供甜点服务。

Scene：Sun Li is taking a dessert order for Mr. and Mrs. Wang.

S：Sun Li（孙莉）　　W1：Mr. Wang（王先生）　　W2：Mrs. Wang（王太太）

S：您好，今晚的菜品怎么样？吃得惯吗？Hello, how was your meal this evening? Do you like it?

W1：是的，谢谢。非常好。Yes, thank you. It was absolutely perfect.

S：您要看一下甜点单吗？Would you like to see the dessert menu?

W1：好吧。Oh, yes, please.

W2：哦，我不确定还能吃下去。或许我们点一个分着吃。Oh, I'm not sure if I can eat any more. Perhaps we could share one between us.

S：没问题。今晚的甜点单上有面包布丁、巧克力慕斯蛋糕和朗姆苹果酥。Yes, absolutely. On this evening dessert list, we have bread pudding, chocolate mousse cakes and rum apple crisps.

W2：什么是面包布丁？What is bread pudding?

S：面包布丁有葡萄干，加鸡蛋布丁一起烤。It's sweet bread with raisins baked in an egg pudding mix.

W2：听上去不错，不过可能会有点腻，有没有清淡一点的？That sounds good, but maybe a little too heavy. Can you recommend something lighter?

S：朗姆苹果酥就不错。A rum apple crisp is a good choice.

W2：那就来个苹果酥吧。We'll go for the apple crisp.

S：好的，这份甜点两人分享。要不要再点一个两人分享？OK. One dessert will serve two. So would you like to split a second one?

W1：好的，再来一份巧克力慕斯蛋糕。Oh, go on then. We'll get a piece of chocolate mousse cake.

S：好的。再来点儿咖啡配甜点怎么样？OK. How about some coffee with your dessert?

W：好的。Yes, please.

S：好的，马上为您拿来甜点和咖啡。Very good. I'll bring your desserts and coffee to you in a moment.

对话3 Dialogue 3 上菜服务 Serving Dishes

场景：孙莉正在为王先生、王太太提供上菜服务。

Scene：Sun Li is serving dishes for Mr. and Mrs. Wang.

S：Sun Li（孙莉）　　W1：Mr. Wang（王先生）　　W2：Mrs. Wang（王太太）

S：晚上好，王太太、王先生，可以为您二位上菜了吗？Good evening, Mr. and Mrs. Wang. May I serve your dinner now?

W1：好的，请上吧。Yes, please.

S：王太太，这是您的挪威烤鲑鱼。Mrs. Wang, this is Norwegian grilled salmon.

W2：不好意思，这道菜是我先生点的。I'm sorry, that is my husband's meal.

S：对不起，王太太！I'm so sorry, Mrs. Wang!

W2：没关系的。That's fine, really.

S：五分熟的牛排。This is the steak cooked medium.

W2：好的，谢谢！OK, thank you!

S：王先生，您还点了意大利酱沙拉配芦笋，现在要上吗？Mr. Wang, you ordered a salad with Italian dressing and a side order of asparagus. May I serve them to you?

W1：好的，谢谢！That would be nice, thank you!

S：王太太、王先生，你们的餐已经上完了，请慢用！Mr. and Mrs. Wang, your meal is ready. Please enjoy your meal!

（过了一会儿……After a while…）

S：王太太、王先生，今晚的菜品怎么样？吃得惯吗？Mr. and Mrs. Wang, how was your meal this evening? Do you like it?

W2：今天的菜真好吃！The food today is quite delicious!

对话4 Dialogue 4 客房送餐服务 Room Service

场景：1206的客人想在客房用早餐。

Scene：A guest in 1206 would like to have breakfast in his room.

W：Waiter（服务员）　G：Guest（客人）

W：你好！这里是送餐部。请问有什么能为您效劳的吗？Hello! Room Service. How can I help you?

G：我想订一份今天的早餐。I'd like to order breakfast today, please.

W：好的，您需要英式早餐还是美式早餐？Certainly. Would you like to order English or American breakfast?

G：我要全套英式早餐。A full English breakfast, please.

W：鸡蛋是要炒的、煎的、水波蛋，还是全熟煮鸡蛋？How would you like the eggs to be cooked, scrambled, fried, poached or boiled?

G：全熟煮鸡蛋。Boiled.

W：好的，喝茶还是咖啡呢？OK. Tea or coffee?

G：咖啡。Coffee.

W：您喜欢水果还是麦片呢？Would you prefer fruit or cereal?

G：麦片和时令水果都要。Both cereal and fruit in season, please.

W：没问题。请问需要几点送餐？OK. What time would you like it to be delivered?

G：八点半吧。8:30, please.

W：好的，是1206房间，对吗？No problem. Room 1206. Is that right?

G：是的，谢谢。Yes, thank you.

W：先生，八点半准时送到您的房间。Sir, it will be delivered to your room at 8:30 on time.

（40分钟后 40 minutes later）

W：（敲门）送餐部。可以进来吗？(Knock) Room Service. May I come in?

G：请进！Come in, please!

W：（推着餐车走进来）早上好，先生，您订的餐给您送来了。(Wheel the cart into the room) Good morning, sir. I have your room service order.

G：非常感谢！Thank you very much!

W：我把托盘放在桌子上，好吗？Shall I set the tray down on the table?

G：太好了，谢谢。That would be great. Thank you.

W：还需要什么其他的东西吗？Is there anything else you would like?

G：不了，谢谢。No, thanks.

W：您需要我回来收拾盘碟吗？Would you like me to come back for the tray?

G：好的。Sure.

W：大概一个小时之后，可以吗？In about an hour, then?

G：说实话，我也不知道需要多长时间。Actually, I don't know how long it will take.

W：好的，先生。如果您不想被打扰的话，可以在餐后将盘碟放在门外，我会来收的。您也可以用餐完毕后打电话给我。Yes, sir. You can leave this tray outside your door if you don't wish to be disturbed. I will come and get it later. Or you can give me a call when you finish your meal.

G：哦，太好了，谢谢你！Great. Thank you!

W：请在这里签单。Could you sign the bill here?

G：好的。OK.

W：谢谢。祝您用餐愉快。Thank you. Enjoy your meal.

补充阅读 Supplement Reading

众所周知，中国素有"茶的故乡"之称。在世界三大饮料——茶、咖啡和可可中，茶的品尝人数居世界首位。中国人饮茶历史悠久，茶在中国人的生活中是不可缺少的，俗语说："开门七件事——柴米油盐酱醋茶。"

中国的茶分为绿茶、红茶、乌龙茶、白茶、黄茶以及黑茶。绿茶来自茶树上的新鲜芽尖，大部分产于中国的南方省份。红茶是一种完全发酵的茶，是在绿茶基础上发展出来的一种茶。乌龙茶是一种半发酵的茶，混合了绿茶和红茶的特点和品质。白茶是一种未经发酵、快速烘干的茶，产于福建省。与其他茶叶品种相比较，白茶的颜色浅淡，味道清淡。黄茶的制作需要将潮湿的茶叶放在潮湿的地方，等到其自然发黄。

As we all know, China is the homeland of tea. And of the three major drinks of the world—tea, coffee and cocoa, tea is consumed by the largest number of people in the world. People have a long history of drinking tea in China, and tea is essential in Chinese daily life. As a Chinese saying goes, "There are seven most important things for a family: wood, rice, oil, salt, sauce, vinegar and tea."

Chinese tea is divided into green tea, black tea, oolong tea, white tea, yellow tea and dark tea. Green tea is made from the new shoots of appropriate tea trees. The production areas of green tea are mainly southern provinces in China. Black tea is a completely fermented tea, a later variety developed on the basis of the green tea. Oolong tea is a semi-fermented leaf. It combines the characteristics and qualities of green tea and black tea. White tea is a kind of unfermented and fast-dried tea, which is produced in Fujian Province. Compared with other kinds of tea, white tea is lighter in color and flavor. Yellow tea is produced by putting damp tea leaves in a wet place and making them turn yellow naturally.

练一练 Activities

一、用汉语写出下图的菜名

A.

B.

C.

D.

二、连线题

（1）烤鲑鱼　　　　　（A）pudding

（2）甜点　　　　　　（B）fried asparagus

（3）布丁　　　　　　（C）mashed potatoes

（4）焗蜗牛　　　　　（D）grilled salmon

（5）煎芦笋　　　　　（E）appetizer

（6）土豆泥　　　　　（F）desserts

（7）开胃菜　　　　　（G）baked snail

三、翻译下列句子

1. 我们来一份巧克力慕斯蛋糕。

2. 您的餐已经上完了，请慢用！

3. 我今天想订晚餐，请送到我的房间。

4. 您可以将盘碟放在门外。

5. 这道菜太好吃了！

6. 您现在准备好点菜了吗？

Unit 5　酒水服务 Drinks Service

导言 Preview

斟酒的要领是：

The key points of pouring wine are：

●斟酒的姿势与位置：侧身站在宾客的右后侧，左手托盘，或者用席巾垫住瓶口，由主宾开始，顺时针方向。若同时有几种酒水，应询问客人饮用何种酒水。

The posture and position of pouring：Stand on the right rear side of the guest, holding a tray in the left hand, or using a napkin to cover the bottle neck. Start with the guest of honor and go clockwise. If there are several types of beverages, ask guests which one they prefer.

●斟酒时的动作和要求：斟酒时瓶口不要搁在杯上，以防碰倒而且也不卫生。也不要太高，以防溅出，一般为2cm左右，倒适量后抬高瓶口轻轻一转，以防酒水洒落。

Actions and requirements of pouring：Do not place the bottle neck on the cup when pouring wine, to prevent knocking over the cup or unhygienic practices. Do not pour too high to prevent splashing. Pour the wine to a depth of approximately 2cm and then gently tilt the bottle slightly away to prevent spillage.

●斟酒的分量：软饮料如果汁、汽水、啤酒等斟八分满，烈酒类3/4，葡萄酒类2/3，像威士忌这样的洋酒类以1盎司为准。中国白酒八分满。

The amount of wine of pouring：For soft drinks such as juice, soda, and beer, pour them 8/10 full. For liquors, pour them 3/4 full. For wine, pour it 2/3 full. For spirits such as whiskey, pour them about 1 ounce. For Chinese Baijiu, pour it 8/10 full.

词库 Word Bank

饮品 Drinks			
汉语 Chinese	英语 English	汉语 Chinese	英语 English
白酒 bái jiǔ	Baijiu	黄酒 huáng jiǔ	yellow-rice wine

续表

红葡萄酒 hóng pú tao jiǔ	red wine	白葡萄酒 bái pú tao jiǔ	white wine
香槟 xiāng bīn	champagne	啤酒 pí jiǔ	beer
果汁 guǒ zhī	juice	矿泉水 kuàng quán shuǐ	mineral water
酸奶 suān nǎi	yogurt	牛奶 niú nǎi	milk
常用词汇 Common vocabulary			
汉语 Chinese	英语 English	汉语 Chinese	英语 English
加冰 jiā bīng	on the rocks	冰块 bīng kuài	ice
鸡尾酒 jī wěi jiǔ	cocktail	开胃酒 kāi wèi jiǔ	aperitif
小食 xiǎo shí	snack	相配 xiāng pèi	match
常温 cháng wēn	at room temperature	佐酒 zuǒ jiǔ	(of food) go with wine
好年份 hǎo nián fèn	a good year/vintage	醒酒 xǐng jiǔ	let it breathe

常用句型 Useful Expressions

推荐饮料 Recommend Drinks

1. 我可以向您推荐青岛啤酒配餐吗？它非常合适。May I suggest Tsingtao Beer with your meal? It goes well.

2. 如果您需要一些清新的饮料，我向您推荐矿泉水。I suggest mineral water if you would like something refreshing.

3. 您在用餐前要喝饮料吗？Would you care for something to drink before your meal?

4. 您是否要看饮料单/酒单？Would you like to see the beverage/wine list?

5. 您喝利口酒还是白兰地？Would you care for a liqueur or brandy?

6. 您是否要喝一些开胃酒？Would you care for some aperitifs?

7. 请问您喝哪种葡萄酒？What kind of wine do you prefer?

8. 今晚我们的饮料有促销活动，五星啤酒怎么样？We have a special drink promotion this evening. May I suggest the Five Star Beer?

9. 我向您推荐口感优质的中国红葡萄酒。We have excellent Chinese red wine which I can recommend.

10. 我想尝试一些新的东西。但是我不知道今天该喝什么。I'd like try something new. But I don't know what to drink today.

11. 你有什么建议吗？/你能给我一些建议吗？Do you have any recommendations? / Can you give me some suggestions?

12. 您想尝尝中国白酒吗？Would you like to try some Chinese Baijiu?

13. 先生，您想喝点什么？What would you like to drink, sir?

14. 先生，你决定喝点什么了吗？Have you decided what to drink, sir?

15. 您想在喝葡萄酒的时候配点什么小食吗？Would you like to have some snacks with your wine?

16. 来一杯夏布利怎么样？它和您点的虾很配。How about a Chablis? It goes very well with shrimps you ordered.

17. 这是酒单，先生。Here is the wine list, sir.

18. 晚饭前请问喝什么饮料？What would you like to drink before your dinner, please?

19. 加冰威士忌还是直接威士忌？/有冰还是没有冰？Whisky on the rocks or straight up? / With or without ice?

20. 常温还是冰镇？At room temperature or chilled?

21. 您要小份的还是大份的？Would you like a small or large portion?

22. 波尔多白葡萄酒是一种干白葡萄酒。Bordeaux Blanc is a dry white wine.

23. 我推荐茅台，它是中国众多名酒之一。虽然酒劲儿大，但永远不会上头。I recommend Maotai, one of the many famous liquors in China. It's strong but never goes to the head.

24. 这款酒口感醇厚细腻，不干涩。This wine is rich but delicate and not too dry.

25. 您想要哪种牌子的啤酒？Which brand of beer would you like?

情景对话 Situational Dialogues

对话 1 Dialogue 1 聊中国白酒 Talking about Chinese Baijiu

场景：王先生再一次来到酒吧，酒吧服务员前来服务。

Scene: Mr. Wang once again comes to the bar and the barman comes to serve him.

B：Barman（酒吧服务员）　　W：Mr. Wang（王先生）

B：晚上好，王先生。很高兴再次见到您。Good evening, Mr. Wang. Glad to see you again.

W：我也很高兴见到你。Glad to see you too.

B：您今天想喝点什么酒？Which wine would you like tonight?

W：一杯威士忌，谢谢。A glass of whiskey, please.

B：加冰威士忌还是不加冰？Whisky on the rocks or straight up?

W：一杯加冰的。Whisky on the rocks.

B：给您，先生。Here you are, sir.

W：太好了。这儿的人通常喝什么酒？Great. What do people usually drink here?

B：大多数中国人喜欢白酒。它很受欢迎，尤其是在中国的北方地区。中国最好的酒是茅台酒，是我国国宴用酒。Most Chinese people like Baijiu. It's very popular, especially in the north part of China. The best liquor in China is Maotai liquor, which is used for national banquets.

W：下次我去中国餐馆时试试。请问还有哪些中国酒？I'll try it next time when I go to a Chinese restaurant. What are some other Chinese liquors, please?

B：最常见的是绍兴米酒，它是用大米酿造的，没有茅台那么烈。绍兴酒比较温和，在中国南方很受欢迎。有些人喜欢温一下再喝。The most common one is Shaoxing rice wine, which is made from rice and is not as strong as Maotai. Shaoxing wine is quite mild and it's popular in the southern part of China. Some people like to warm it before drinking.

W：喝温酒？我还是第一次听说。听起来很有趣。就我个人而言，我很少喝不加冰的酒。干杯！To drink warm wine? It's the first time I have heard of that. It sounds very interesting. Personally, I seldom drink wine without ice. Cheers!

对话2 Dialogue 2 点酒 Taking a Wine Order

场景：王先生和史先生走进一家酒吧。酒吧服务员正在为他们点单。

Scene：Mr. Wang and Mr. Shi walk into a bar. A barman is taking order and serving them.

B：Barman（酒吧服务员）　　W：Mr. Wang（王先生）　　S：Mr. Shi（史先生）

B：先生们，晚上好！Good evening, gentlemen.

W：晚上好。Good evening.

B：你们想坐哪里？Where would you like to sit?

S：我们想坐在靠近窗户的桌子，可以看见外滩夜景。We would like to sit at a table near the window, with a night view of the Bund.

B：这边请。This way, please.

B：这是酒单，先生。请问要喝点什么吗？Here is the wine list, sir. Would you like something to drink, please?

W：给我一杯威士忌。A glass of whiskey, please.

B：那您想怎么喝威士忌，直接喝还是加冰？How would you like your whiskey, straight up or on the rocks?

W：加纯净水。With plain water.

B：您呢，先生？And you, sir?

S：请给我一杯鸡尾酒。A cocktail for me, please.

B：玛格丽特怎么样，先生？配料是龙舌兰、君度、青柠汁和冰块。How about a Margarita, sir? With tequila, Cointreau, lime juice and ice.

S：听起来不错。That sounds fine.

B：需要配点小吃来佐酒吗？Would you like some snacks with the drink?

W：好的，来块苹果派。Yes, a piece of apple pie, please.

S：给我来点薯片。Some chips for me.

B：好的，先生。还要别的吗？Yes, sir. Anything else, please?

W：不用了，谢谢。No, thank you.

B：我的荣幸。您点的酒和小吃马上就上。My pleasure. Your order will be served right away.

对话 3 Dialogue 3 点酒和上酒 Taking and Serving a Wine Order

场景：孙莉正在为王先生和王太太点酒水、上酒。

Scene：Sun Li is taking and serving a wine order for Mr. and Mrs. Wang.

S：Sun Li（孙莉）　W1：Mr. Wang（王先生）　W2：Mrs. Wang（王太太）

S：晚上好，王太太、王先生，二位想好了要点什么酒吗？Good evening, Mr. and Mrs. Wang. Have you decided which wine you would like?

W1：我想要雷司令配我点的虾。I think this Riesling would go with the shrimp that I ordered.

S：可以的，但长相思配虾味道可能更好。It would, but maybe Sauvignon Blanc would go better with the shrimp.

W1：太棒了！那我们就要这个了。Great! We will go with that one then.

S：王太太，您是否要来杯开胃酒？Mrs. Wang, would you care for an aperitif?

W2：不用了，谢谢。No, thank you.

S：好的，这是2011年（把酒瓶拿给王先生看）。Certainly. Here is 2011 (Show the wine bottle to Mr. Wang).

W1：好的，打开让我尝尝。Go ahead and open it so I can taste it.

S：（开瓶，把瓶塞递给王先生后倒出一小杯酒）请品尝，先生。(Open the bottle, hand the cork to Mr. Wang, and pour a little into a wine glass) Please taste the wine, sir.

W1：嗯，闻起来很香，口感也不错！Yes, a nice bouquet when I smell it; and it tastes lovely!

S：王太太，我可以为您斟酒了吗？Would you like me to pour the wine now, Mrs. Wang?

W2：谢谢，但我想等我的菜上来再倒。Thank you, but I think I'll wait until my main course is served.

S：好的，那您呢，先生？Very good. How about you, sir?

W：不不，我不想等，把酒倒上吧！No, no, I don't want to wait. Pour away!

S：好的，愿意效劳！OK, sir. My pleasure!

补充阅读 Supplement Reading

中国是世界上最早酿酒的国家之一，据传，中国人在七千年前就开始用谷物酿酒。酒作为一种特殊的文化，一直占据着重要地位。

中国有很多种类的酒，如白酒、黄酒、果酒、啤酒、药酒等，这里介绍一下白酒和黄酒。

白酒无色透明，由高粱、玉米、大麦或小麦制成，其中大部分易于发酵。白酒的酒精含量通常在 30% 以上。

中国米酒，也叫黄酒，早在公元前 2500 年就开始酿造了。黄酒是一种很受人们欢迎的酒精饮料，特别是在中国南方。黄酒的酿造一般要经过八个步骤：浸米、蒸饭、晾饭、落缸发酵、开耙、坛发酵、煎酒和包装。

China is one of the first countries in the world to make wine. According to legend, the Chinese people began to make wine from grains seven thousand years ago. Wine, as a special culture, has always occupied an important position.

There are many kinds of wine in China, such as Baijiu, yellow-rice wine, fruit wine, beer, medicinal wine and so on. Here we introduce Baijiu and yellow-rice wine.

Baijiu, colorless and transparent, is made from sorghum, corn, barley or wheat, most of which are easy to ferment. Typically, Baijiu contains more than 30% alcohol by volume.

Chinese rice wine, also called Huang Jiu, has been made in China since 2500 B.C. Chinese rice wine has been one of the popular alcoholic beverages, especially in southern China. The brewing of Chinese rice wine generally needs to go through eight steps: soaking rice, steaming rice, drying rice, falling fermentation, raking, jar fermentation, frying wine and packaging.

练一练 Activities

一、写出下列酒的称谓

A.

B.

C.　　　　　　　　　　　　　　　D.

二、连线题

（1）香槟　　　　　　（A）ice
（2）矿泉水　　　　　（B）juice
（3）牛奶　　　　　　（C）snack
（4）冰块　　　　　　（D）yogurt
（5）酸奶　　　　　　（E）milk
（6）果汁　　　　　　（F）mineral water
（7）小吃　　　　　　（G）champagne

三、翻译下列句子

1. 我想尝试一些新的东西，你有什么建议吗？
2. 您想喝点什么？尝尝中国白酒？
3. 您想要哪种牌子的啤酒？
4. 中国最好的酒是茅台酒，是国宴用酒。
5. 您是否要来杯开胃酒？
6. 是的，闻起来很香，口感也不错！

Unit 6　结账 Settling the Bill

导言 Preview

　　酒店餐厅结账业务是客人在用餐结束后，付款结账的过程。当客人用餐完毕后，服务员会将结账单给客人，上面会显示消费的项目、数量、价格等信息。客人可选择用现金、信用卡或移动支付等方式付款。如果用现金支付，客人需将现金交给服务员。服务员要当面清点现金，并及时送至收银台，由收银员收钱并找零。如果用信用卡或移动支付，客人需用卡片或手机扫码支付，并确认付款金额。待付款完成后，服务员会提供收据或发票给客人作为付款凭证。酒店餐厅结账业务旨在方便客人支付的同时保证账务的准确性和安全性。

The hotel restaurant payment process refers to the procedure where guests settle their bills after dining. After finishing their meal, the waiter will provide the guest with a bill that includes details of the items consumed, quantity, and prices. Payment can be made in various forms such as cash, credit card, or mobile payment. If paying in cash, the guest hands the money to the waiter. The waiter should count the cash in front of the guest and promptly deliver it to the cashier's desk, and the cashier will then accept the money and provide the change. For credit card or mobile payment, the guest swipes his card or scans a QR code and confirms the payment amount. Once the payment is completed, the waiter provides a receipt or invoice to the guest as proof of payment. The hotel restaurant payment process aims to facilitate guest payments while ensuring the accuracy and security of the accounting.

词库 Word Bank

常用词汇 Common vocabulary			
汉语 Chinese	英语 English	汉语 Chinese	英语 English
签名 qiān míng	sign	找零 zhǎo líng	change
账单 zhàng dān	bill	结账 jié zhàng	settle the bill
正确的 zhèng què de	right	服务费 fú wù fèi	service charge
AA 制 AA zhì	go Dutch	合计 hé jì	total
收银台 shōu yín tái	cashier's desk	小费 xiǎo fèi	tip

常用句型 Useful Expressions

1. 能把账单给我吗？Could you bring me the bill, please?
2. 服务员，买单。Waiter, check please.
3. 我们可以买单吗？Can we have the bill, please?
4. 请给我结账。I'd like to settle my bill, please.
5. 这是账单。Here's the check/bill.
6. 总共多少钱？What does this amount to?
7. 有 10% 的服务费包括在内。There's a 10% service charge included.
8. 恐怕这个账单有点问题。I'm afraid there is a mistake on the bill.
9. 你可以核实一下吗？Could you check it?
10. 你们是一起结账还是分开结账？Do you want one bill or separate bills?

11. 你们想怎么结账？How would you like to pay your bill?

12. 我可以用信用卡付账吗？Can I pay for the bill by credit card?

13. 您是现金还是刷卡？Are you paying in cash or by card?

14. 我付现金。I'll pay in cash.

15. 两种都可以，您可以随便选。Both are OK. You may choose.

16. 您介意在这儿签名吗？Would you mind signing your name here?

17. 有收据吗？Do you have the receipt?

18. 我来付账。I'll get the check.

19. 我们分开结账。We'd like to pay separately.

20. 让我们 AA 吧。Let's go Dutch.

21. 让您久等了，×××先生。这是您的账单，您要核对一下吗？Thank you for waiting, Mr. ×××, and here is your bill. Would you like to check it?

22. 能给我收据吗？Could I have a receipt, please?

情景对话 Situational Dialogues

对话 1 Dialogue 1 结账（1）Settling the Bill（1）

场景：孙莉正在餐厅为王先生、王太太结账。

Scene：Sun Li is settling the bill for Mr. and Mrs. Wang in the restaurant.

S：Sun Li（孙莉）　　W1：Mr. Wang（王先生）　　W2：Mrs. Wang（王太太）

S：有什么能为您效劳的吗？How can I help you?

W1：我们可以买单吗？Can we have the bill please?

S：好的，王先生。这是您的账单。Certainly, Mr. Wang. Here is your bill.

W1：谢谢！Thanks!

S：请问您想用什么方式付款？How would you like to settle the bill?

W1：可以用信用卡结账吗？Do you take credit cards?

S：可以，王先生。Certainly, Mr. Wang.

W2：亲爱的，我想我们还是把账挂到我们的房费上吧，（然后问孙莉）这样可以吗？Darling, I think it would be better to put this on our room account.（Then turn to Sun Li）Can we do that?

S：没问题！Certainly!

W1：那就这么办吧。Let's do that then.

S：您带房卡了吗？Do you have your room card available?

W1：是的，给你。Yes, here it is.

S：好的，是 1208 房间，对吗？Very good. Room 1208, is that correct?

W1：对的。Yes, that's correct.

S：可以请您核实账单，确认无误后在这里签上您的名字吗？May I ask you to just check the bill and sign here if everything is correct?

W1：好的。Sure.

S：谢谢！Thanks a lot!

对话 2 Dialogue 2 结账（2）Settling the Bill (2)

场景：结账时客人对自己的账单金额有疑问，餐厅服务人员为他解释。

Scene：When settling the bill, a guest has a question about the amount of his bill, and a waiter explains it to him.

W：Waiter（服务员）　G：Guest（客人）

W：先生有什么需要？What can I do for you, sir?

G：我想结账。I'd like to settle my bill, please.

W：请稍等。这是您的账单。One moment, please. Here is your bill.

G：这比我们点的要多。请为我解释一下。It's more than we've ordered. Can you explain the bill?

W：好的。盐水鸭，80 元；蟹粉豆腐，50 元；西兰花虾仁，55 元；番茄汤，20 元。是这样吗？Well. Salted Duck, CNY 80; Bean Curd with Crab Flour, CNY 50; Shrimp with Broccoli, CNY 55; Tomato Soup, CNY 20. Is that right?

G：对的。酒水的费用呢？Exactly. What about the cost of drinks?

W：一瓶啤酒 25 元，一瓶果汁 40 元。A bottle of beer, CNY 25; a bottle of juice, CNY 40.

G：等等，我们问过果汁，但最终没有点。Wait, we asked about juice, but did not order it.

W：非常抱歉，是我们弄错了，我会扣除这一项，然后给您重打一张账单。I'm sorry, this is our mistake. I will deduct it and reprint the bill.

对话 3 Dialogue 3 现金结账 Paying by Cash

场景：一名客人用完晚餐后准备用现金结账。

Scene：A guest is going to settle the bill in cash after dinner.

W：Waiter（服务员）　G：Guest（客人）

G：服务员，结账。Waiter, the bill, please.

W：好的，先生。这是您的账单。OK, sir. Here's your bill.

G：总共多少钱？What does this amount to?

W：您的账单总额为 360 元人民币。Your bill totals CNY 360.

G：恐怕这个账单有点问题。你能解释一下账单吗？I'm afraid there is a mistake on the bill. Can you explain the bill?

W：当然，先生。这里包括您点的菜：炸虾 100 元，蒸蟹 80 元，炒豆芽 20 元。Of course, sir. This includes the dishes you ordered: Fried Prawn, CNY 100; Steamed Crab, CNY 80; Fried Bean Sprout, CNY 20.

G：对的。那酒水呢？Right. How about drinks?

W：一瓶啤酒 60 元，一瓶牛奶 40 元。A bottle of beer is CNY 60, and a bottle of milk is CNY 40.

G：总共只有 300 元人民币。So that makes only a total of CNY 300.

W：是的，先生。您是对的。但是要收取 20% 的服务费。总金额为人民币 360 元。Yes, sir. You are right. But there is a 20% service charge. So the total comes to CNY 360.

G：哦，我明白了。给你。Oh, I see. Here you are.

W：400 元。请稍等。CNY 400. Please wait a minute.

W：这是您的零钱和收据，谢谢。晚安。希望再次见到您。Here is your change and your receipt, thank you. Good night. Hope to see you again.

G：谢谢。这是你的小费。Thank you. This is your tip.

W：谢谢您，先生。但我们不接受小费。Thank you, sir. But we don't accept tips.

对话 4 Dialogue 4 微信结账 Paying by WeChat

场景：一名客人用晚餐后准备用微信结账。

Scene：A guest is going to settle the bill by WeChat after dinner.

W：Waiter（服务员）　　G：Guest（客人）

G：结账。I'd like to settle my bill, please.

W：好的，我马上过来。OK, I'll be right with you.

W：这是账单。Here's the bill.

G：好的，请问可以用微信支付吗？Yes, can I use WeChat Pay?

W：当然可以！您可以打开微信，使用扫一扫功能扫描桌上的二维码进行支付。请确认结账金额。Of course! You can open WeChat and use the scan function to scan the QR code on the table for payment. Please confirm the total amount.

G：好的，让我扫描一下。确认了，金额是 200 元。OK, let me scan. Confirmed, it's 200 yuan.

W：非常感谢。请您进行确认支付，支付成功后我们会提供支付凭证。Thank you very much. Please proceed with the payment confirmation. Once the payment is successful, we will provide a payment receipt.

（顾客在微信中确认支付。The guest confirms the payment on WeChat.）

W：支付成功！这是您的支付凭证，同时也是最终账单。谢谢光临！Payment successful! Here's your payment receipt, which also serves as the final bill. Thank you for coming!

补充阅读 Supplement Reading

伴随着手机的普遍使用，以及移动互联网等通信技术的快速发展，用户对快捷安全的支付手段具有强烈的需求。扫码支付就是基于账户体系搭建起来的无线支付方案，具有简单、快捷、高效和安全等特点。携带一部手机出门，即可完成餐馆就餐、购物等日常活动，这极大地方便了普通人的交通出行，提升了消费体验，真正实现了无现金生活，得到了中国人的广泛使用和外国来华游客的赞许。对于消费者而言，只需要拥有一部可以上网的互联网手机，绑定个人的银行卡账户，在手机上安装二维码识别软件，随时随地都可以在贴有二维码的地方简单扫描一下完成实时交易，既缩短了支付时间，也避免了携带钱包外出而遗失银行卡或者现金等情况的发生。

With the widespread use of mobile phones and the rapid development of communication technologies such as mobile Internet, users have a strong demand for fast and secure payment methods. Scan-to-pay is a wireless payment solution based on an account system, characterized by its simplicity, speed, efficiency, and security. With just a mobile phone in hand, users can easily complete daily activities such as dining in restaurants and shopping, greatly facilitating people's transportation and enhancing the consumer experience. It truly realizes a cashless life, and has been widely used by Chinese people and praised by foreign tourists visiting China. For consumers, all they need is an Internet-enabled mobile phone, a linked personal bank account, and a QR code recognition software installed on their phones. They can scan the QR code anywhere and anytime to complete real-time transactions, reducing payment time and avoiding situations such as carrying a wallet and losing bank cards or cash.

练一练 Activities

一、连线题

(1) 账单　　　　　(A) sign

(2) 小费　　　　　(B) go Dutch

(3) 签名　　　　　(C) cashier's desk

(4) 找零　　　　　(D) bill

(5) AA 制　　　　(E) total

(6) 收银台　　　　(F) tip

(7) 合计　　　　　(G) change

二、根据语意排列句子顺序

A. 先生，让您久等了。收据已开好，确认无误后在这里签上您的名字。

B. 好的，您二位每人需要扫码支付 80 元。

C. 服务员，结账。

D. 抱歉，我们的电脑突然出问题了，需要等一刻钟。

E. 你们想怎么结账，现金、微信还是刷卡？

F. 微信吧，我们 AA 结账。

G. 请稍等。这是您的账单。

H. 能给我收据吗？

Chapter 4　康乐服务 Health and Recreation Service

　　康乐服务提供多种项目和活动，如健康活动、娱乐活动、休闲活动、美容活动等，以满足人们对健康娱乐的要求。中心内设有健身俱乐部、美容院、游泳池、健身房等设施。良好的娱乐设施有助于吸引更多的客人，娱乐设施的标准是衡量酒店的重要因素。如今，一些酒店的康乐中心成为其总收入的重要来源。

　　Health and recreation service provides many programs and activities, such as health activities, entertainment activities, leisure activities, beauty activities and so on, so as to meet people's requests of health and entertainment. Inside the center, there are health clubs, beauty salons, swimming pools, gymnasiums, and other facilities. Good entertainment facilities help attract more guests, and the standard of entertainment facilities is an important element to measure a hotel. Nowadays, the health and recreation center in some hotels becomes a significant source of their total income.

康乐服务项目
Health and Recreation Service Items

序号	中文名称	英文全称
1	游泳池（yóu yǒng chí）	swimming pool
2	夜总会（yè zǒng huì）	nightclub
3	桑拿（sāng ná）	sauna
4	健身中心（jiàn shēn zhōng xīn）	fitness center
5	美容美发中心（měi róng měi fà zhōng xīn）	beauty salon center
6	保龄球室（bǎo líng qiú shì）	bowling alley

Unit 1　歌厅 KTV

导言 Preview

　　KTV 代表 Karaoke Television。Karaoke 是一个日英混合词，其中"Kara"在日语中意为"空"。KTV 从狭义上可以理解为一个提供卡拉 OK 视听设备和唱歌空间的地方，广义上可以理解为提供卡拉 OK 和酒精饮料的场所，这是许多夜间娱乐场所的主要业务。KTV 也可以说是一个小型唱吧，你可以在那里跳舞、唱歌以及喝酒，对于小型聚会来说，它是首选之地。

KTV stands for Karaoke Television. Karaoke is a Japanese-English hybrid, where "Kara" means "empty" in Japanese. KTV, in a narrow sense, is a place that provides karaoke audio-visual equipment and a space for singing. KTV is broadly understood as a venue offering karaoke along with alcoholic beverages, which is the main business of many night entertainment venues. KTV can also be described as a small singing bar where you can dance, sing, and drink, making it the first choice for small parties.

词库 Word Bank

常用词汇 Common vocabulary			
汉语 Chinese	英语 English	汉语 Chinese	英语 English
卡拉 OK kǎ lā OK	KTV（Karaoke TV）	音高 yīn gāo 程度 chéng dù	pitch
音调 yīn diào	key	音质 yīn zhì 音品 yīn pǐn	timbre
扩音器 kuò yīn qì 麦克风 mài kè fēng	microphone	语气 yǔ qì 音色 yīn sè	tone
噪音 zào yīn 响声 xiǎng shēng 杂音 zá yīn	noise	曲调 qǔ diào	tune
音响效果 yīn xiǎng xiào guǒ	acoustics	美声 měi shēng	bel canto

常用句型 Useful Expressions

1. 你唱歌拿手吗？Are you good at singing?

2. 我想点首歌。I'd like to request a song.

3. 你先唱。You sing first. / Go ahead. / After you.

4. 大家快乐地玩吧！Let's enjoy ourselves!

5. 约翰，你来唱一首吧。How about a song, John?

6. 你打算唱什么歌？What are you going to sing?

7. 来个二重唱吧。Let's sing a duet.

8. 现在轮到我了。Now it's my turn. / It's finally my turn.

9. 我不敢在大家面前唱歌。I don't have the nerve to sing in front of people. / I don't

have the guts to sing in front of people.

10. 我跟不上新歌的速度。I can't keep up with the new songs. / I can't keep the new music. / I can't learn the new songs fast enough.

11. 我五音不全。I'm tone-deaf. / I have no ear for music. / My singing is out of tune.

12. 你有什么拿手的歌吗？What's your karaoke speciality? / What's your best song? / Which song do you sing best?

13. 我从来没听说过那首歌。I've never heard of that song.

14. 你唱得真好！You're a good singer! / You sing very well!

情景对话 Situational Dialogues

对话1 Dialogue 1 练歌房（1） KTV（1）

场景：练歌房唱歌

Scene：Sing in a KTV room

L：Lulu（露露）　　K：Kate（凯特）

L：嘿，凯特。我们到了，你们在哪个房间呢？Hey, Kate. Here we are. Which room are you in?

K：457包房。Room 457.

L：好，一会儿见。Yeah, see you later.

（在457包房 In room 457）

L：哇，这个包间真是舒服呀，这音响的音色也很好。Wow, the private room is so comfortable, and the timbre of audio equipment is also excellent.

K：这是最好的了。This is the best one in this area.

L：这是点歌单，我们还在等谁呀？Here is the song list. Who are we waiting for?

K：杰克和苏一会儿就会来。Jack and Su will come here.

L：苏？她会来？太棒了。苏是有名的女高音呢。她很擅长美声唱法。Su? Is she coming here? That's great. Su is a famous soprano. She is good at bel canto.

K：是吗？杰克怎么样呀？Really? How about Jack?

L：哦，他是个麦霸，而且唱歌经常跑调。Oh, he always hogs the microphone and his singing is often out of tune.

K：太可怕了。来吧，在他们来之前，我们先点些歌唱吧。That's terrible. Come on, let's pick some songs to sing before they arrive here.

L：好。OK.

对话2 Dialogue 2 练歌房（2） KTV（2）

场景：练歌房唱歌

Scene：Sing in a KTV room

C：Clerk（店员）　　G：Guest（顾客）

C：晚上好。欢迎光临我们的 KTV。我能为您做些什么？Good evening. Welcome to our KTV. What can I do for you?

G：晚上好。请给我们安排一个包间。Good evening. Please arrange a private room for us.

C：没问题。我们有很多 KTV 包间。有多少人？No problem. We have many KTV rooms. How many people are there?

G：五到六人。Five to six.

C：中型房间怎么样？How about a medium-sized room?

G：你觉得对我们来说够大吗？Do you think it is big enough for us?

C：是的，我们的房间非常宽敞。Yes, our rooms are very commodious.

G：好。你们有英文歌吗？因为我有几个朋友是外国人。Well. Do you have English songs? A couple of my friends are foreigners.

C：是的。这是歌单。除了英文歌曲，我们还有日语歌曲、韩语歌曲、西班牙语歌曲和其他外国歌曲。Yes. This is the song list. Besides English songs, we also have Japanese songs, Korean songs, Spanish songs and other foreign songs.

G：那很好。That's fine.

C：您住在我们酒店吗？Do you stay in our hotel?

G：是的，我住在 712 房间。一小时多少钱？Yes, I am in Room 712. How much for one hour?

C：登记的客人，每小时 20 元。For registered guests, it is 20 yuan an hour.

G：这是合理的。顺便问一下，你能告诉我们如何点歌吗？It's reasonable. By the way, can you tell us how to order songs?

C：请稍等。我来帮您。Please wait for a moment. Let me help you.

对话 3 Dialogue 3 练歌房（3）KTV (3)

场景：练歌房唱歌

Scene：Sing in a KTV room

H：Helen（海伦）　　K：Kate（凯特）

K：到你了，海伦。It's your turn now, Helen.

H：好的。我来了。OK. I'm coming.

K：你的招牌歌。我点给你的。This is your song. I picked it for you.

H：感谢。你想得真周到。Thank you. You are so considerate.

K：按麦克风上的红色按钮打开麦克风。Push the red button on the microphone to

turn it on.

　　H：好的。这调子对我来说太高了。OK. This key is too high for me.

　　K：我想那对你来说是小菜一碟。I think it's a piece of cake for you.

　　H：好吧。我试试…… OK. Let me have a try...

　　K：唱得好！真希望有一天我能唱得和你一样好。Well done！I hope I can sing as well as you one day.

　　H：感谢。我确定你会的。Thank you. I'm sure you will.

　　K：希望如此。感谢你这么说。I hope so. Thank you for saying so.

补充阅读 Supplement Reading

中国的 KTV

　　卡拉 OK 最早是 20 世纪 70 年代在日本发展起来的一种情感发泄方式，然后迅速风靡东亚。

　　"我喜欢它。你可以放松自己，然后……练习唱歌。"

　　这种娱乐方式于 20 世纪 90 年代传入中国，并更名为 KTV。在 KTV 中，参与者可以观看音乐视频、跳舞，或者只是在封闭的房间里互相交谈。在北京，周末很难订到房间，而随着新年的临近，这就变得更加困难了。

　　中国的 KTV 与西方的 KTV 不同。通常情况下，中国的 KTV 包间装饰豪华，你不必在陌生人面前尴尬。

　　"中国的 KTV 更像是一场派对。在这里你可以和朋友一起去，而在美国，这是在公共场所进行的。你去酒吧，在大家面前唱你的歌。这里更私密，更像是社交活动。"

　　"我更喜欢中式 KTV，那种亚洲风格的 KTV。"

　　"这是一种社交方式。当你来的时候，你通常会被提供一些食物。对于像我这样的人来说，来这儿是学习中文歌曲的好方法。有时间和朋友出去逛逛。这不仅是关于唱歌，而且是关于聊天，是与朋友共度时光。"

　　所以在朋友面前，你也可以成为一个摇滚明星，无论你唱得多么糟糕，观众都会给你最热烈的掌声。然而，唱什么是很多去 KTV 的人关心的问题。俗话说，无论你多么努力地表现出温柔和年轻，当你开始唱歌时，你的真实年龄马上就会显露出来——人们很容易根据你最喜欢的歌曲来判断你的年龄。

　　"我认为唱歌是一种年龄哲学。因为只有当你到了一定的年龄，你才能明白你喜欢的歌手在唱什么。"

　　作为一种放松、与朋友聚会、结交新朋友的好方法，去 KTV 已经成为中国节日期间重要的娱乐活动。

　　因此，随着新年和春节的临近，你可能也想试试你的歌唱才能。

KTV in China

Karaoke first evolved in Japan as an emotional outlet in the 1970s, and then it immediately swept East Asia.

"I love it. You can relax yourself, and then... practice singing."

The entertainment came to China in the 1990s and got the new name of KTV. The participants can watch the music videos, dance, or just talk to each other in enclosed rooms. In Beijing, it is hard to book a room on weekends, and when the New Year is approaching, it becomes even more difficult.

The KTV in China is different from its counterparts in the west. More often than not, the KTV rooms in China feature deluxe decorations and you don't have to embarrass yourself in front of strangers.

"Here it's more like a party in China. Here you get to go with friends, while in America, it's done in a public space. You go to a bar, and sing your song in front of everybody else. Here it's more private, more of a social event."

"I like Chinese KTV better, the Asian style of KTV."

"It's a way to socialize. When you come, you usually get food included. It's a good way for people like me to learn some Chinese songs here. Just hang out with friends when having time. It's not only about singing, but also about chatting and spending time with friends."

So in front of friends, you can also become a rock star and the audience will always give the warmest applause no matter how badly you sing. However, what to sing is a concern for a lot of people who go to the KTV. A popular saying goes that no matter how hard you try to appear tender and young, your real age reveals itself immediately when you begin to sing—people could easily tell your age according to the songs you like most.

"I think singing is a philosophy of age. Because only when you reach a certain age, you can understand what the singers you like are singing about."

As a good way to relax, catch up with friends, and make new friends, going to KTV has become an important entertainment during the holiday seasons in China.

So with the New Year and Spring Festival approaching, you may also want to try out your singing talent.

练一练 Activities

一、朗读下列词汇

音响　音质　音色　麦霸　美声　通俗

二、按照谈话顺序排列下列句子

（A）最近新开的一家 KTV 很不错，咱们去唱歌，怎么样？

（B）完全同意。几点集合？

（C）晚上有什么安排吗？

（D）晚上六点吧，我们先一起吃晚餐，再去唱歌。

（E）正合我意！好久没当麦霸了。

（F）今天的工作太累了，真想放松一下，你有好的建议吗？

（G）再把王凯和张明一起叫上，人多热闹。

（H）好的，晚上见！

Unit 2　水疗服务 SPA Service

导言 Preview

这个词来源于比利时 SPA 小镇的名字，这个小镇的名字可以追溯到罗马时代。

The term is derived from the name of the town of SPA in Belgium, whose name dates back to Roman times.

身体治疗、SPA 治疗或美容治疗是有助于身体健康的非医疗程序。

A body treatment, SPA treatment, or cosmetic treatment is a non-medical procedure to help the health of the body.

词库 Word Bank

常用词汇 Common vocabulary			
汉语 Chinese	英语 English	汉语 Chinese	英语 English
按摩 àn mó	massage	浴巾 yù jīn	bath towel
按摩床 àn mó chuáng	massage bed	香油 xiāng yóu	balm
治疗 zhì liáo	treatment	拖鞋 tuō xié	slipper
温度 wēn dù	temperature	浴袍 yù páo	robe

续表

膝盖 xī gài	knee	睡衣 shuì yī	pajamas
凭证 píng zhèng	voucher	草本的 cǎo běn de	herbal
轻点 qīng diǎn	softer	花的 huā de	floral
冷/热毛巾 lěng/rè máo jīn	cold/hot towel	舒适的 shū shì de	comfortable
枕头 zhěn tou	pillow	浓缩的 nóng suō de	concentrated

常用句型 Useful Expressions

1. 先生/夫人，早上/中午/晚上好！欢迎来到水疗中心。Good morning/afternoon/evening, sir/madam! Welcome to the SPA center!

2. 我是您的按摩/理疗师，我可以帮您吗？I am your therapist. How may I help you?

3. 请随我来好吗？这边请！您先请！I'll show you the way. This way please! After you!

4. 直走！请向左/右转！上楼/下楼！Go straight ahead! Turn left/right, please! Go upstairs/downstairs!

5. 小心脚下！请当心！Watch your step! Please be careful!

6. 我叫……，您可以随时叫我，我很乐意为您服务。My name is…, and you can call me anytime. I am always at your service.

7. 这是您的拖鞋。Here are your slippers.

8. 这些新的毛巾和茶是为您准备的。Here are some fresh towels and tea for you.

9. 我会立即给您拿过来。I will bring/send it to you immediately.

10. 这是草本/姜茶，请享用。This is herbal/ginger tea. Please enjoy it.

11. 请您穿上您的衣服后，喝杯草药茶。Please put on your clothes and have a cup of herbal tea.

12. 为了使您更好地享受按摩护理，请您关掉手机，并保持安静。谢谢！For your enjoyable massage, please turn off your phone and keep silent, thanks!

13. 这是我们的四种香薰按摩油，您可以闻一下然后选出您喜欢的。These are four kinds of aroma massage oil. You may smell and choose the one which you like.

14. 这个冷/热毛巾是给您敷脸的。This is the cold/hot towel for your face.

15. 在开始水疗之前，我会给您先来个植物香足浴。Before starting your treatment, I will give you a floral foot bath.

16. 请把脚放在水里面。Please put your feet in the water.

17. 这个温度可以吗？Is the temperature OK?

18. 这个音量可以吗？Is the volume OK?

19. 您舒服吗？力度怎么样？如果您想力度大点或轻点，请告诉我。Are you comfortable? How is the pressure? If you like stronger or softer, please let me know.

20. 请把脸朝下。Please lay your face down.

21. 麻烦您翻过来好吗？Could you please turn over?

22. 我先去洗手，马上回来。I am going to wash my hands and will be right back.

23. 请您闭上眼睛享受护理。Please close your eyes and enjoy your treatment.

24. 我会在浴室的外面给您挂一条干净的毛巾。I will hang a clean towel outside the bathroom for you.

25. 我已经在浴室里给您挂了一条干净的毛巾。I have hung a clean towel inside the bathroom for you.

26. 劳驾一下，这次的水疗结束了。Excuse me, I have finished the treatment.

27. 您对这次水疗满意吗？Do you enjoy your treatment?

28. 按摩油会在您身上作用一个小时，所以请您一小时后再沐浴。The massage oil will be working on your body for one hour, so please take your shower after one hour.

29. 让我来帮您脱下外袍好吗？May I help you with your robe?

30. 请让我扶您下床好吗？Please allow me to assist you off the bed.

31. 沐浴更衣后，我会在外面准备一些热茶。After you take a shower and change clothes, I will have some warm tea waiting for you outside.

32. 您希望怎么结账呢，用现金还是刷卡？How would you like to pay, by cash or credit card?

33. 夫人，这是您的账单。Here is your bill/your check, madam.

情景对话 Situational Dialogues

对话1 Dialogue 1 保健服务（1）Health Service（1）

场景：咨询水疗服务

Scene：Consult SPA services

S：Staff（员工）　　G：Guest（宾客）

S：您好，请问您需要什么服务？Hello, can I help you?

G：我想做水疗。你们这儿怎么收费？Yes, I'd like to get a SPA treatment. How much do you charge here?

S：一次一百。如果办一张十次的卡，只收八百。RMB 100 once. But if you buy a card that allows you ten treatments, we only charge you 800.

G：那我办一张卡吧。OK. I'll go for that card.

S：好的，请您先登记一下。OK, please register here first.

对话 2 Dialogue 2 保健服务（2）Health Service（2）

场景：咨询水疗服务

Scene：Consult SPA services

S：Staff（员工）　　G：Guest（宾客）

G：我觉得不太对劲儿，全身酸痛！I don't feel well. My whole body aches!

S：真的啊……我知道了，您需要去做个水疗了。Oh... I know, you need a SPA.

G：我们宾馆有水疗中心吗？Is there a SPA center in the hotel?

S：是的。在十楼。Yes. It is on the 10th floor.

G：效果怎么样呢？必须和别人一起泡吗？How does it work? Do I have to soak with other people?

S：您可以选择租私人房间或者洗大众浴池。有公共的，也有私人的设施。You can rent your own room or go to the public baths. There are both public and private facilities.

G：哪一种比较好呢？Which is better?

S：这个嘛……公共浴池当然比较便宜，但是私人房间雅致多了，也干净多了。我保证您泡完温泉一定会感觉脱胎换骨！Well, the public baths, of course, are cheaper, but the private ones tend to be nicer and cleaner. I guarantee you'll feel like refreshed afterwards!

G：好的。我要个私人间。OK. I'll rent a private room.

对话 3 Dialogue 3 娱乐服务 Entertainment Service

场景：了解更多的娱乐设施

Scene：Learn more about recreational facilities

N：Nicole（妮可）　　D：Diana（戴安娜）

N：早上好，戴安娜，好久不见了。Good morning, Diana, long time no see.

D：早上好，妮可。Morning, Nicole.

N：听说你去度假了。I heard you went on vacation.

D：是的。前段时间工作很累，所以上周去度假村休息了几天。Yes. I was really tired from work in the past few days, so I spent a few days at a resort to relax.

N：度假村里有什么娱乐设施吗？Are there any entertainment facilities in it?

D：这家超豪华的旅游度假酒店坐落于盐田区大梅沙，位于被称为深圳旅游一大亮点，拥有主题公园、两个高尔夫球场、水疗、可容纳一千人的剧场、茶园以及其他游览景点的东部华侨城旅游景区内。This super luxury hotel and resort is located at Dameisha, Yantian District and is part of the OCT East Resort, which has become a major highlight of

Shenzhen's tourism industry. It boasts theme parks, two golf courts, SPA, a 1,000-seat theater, an extensive tea garden, and numerous other attractions.

N：哇，听上去太棒了！我真是羡慕你！Woo, it seems so great! I admire you!

D：是的。里面的设施非常完善，是一个娱乐放松的地方。Yes. The facilities there are perfect, and it is a superexcellent place for amusement and relaxation.

N：度假村的水疗应该很棒吧，你去做过吗？The SPA there must be great, and have you ever done that?

D：当然，我平日里就经常做水疗，当然不会错过这个机会。Sure, I often do SPA in my daily time, and can't miss this opportunity.

N：感觉怎么样？How do you feel?

D：太棒了！整个过程都非常享受，全身都感到非常轻松。Perfect! I enjoyed the whole process and felt relaxed all over.

N：现在有些人选择在家里做水疗，效果也不错。Some people choose to do SPA at home, which bears a relatively good effect.

D：不过我还是更喜欢去水疗中心做。咱们公司附近就有一家不错的水疗中心。However, I prefer to do SPA at the SPA center. There is a good one near our company.

N：是吗？我们可以一起去。Really? We can go there together.

D：好主意。Good idea.

补充阅读 Supplement Reading

水 疗

走在大街上总能看到各种各样的 SPA 广告和招牌。大家可能知道 SPA 这个词肯定跟身体护理和保健有关。但它背后真正的意思你知道吗？

SPA 指水疗，凡是与 SPA 相关的地方（包括温泉度假村）一般都提供各种各样的身体保健项目。

SPA 这个词来源于比利时一个叫 SPA 的小镇，这个小镇在罗马时代就存在了，当时叫作 Aquae Spadanae，有时也被误当作拉丁文的 spargere，即"抛洒、滋润"的意思。这个小镇的泉水因为有治疗功效而为人所知。

1626 年，"English SPA"这样的说法首次出现。到了 1777 年，SPA 小镇已经声名远扬，以至于任何有温泉且能驱除疾病的地方都取名为 SPA。不过，人们在没有温泉的地方开设保健中心并取名叫 SPA 却是 1960 年的事情了。自那以后，SPA 开始遍地开花。到了 1974 年，你可以在自家浴缸里泡个热水澡，并称之为 SPA。

SPA 可以愉悦身心，为体内囤积的压力找到一个出口，令人的身、心、灵达到和谐与平衡的享受。现代 SPA 主要是水资源及水设备的不同，常见的有桶浴、湿蒸、干蒸、淋浴及水力按摩浴等，也常常选用矿物质、海底泥、花草萃取物、植物精油等来改善水质并作用于人体。SPA主要具有美容养颜、放松身体、舒缓身心、保养皮肤、治疗疾病等功效。

　　SPA有不同的主题吸引力，有的偏重放松、舒缓、排毒的疗程，有的以健美瘦身为重点，还有的重芳香精油、海洋活水或纯草本疗法等。但无论是哪种类型的SPA，都脱离不了满足客人听觉（疗愈音乐）、嗅觉（天然花草薰香）、视觉（自然景观）、味觉（健康餐饮）、触觉（按摩护理）和思考（内心放松）六种愉悦感官的基本需求。

SPA

　　Walking on the street, you can always see a variety of SPA advertisements and signs. You probably know the word SPA and it's certainly associated with physical care and wellness. But do you know what it really means?

　　SPA refers to hydrotherapy, and spa-related places (including hot spring resorts) generally offer a variety of physical health programs.

　　The word SPA comes from a Belgian town named SPA, which has been around since Roman times, when it was called Aquae Spadanae, sometimes misinterpreted as the Latin word "spargere", meaning "to pour or moisten". The town's spring water is known for its healing properties.

　　The term "English SPA" first appeared in 1626. By 1777, the town of SPA had become so famous that any place with a hot spring to get rid of diseases was called a SPA. However, it wasn't until 1960 that people opened health centers in places without hot springs and called them SPAs. Since then, SPAs have sprung up everywhere. By 1974, you could take a hot bath in your own bathtub and call it a SPA.

　　SPA can delight the body and mind, find an outlet for the pressure stored in the body, and make the body, mind and spirit enjoy harmony and balance. Modern SPA is mainly the difference between water resources and water equipment, and common types include bucket bath, wet steaming, dry steaming, shower and hydraulic massage bath, etc. Modern SPA often chooses minerals, submarine mud, flower extracts, plant essential oils, etc., to improve water quality and use them on the human body. SPA mainly can enhance the beauty, relax the body, soothe the body and mind, health the skin, treat the disease and has other effects.

　　SPA has different theme appeals. Some focus on relaxation, soothing, and detoxification treatments; some focus on bodybuilding and slimming; some focus on aromatic essential oils, sea water or pure herbal remedies. But no matter what type of SPA, it can not be separated from meeting guests' six basic needs of pleasure senses of hearing (curative music), smell (natural flowers and flowers aromatherapy), vision (natural landscape), taste (healthy dining), touch (massage care) and thinking (inner relaxation).

练一练 Activities

一、用汉语写出下图的名称

A.

B.

C.

D.

二、连线题

（1）水疗　　　　　　　（A）foot bath

（2）按摩油　　　　　　（B）private room

（3）足浴　　　　　　　（C）on vacation

（4）私人间　　　　　　（D）herbal tea

（5）度假　　　　　　　（E）massage oil

（6）草药茶　　　　　　（F）SPA

Unit 3　健身房 Fitness Center

导言 Preview

酒店健身房起源于欧美健身俱乐部。在当今西方发达国家，健身已经不再是追求时尚，更重要的是获得健康。它已逐渐地成为人们生活中的一部分，成为生活必需品。健身运动已被越来越多的人所接受。

Hotel gyms originated from health clubs in Europe and the United States. In today's developed Western countries, fitness is no longer the pursuit of fashion, and more important is to get healthy. It has gradually become a part of people's lives, and a necessity of life. Fitness has been accepted by more and more people.

词库 Word Bank

常用词汇 Common vocabulary			
汉语 Chinese	英语 English	汉语 Chinese	英语 English
健身房 jiàn shēn fáng	gym	减少 jiǎn shǎo	reduction
保持体态 bǎo chí tǐ tài	get fit	脂肪 zhī fáng	fat
减肥 jiǎn féi	lose weight	消除脂肪 xiāo chú zhī fáng	reduce the fat/ get rid of the fat
增重 zēng zhòng	gain weight	低脂饮食 dī zhī yǐn shí	low-fat diet
增强肌肉 zēng qiáng jī ròu	build muscle	健身 jiàn shēn	work out
健身中心 jiàn shēn zhōng xīn	fitness center	体脂肪 tǐ zhī fáng	body fat
健身教练 jiàn shēn jiào liàn	trainer	卡路里 kǎ lù lǐ	calorie
私人教练 sī rén jiào liàn	personal trainer	燃烧卡路里 rán shāo kǎ lù lǐ	burn calorie
运动鞋 yùn dòng xié	sneaker	曲线 qū xiàn	curve
置物柜 zhì wù guì	locker	热身 rè shēn	warm up
入会费 rù huì fèi	membership fee	肌肉 jī ròu	muscle
参加健身课程 cān jiā jiàn shēn kè chéng	enroll in fitness classes	伸展 shēn zhǎn	stretch
局部瘦身 jú bù shòu shēn	spot reduction	收缩 shōu suō	contract
部位 bù wèi	spot	柔韧度 róu rèn dù	flexibility

常用句型 Useful Expressions

1. 当您完成入会手续后，我们会跟您收取两万三千元的入会费。After you complete the membership procedures, we will charge you a membership fee of 23,000 yuan.

2. 我每天健身，为的就是增加我胸部和手臂的肌肉，并消除腰部的脂肪。I work out every day in order to build muscle in my chest and arms and get rid of the fat around my waist.

3. 现代人在健身房健身已慢慢成为一种趋势。It's gradually becoming a trend for

modern people to work out in the gym.

4. 这个模特儿每个星期到健身房健身五次。The model goes to the gym for a workout five times a week.

5. 你最好做点运动。You'd better have/get some exercise.

6. 控制热量的饮食对想减肥的人很有帮助。A calorie-controlled diet will help those who want to lose weight.

7. 她的曲线尽显！每个男人都为她着迷。She's got all that perfect curves. Every guy is so crazy about her.

8. 开始做运动前，我们都应该热身。We all should warm up before doing some exercise.

9. 我们把汽车发动机热一下，再开车吧！Let's warm up the car engine before we start driving!

10. 做任何运动前，热身的伸展运动都是非常重要的。Warm-up stretches are extremely important before any exercise.

11. 热身十分钟后，他开始慢跑。After a warm-up of ten minutes, he started jogging.

12. 每次健身的前后，都应该做些伸展的动作。Every time you work out, you should begin and end with some stretching exercises.

13. 把你的手臂往上伸展。Stretch your arms up.

14. 健身之前和健身过程中，一定得做伸展的动作。Always stretch before and during workouts.

15. 既然你的柔韧度不是很好，那么你急需固定做些伸展的运动。Since your flexibility level is not good, you are in desperate need of doing some stretching exercises regularly.

情景对话 Situational Dialogues

对话1 Dialogue 1 健身服务（1）Fitness Service（1）

场景：一位宾客在俱乐部的练习情况

Scene: A guest's practice at the club

S：Staff（员工） G：Guest（宾客）

S：早上好。欢迎来到健康俱乐部。先生，您是游泳还是健身？Good morning. Welcome to Health Club. Are you going to swim or work out, sir?

G：我要游泳，可能也会健身。I'm going to swim, maybe do some workout then.

S：先生，您是宾馆的客人吗？Are you our hotel guest, sir?

G：不，但我是俱乐部会员。No, but I'm the club member.

S：您能出示下会员卡方便我们登记吗？Could you show me your member card so that we can register for you?

G：给你。Here you are.

S：谢谢。您能在这签名吗？Thank you. Can you sign here?

G：好的。OK.

S：谢谢。祝您玩得愉快。Thank you. I wish you have a good time here.

对话2 Dialogue 2 健身服务（2）Fitness Service（2）

场景：员工介绍俱乐部会员情况。

Scene：The staff introduces the club membership.

S：Staff（员工）　G：Guest（宾客）

S：先生，下午好。Good afternoon, sir.

G：下午好。我想成为健康俱乐部的会员。你能给我讲下细节吗？Good afternoon. I want to be the member of Health Club. Could you tell me the details?

S：好的，我们有三种卡。一种是只能游泳的，一种是只能健身的，还有一种是二者均可的。只能用于游泳或健身的是700元30次，3个月内有效。通卡是900元30次，3个月有效。OK, we have 3 kinds of cards. One is only for swimming, one is only for fitness and another is for both. The card for 30 times swimming or fitness is 700 yuan and available for 3 months, and the card for both is 900 yuan and available for 3 months, too.

G：明白了，泳池的水温和水深如何？I see. What about the water temperature and depth of the pool?

S：我们有一个温水按摩池，温度是36℃。水深是1.4米。我带您看下俱乐部怎样？We have a warm massage pool, and the temperature is 36℃. The depth is 1.4 meter. Would you like me to show you our club?

G：好的，谢谢。OK, thank you.

S：请这边走。This way, please.

对话3 Dialogue 3 健身服务（3）Fitness Service（3）

场景：员工介绍俱乐部会员情况。

Scene：The staff introduces the club membership.

R：Receptionist（接待员）　G：Guest（顾客）

R：下午好。有什么能为您效劳吗？Good afternoon. Can I help you?

G：我想做运动。能不能告诉我这里有什么运动设施？I'd like to take some exercise. Could you tell me what facilities you have here?

R：当然可以，先生。我们体育馆设备齐全，有许多最新的运动设施，像运动脚踏车、举重设备、游泳池、网球场之类的。您从这张地图能知道更多细节。Certainly, sir. We have a well-equipped gym with many latest fitness facilities, such as exercise bicycles, weightlifting equipment, swimming pools, tennis courts and so on. You may find more details on this map.

G：听起来棒极了！That sounds terrific!

R：我们还有一个不错的桑拿浴室，免费提供毛巾和浴皂。Then we have an excellent sauna, with a free supply of towels and soap.

G：太好了！我想去游泳。顺便问一下，你们这里有游泳裤卖吗？我的游泳裤放在家里了。Great! I'd like to go swimming. By the way, do you sell swimming trunks here? I've left mine at home.

R：是的，旁边的商店里就卖。Yes, you can find them at the shop nearby.

补充阅读 Supplement Reading

健身六个常识误区

1. 流汗越多，消耗的脂肪越多。

这个错误的观点鼓励人们在极热的环境下运动，或者穿好几层衣服、穿橡胶或塑料减肥服，希望通过流汗将脂肪排出。不幸的是，排出去的是水而不是脂肪。

作为一种能量来源，脂肪只在运动时才消耗，而且在运动初始阶段并不能奏效。当你开始运动时，你消耗的是碳水化合物，或者糖类。平缓进行有氧运动大约20分钟才会由消耗糖类向消耗脂肪过渡。有氧运动就是有节奏的、持续的活动。它需要耗氧并且锻炼像手臂和腿部的大块肌肉，例如骑自行车、跳绳、步行、慢跑、跳舞和游泳。所以说，要消耗脂肪，至少要运动40分钟。

2. 如果你停止锻炼，你的肌肉将变成脂肪。

如果你减少运动量，并且继续吃相同或更多的食物，你过去努力锻炼而减去的脂肪很可能会卷土重来。然而，这并不是因为你的肌肉变成了脂肪。肌肉可能萎缩或失去弹性，但是它们不能变成脂肪。肌肉就是肌肉，脂肪就是脂肪。

3. 锻炼增加食欲。

对于持续进行了1个小时或者更长时间的剧烈运动的人来说确实如此。然而，不到1个小时的平缓运动很可能在1至2个小时内降低你的食欲。

通常锻炼会降低血糖，在开始锻炼前你最好先吃点东西做准备。然而，如果你的血糖量高于250毫克/分升，锻炼会使你的血糖量升得更高。

4. 每周进行10分钟的锻炼，你就能变得健康。

这种观点和类似的观点很普遍，但不正确。健康之路无捷径。要想变得健康就需要锻炼，通常的规则是每周进行3次、每次20分钟的有氧运动。坚持是关键。如果你错过了一两天，不要通过加倍的运动来弥补。

5. 不劳则无获。

有些人倾向于过度锻炼以达到更好的效果，然而这样做可能造成伤害或引起肌肉疼痛。最佳的方式就是缓慢地开始锻炼，然后逐渐增加运动量。

开始锻炼时，先用一刻钟的时间进行伸展运动，然后进行30到40分钟的步行或步行加慢跑，最后以10分钟的伸展运动结束。以这样的方式开始运动就会有个良好的开端，不会感到疼痛，也不会受到伤害。

6. 用电疗代替锻炼。

电疗可能有助于肌肉收缩，稍微变得结实，但是这种疗法不能代替锻炼，也不能帮助你减肥。如果你想减少脂肪，必须做有氧运动。

Six Common Misconceptions about Fitness

1. The more you sweat, the more fat you burn.

This misconception encourages people to exercise in extreme heat or wear layers of clothing or rubber or plastic weight-loss suits in the hope of sweating fat off. Unfortunately, it's water, not fat, that goes out.

As a fuel source, fat is consumed only during exercise. And it doesn't work in the initial stages of exercise. When you start exercising, you consume carbohydrates, or sugars. It takes about 20 minutes of gentle aerobic exercise to transition from burning sugar to fat. Aerobic exercise is a rhythmic, continuous activity. It uses oxygen and works large muscles like the arms and legs, for example, cycling, jumping rope, walking, jogging, dancing and swimming. So, to burn fat, you need to do exercise for at least 40 minutes.

2. If you stop exercising, your muscles will turn to fat.

If you cut back on exercise and continue to eat the same or more food, the fat you lost from working out hard in the past is likely to come back. However, it's not because your muscles turn to fat. Muscles may atrophy or lose their elasticity, but they cannot become fat. Muscle is muscle and fat is fat.

3. Exercise increases appetite.

This is true for people who engage in vigorous exercise for an hour or more. However, less than 1 hour of gentle exercise is likely to reduce your appetite for 1 to 2 hours.

Exercise always lowers blood sugar, so it's best to prepare by eating before you start. However, if your blood sugar level is higher than 250 mg/dl, exercise can cause your blood sugar to rise even higher.

4. Do exercise 10 minutes every week, and you can become healthy.

This claim and similar claims are common, but are not true. There is no shortcut to health.

Getting fit requires exercise, and the general rule is doing 20 minutes of aerobic exercise three times a week. Persistence is the key. If you miss a day or two, don't try to make up for it by doubling up on your exercise.

5. No pains, no gains.

Some people tend to over-exercise for faster results, but doing so can cause injury or muscle pain. The best way is to start slowly and then gradually increase the amount of exercise.

Start your workout with a quarter of an hour of stretching, then with 30 to 40 minutes of walking or walking and jogging, and finish with 10 minutes of stretching. Starting in this way will give you a good start. There's no pain, and no injury.

6. Use electrotherapy instead of exercise.

Electrotherapy may help muscles contract and tone up slightly, but this treatment is not a substitute for exercise, nor will it help you lose weight. If you want to lose fat, you must do aerobic exercise.

练一练 Activities

一、朗读下列词汇

减肥　　健身　　曲线　　伸展　　热身

二、翻译下列句子

1. 开始做运动前，我们都应该热身。
2. 把你的手臂往上伸展。
3. 请您出示下会员卡。
4. 泳池的水温和水深如何？
5. 我们还有一个不错的桑拿浴室，免费提供毛巾和浴皂。

Unit 4　美容院 Beauty Salon

导言 Preview

美容沙龙，也叫美容院，在酒店中扮演着重要的角色。对于一些酒店来说，这是一个突出的特点，也是吸引客人的主要因素。

大多数酒店都可以为客人提供发型设计。当客人需要参加正式的活动时，他们可以去酒店的理发店，根据他们的要求做头发。这项服务受到客人的欢迎。

在美容院，人们不仅可以做头发，还可以享受按摩。如泰国的一些酒店，以按摩而闻名。很多客人来这些酒店只是为了按摩。这是放松的好方法。

Beauty salon, which is also called beauty parlor, plays an important role in a hotel. And for some hotels, it is an outstanding characteristic and the main attraction to guests.

Most hotels could provide hairstyle designs to their guests. When guests need to take part in the formal activities, they could go to the barber's in the hotel and get their hair styled at their request. This service is welcomed by guests.

In a beauty salon, people could not only have their hair styled, but also enjoy massage. Some hotels such as those in Thailand are very famous for their massage. Lots of guests come to these hotels just for their massage. It is a good way to relax.

词库 Word Bank

常用词汇 Common vocabulary			
汉语 Chinese	英语 English	汉语 Chinese	英语 English
满意的 mǎn yì de	satisfactory	给（某人或身体某部位）按摩（或推拿）gěi (mǒu rén huò shēn tǐ mǒu bù wèi) àn mó (huò tuī ná)	massage
调色剂 tiáo sè jì 增色剂 zēng sè jì	toner	循环 xún huán 环流 huán liú 运行 yùn xíng	circulation
滋补 zī bǔ 滋润 zī rùn 使活跃 shǐ huó yuè 使健壮 shǐ jiàn zhuàng	invigorate	给（皮肤、空气等）增加水分 gěi (pí fū、kōng qì děng) zēng jiā shuǐ fèn	moisturize
剥落 bō luò 剥落物 bō luò wù	exfoliation	滋补的 zī bǔ de	tonic
剥皮 bāo pí	peel	使清洁 shǐ qīng jié 清洗 qīng xǐ	cleanse
擦洗 cā xǐ 擦净 cā jìng	scrub		

常用句型 Useful Expressions

1. 先生，下午好，请坐这儿。Good afternoon, sir. Take this chair, please.
2. 下午好，请替我理发，并修面。Good afternoon. I want a haircut and a shave,

please.

3. 好的，您想剪什么发式？Very well, how would you like your hair cut?

4. 照这样吗？Would you keep the same style?

5. 请看一下，效果好吗？Please have a look, and is it all right?

6. 您要洗头吗？Would you like to have a shampoo?

7. 胡须要不要给您刮掉？Do you want me to shave off your beard?

8. 要不要把您的胡须修剪一下？Would you like to trim your moustache?

9. 夫人，您的头发是想电烫、冷烫，还是洗一洗再做？How would you like your hair done, madam? Permanent, cold wave, or washed and styled?

10. 您能否给我看一些发型的式样？Can you show me some patterns of hairstyles?

11. 我想理个发。I'd like to have my hair cut.

12. 您想理什么式样的？How do you want it?

13. 修剪一下就行了。两边剪短些，但后面不要剪得太多。Just a trim, and cut the sides fairly short, but not so much at the back.

14. 顶上不剪吗？Nothing off the top?

15. 嗯，稍微剪一点。Well, a little off the top.

16. 您要不要修面或洗头？Would you like a shave or shampoo?

17. 我想理发和修面。I want a haircut and a shave, please.

18. 好的，您喜欢什么发式？OK, what hairstyle do you prefer?

19. 要我为您修剪一下小胡子吗？Do you want me to trim your moustache?

20. 好，能不能把两边鬓角再剪短些？Well, could you cut a little more off the temples?

21. 您看这样满意吗？Is that satisfactory?

22. 还要我为您做些什么吗？Anything else I can do for you?

23. 我想做面部美容。I want a facial.

24. 面部美容大都是先彻底清洁面部皮肤。Most facials start with a thorough cleansing.

25. 我要做半小时美容外加化妆。I'll take the half-hour facial with make-up.

情景对话 Situational Dialogues

对话1 Dialogue 1 美容美发（1）Beauty Salon (1)

场景：向理发师说明情况

Scene：Explain the situation to the barber

B：Barber（理发师）　　C：Customer（顾客）

B：早上好，先生。请坐。Good morning, sir. Take a seat, please.

C：谢谢。我想理发。Thank you. I'd like to have my hair cut.

B：您要怎么剪？How do you want it?

C：稍微修一下，两边剪短一点，但后面不要剪得太多。Just a trim, and cut the sides fairly short, but not so much at the back.

B：上面不要剪掉吗？Nothing off the top?

C：嗯，上面剪掉一点。Well, a little off the top.

B：前面怎么样？How about the front?

C：前面保持原样。Leave the front as it is.

B：您要刮脸还是洗头？Would you like a shave or shampoo?

C：不，谢谢。我可以自己做这些事。No, thanks. I can do these things by myself.

对话2 Dialogue 2 美容美发（2）Beauty Salon（2）

场景：与理发师探讨最近流行的发型

Scene：Discuss the latest popular hairstyles with the hairdresser

H：Hairdresser（理发师）　　C：Customer（顾客）

C：我准备换个新发型，你有什么建议吗？I'm ready for a new hairdo. Do you have any suggestions?

H：您最近有没有看到什么新的发型？Have you taken a look at some of the new styles lately?

C：有，我带了一本杂志给你看。我喜欢这个发型。Yes, I have brought a magazine to show you. I like this one.

H：哦，它很漂亮。您的头发要继续留这么长吗？还是要剪短一点？我认为您剪短发一定很好看。或许您该剪得比杂志上更短些才好。Oh, that is pretty. Do you want to keep your hair this long? Or do you want to take it shorter? I think you would look cute with short hair. Perhaps it should go even shorter than in the picture.

C：你来决定吧。我说过的，我已准备好要改变一下自己。I'll leave it up to you. As I said, I'm ready for a change.

H：好。您应该认真考虑一下挑染。OK. You should really think about highlighting the surface of your hair, too.

C：你认为那样会好看吗？我担心那会使我的头发看起来不自然。Do you think that would look good? I'm worried that it will make my hair look unnatural.

H：不会。只是稍微染一下。这次我们可以稍微染一点。如果您喜欢的话，下一次可以染多一点。要不然，染过的颜色四个星期就会淡了。No, it won't. The highlights are very subtle. We can do a little bit this time. If you like it, we can do more next time.

Otherwise, the highlights would fade out in about four weeks.

C：好的，我听你的。顺便问一下，洗头、做头发要多少钱？OK, I count on you. By the way, how much do you charge for a shampoo and set?

H：一共200元。200 yuan in total.

对话3 Dialogue 3 美容美发（3）Beauty Salon (3)

场景：一位顾客在美容院做面部护理。

Scene: A customer gets a facial at a beauty salon.

A：Assistant（服务员）　C：Customer（顾客）

A：下午好，女士。我能为您做些什么？Good afternoon, madam. What can I do for you?

C：下午好。我想做面部护理。但这是我第一次来这里，所以你能告诉我流程是怎样的吗？Good afternoon. I want a facial treatment. But this is my first time here, so can you tell me how you do it?

A：当然。大多数面部护理都是从彻底清洁开始的。然后我们通常用爽肤水来激活皮肤，接着是去角质治疗，用去皮面膜或磨砂膏去除使皮肤看起来暗淡的死细胞。之后，我们会用油或面霜按摩您的脸部和颈部，以促进血液循环，缓解紧张，然后用面膜滋润和软化皮肤。Sure. Most facials start with a thorough cleansing. Then we usually use a toner to invigorate the skin followed by exfoliation treatment, using a peeling mask or scrub that removes the dead cells that makes the skin look dull. After that, we'll massage your face and neck with oil or cream to improve the circulation and relieve the tension, followed by a mask to moisturize and soften the skin.

C：这正是我想要的。要花多长时间？That's exactly what I want. How long does it take?

A：有半小时和一小时的治疗。半小时的面部护理20元，一小时的30元。如果您想化妆，再加10元就可以了。There are half-hour and one-hour treatments. The half-hour facial costs twenty yuan and the one-hour costs thirty yuan. If you want a makeup, another ten yuan will do.

C：好。我要做半小时的化妆面部护理。Good. I'll take the half-hour facial makeup treatment.

补充阅读 Supplement Reading

美容美发沙龙知识加油站

1. 在给客人进行美容之前，应详细介绍美容内容，并可适时介绍产品供顾客选择。如：

面部美容大都是先彻底清洁面部皮肤。

小姐，您的皮肤太干了，应该用些补水产品。

您可以试一下我们这里的补水套装，效果很好的。

2. 在给客人剪发之前，应主动问清楚顾客想要什么样的发型，以及其他对头发的具体要求，并不断询问顾客是否满意，以免最后剪出的发型让顾客不满。如：

您喜欢头发做成什么式样？

您要染什么颜色？

您看这样满意吗？

3. 如今的美发店在剪发之外也会提供许多其他服务。因此理发师在给客人剪完头发后，可酌情询问顾客是否需要其他服务，以提高客人对本店的满意度。如：

您要不要修面或洗头？

要我为您修剪一下小胡子吗？

还要我为您做些什么吗？

Beauty Salon Knowledge Gas Station

1. Before providing a beauty treatment to the guest, the content and details of the treatment should be introduced thoroughly. Additionally, timely recommendations of products for customers to choose from are essential, for example:

Most facials start with a thorough cleansing.

Miss, your skin is too dry. You'd better use some hydrating products.

You can try our hydrating package. It has good effects.

2. Before cutting guests' hair, you should take the initiative to ask them what kind of hairstyle they want, and other specific requirements for hair. And constantly ask the customers whether they are satisfied, in order to avoid their dissatisfaction with the final hairstyle, for example:

How would you like your hair set?

What color would you like to dye it?

Is this satisfactory?

3. Today's barbershops offer many other services besides haircuts. Therefore, after cutting the hair of customers, the hairdressers can ask them whether they need other services, so as to deepen the customers' satisfaction with the shop, for example:

Would you like a shave or shampoo?

Do you want me to trim your moustache?

Anything else I can do for you?

练一练 Activities

一、连线题

（1）理发　　　　　　　（A）dye
（2）发型　　　　　　　（B）make up
（3）化妆　　　　　　　（C）shave
（4）冷烫　　　　　　　（D）hairstyles
（5）修面　　　　　　　（E）hair cut
（6）染发　　　　　　　（F）cold wave

二、翻译下列句子

1. 我想修剪一下我的胡须。
2. 您要洗头吗？
3. 夫人，您的头发是想电烫、冷烫，还是洗一洗再做？
4. 我想做面部美容。
5. 您最近有没有看到什么新的发型？

Chapter 5　会议服务 Conference Service

会议服务，是一项专门提供会议场地、会议所需设施设备，并涵盖餐饮供应及专业人力服务的综合性业务。一般包括会前准备、会中服务、会后收尾三个步骤。

Conference service is a comprehensive business that specializes in providing conference venues, necessary facilities and equipment, as well as catering services and professional manpower services. Generally, it includes three steps: pre-conference preparation, in-conference service and post-conference winding-up.

会前准备 Pre-conference Preparation

1. 了解会议基本情况：接待人员应了解参加会议的人数，会议类型、名称、时间、会桌的要求，与会者的风俗习惯，付款方式和收费金额，等等。

The knowledge of the basic situation of the conference: The receptionist should know the number of participants, the meeting type, title, time, the requirements of the meeting table, the customs and habits of the participants, the way of payment and the charge amount, etc.

2. 布置会场：接待人员应布置符合主办者的意图和要求的会场，保证会场整洁，会标大小合适、颜色协调，绿植摆放位置合适。

Arrangements of the venue: The receptionist should arrange the venue that meets the intention and requirements of the organizer, ensure that the venue is clean and tidy, the logo size is suitable, the color is coordinated, and the position of green plants is appropriate.

3. 了解物品需求：接待人员应了解物品的特殊要求，确保物品干净整洁，没有破损，并预留出超过与会人数的10%作为备量。

The acquaintance with item requirements: The receptionist should know the special requirements of the items, and ensure that the items are clean and tidy, without damage. And items for more than 10% of the participants should be reserved as backup.

会中服务 In-conference Service

1. 迎宾服务：在会议开始前半小时，迎宾人员应在门口处迎接参会人员。正确引导参会人员到达指定地点是保证良好的会议座次安排的关键。

Welcome service: Participants should be met at the door by a greeter half an hour before the meeting begins. Greeters should correctly guide the participants to the designated place, which is the key to ensure the good seating arrangement for the meeting.

2. 检查设备设施：接待人员在会议开始半小时前就要开启会场灯光，并保持灯光明亮，确保话筒、音响、音视频播放器、投影等设施能正常工作。

Checking the equipment and facilities：The lights of the venue should be turned on half an hour before the meeting, and the receptionist should keep the lights bright. The microphone, audio equipment, audio and video player, projector and other facilities can work normally.

3. 茶歇服务：在会议休息开始前至少5分钟，服务人员将会议茶歇的各种饮品、点心、用具等准备齐全，做好服务准备。会议结束后，服务人员应及时整理餐台，恢复原貌，撤走并送洗餐具。

Tea break service：At least 5 minutes before the meeting break, the service staff prepare all kinds of drinks, snacks and utensils for the meeting break, and prepare for the service. After the meeting, the service staff should tidy up in time to restore the original appearance, and then remove and send the tableware for washing.

会后收尾 Post-conference Winding-Up

1. 送客服务：服务人员应保证会议室所有的门处于打开状态，并及时为客人准备好电梯。

Customer farewell service：The service personnel should ensure that all the doors of the conference room remain open, and prepare the elevator for guests in time.

2. 检查与清理会场：等待所有客人离场之后，服务人员应仔细检查会场是否有客人遗留的物品，并登记归还。之后服务人员应清扫卫生，摆放桌椅归位，撤下设备、设施用品，分类归还。

Checking and cleaning up the venue：After all guests leaving the venue, the service personnel should carefully check whether there are any items left by guests. Register the left items and return them. Then the service personnel should do the cleaning, put the tables and chairs in place, remove equipment and facilities, and return them.

Unit 1　会议设备 Conference Equipment

导言 Preview

会议设施、设备是指在会议室里召开会议时所使用的一系列设施、设备。根据其功能可分为以下几大类：

1. 影音设备

（1）视频和控制设备，包括：投影设备、LED设备、等离子设备、电脑、视频播放器、视频转换器、视频中央控制设备等。

（2）会议发言扩声设备，包括：音响设备、会议系统设备、无线麦克、音效设备等。

2. 办公设备

包括：办公文具、复印机、打印机、扫描仪、网络设备等。

3. 翻译设备

包括：同声传译机。

4. 记录设备

包括：摄影摄像机、速录设备、录音设备等。

5. 灯光设备

包括：电脑灯、帕灯、追光灯、地排灯、激光灯等各种灯光设备及灯效控制设备。

6. 门禁系统

包括：条形码扫描器、统计软件等。

7. 特殊设备

包括：舞台效果设备、会议环节特制设备、投票设备等。

Conference facilities and equipment refer to a series of facilities and equipment used in meetings held in conference rooms. They can be divided into the following categories according to their functions：

1. Video and audio equipment

（1）Video and control facilities include projection equipment, LED equipment, plasma equipment, computers, video players, video converters, video central control equipment, etc.

（2）Meeting speech amplification equipment includes audio equipment, conference system equipment, wireless microphones, sound equipment, etc.

2. Office equipment

Office equipment includes office stationery, copiers, printers, scanners, network equipment, etc.

3. Translation equipment

Translation equipment includes simultaneous interpretation machines.

4. Recording equipment

Recording equipment includes photography and video cameras, quick-recording equipment, audio recording equipment, etc.

5. Lighting equipment

Lighting equipment includes computer lights, PAR lamps, chasing lights, floor lights, laser lights and lighting control equipment.

6. Access control system

Access control system includes barcode scanners, statistical software, etc.

7. Special equipment

Special equipment includes stage effect equipment, special conference equipment, voting equipment, etc.

词库 Word Bank

会议设备 Conference equipment			
汉语 Chinese	英语 English	汉语 Chinese	英语 English
投影仪 tóu yǐng yí	projector	无线麦克 wú xiàn mài kè	wireless microphone
液晶显示屏 yè jīng xiǎn shì píng	LCD screen	打印机 dǎ yìn jī	printer
视频播放器 shì pín bō fàng qì	video player	同声传译机 tóng shēng chuán yì jī	simultaneous interpretation machine
音频播放器 yīn pín bō fàng qì	audio player	摄影机 shè yǐng jī	video camera
音响 yīn xiǎng	audio equipment	激光笔 jī guāng bǐ	laser pointer
常用词汇 Common vocabulary			
汉语 Chinese	英语 English	汉语 Chinese	英语 English
商务中心 shāng wù zhōng xīn	business center	可视电话会议 kě shì diàn huà huì yì	video telephone conference
会议室 huì yì shì	meeting room	会议服务部 huì yì fú wù bù	Convention Service Department
多功能会议厅 duō gōng néng huì yì tīng	multi-purpose meeting room	研讨会 yán tǎo huì	seminar
接待室 jiē dài shì	reception room	礼堂 lǐ táng	auditorium
会议厅 huì yì tīng	convention hall	演讲台 yǎn jiǎng tái	rostrum

常用句型 Useful Expressions

预订会议室 Book a Meeting Room

1. 您能为我们订一间多功能会议室吗？Can you book a multi-purpose meeting room for us?

2. 我们这个星期五要开会，我想订一个大会议厅。We are going to have a meeting this Friday. I'd like to book a convention hall.

3. 请为我们安排好会议室。Please arrange the conference room for us.

4. 您想要什么样的会议室？What kind of meeting room do you want?

5. 你们有能容纳200人的会议大厅吗？Do you have one convention room for 200 persons?

会议设施 Conference Facilities

1. 您需要哪些设施？What facilities do you need?

2. 您想要预订哪种座位风格？Which seating style would you want to book?

3. 对于鸡尾酒会风格，可容纳100人。For cocktail reception style, its capacity can be 100 persons.

4. 您想要固定的椅子，还是可移动的椅子？Do you want fixed chairs, or movable chairs?

5. 你能为我们的会议准备一张圆桌吗？Can you prepare a round table for our conference?

会议设备 Conference Equipment

1. 您需要哪些电子设备？What electronic devices do you need?

2. 您需要投影仪和电脑吗？Do you need a projector and a computer?

3. 大厅里有一个液晶屏幕。There is a LCD screen in the hall.

4. 多功能会议室配备有无线麦克风/视频播放器/并发翻译机/音响设备。The multi-purpose meeting room is equipped with wireless microphones/video players/concurrent translation machines/audio equipment.

5. 我会提前帮您安装好会议室所有设备，请您放心。I will help you install all the equipment in the conference room in advance. Please rest assured.

情景对话 Situational Dialogues

对话1 Dialogue 1 安排会议 Arranging Meetings

场景：一位宾客想要安排一个会议。

Scene: A guest would like to arrange a meeting.

C：Clerk（前台职员）　　G：Guest（宾客）

C：先生，早上好，这是会议服务部，能为您效劳吗？Good morning. This is the Convention Service Department. May I help you, sir?

G：你好，我想在你们酒店举行个会议。Hello, I want to hold a convention in your hotel.

C：您想要举行什么样的会议？What kind of conference will you hold?

G：约200人的研讨会。A seminar for about 200 participants.

C：我们有一个可容纳300人的大型会议厅，会议设施齐全。We have a large

convention hall for holding 300 people, fully equipped with facilities.

G：太好了，会议大厅里有演讲台吗？That's good. Do you have a rostrum in the convention hall?

C：是的，我们有。演讲台可按照您的要求进行布置。Yes, we do. The rostrum can be arranged according to your requirements.

G：好的，我会仔细考虑一下，然后联系您。谢谢。OK, I will think it over and then contact you. Thanks.

C：不客气。我们期待着为您服务。You are welcome. We look forward to serving you.

对话2 Dialogue 2 会场预订（1）Reserving Conference Hall（1）

场景：一位宾客想要预订一个会场。

Scene：A guest would like to reserve a conference hall.

C：Clerk（前台职员）　　G：Guest（宾客）

C：我能为您做些什么呢？What can I do for you?

G：我们想在下周一预订一个大约80人的礼堂。We would like to book an auditorium for about 80 people next Monday.

C：您需要哪些设施？What facilities do you need?

G：我们需要一个投影仪，一个无线麦克风和一台笔记本电脑。We need a projector, a wireless microphone and a laptop.

C：没问题。那天您什么时候需要它们？No problem. When will you need them on that day?

G：请在早上八点半之前。Before 8:30 a.m., please.

C：好的，我们期待着您的到来。再见。OK, we look forward to your arrival. Goodbye.

对话3 Dialogue 3 会场预订（2）Reserving Conference Hall（2）

场景：一位宾客想要预订一个会场。

Scene：A guest would like to reserve a conference hall.

C：Clerk（前台职员）　　G：Guest（宾客）

C：早上好，先生。欢迎来到我们的酒店，能为您效劳吗？Good morning, sir. Welcome to our hotel. May I help you?

G：早上好。我昨天给你们酒店打过电话，我想预订你们酒店的会议大厅。Good morning. I called your hotel yesterday, and I'd like to book the convention hall of your hotel.

C：好的，您需要什么样的设施？OK, what kind of facilities do you need?

G：我们需要一个演讲台，10个无线麦克风，一个投影仪，一个同声传译机和音响。We need a rostrum, 10 wireless microphones, a projector, a simultaneous interpretation machine and audio equipment.

C：好的。您想如何装饰演讲台和大厅？All right. How do you want to decorate the rostrum and the hall?

G：我们希望大厅要简单而幽雅。另外，你们能用鲜花来装饰演讲台吗？We want the hall to be simple but elegant. Besides, could you decorate the rostrum with flowers?

C：没问题。您需要我们为您拍照和录像吗？No problem. Do you need us to take photos and record videos for you?

G：太好了，我们正好缺一位摄影师。That's great. We just need a photographer.

C：好的，研讨会将持续多少天？OK, how many days will the seminar last?

G：需要三天。It will be three days.

C：我知道了，您需要多少个房间？I see, and how many rooms do you need?

G：我们总共需要200间标准间，10间普通套房和10间豪华套房。We need 200 standard rooms, 10 junior suites and 10 deluxe suites in all.

C：好的。您能告诉我会议安排的餐饮要求吗？All right. Could you tell me your requirements for arranging catering for the conference?

G：第一天和最后一天的晚餐都是晚宴。其余都是自助餐。The dinners on the first day and the last day are banquets. Buffets are for other meals.

C：好的。我们期待为您服务。Sure. We look forward to serving you.

对话4 Dialogue 4 会场预订（3）Reserving Conference Hall（3）

场景：一位宾客想要预订一个会场。

Scene：A guest would like to reserve a conference hall.

C：Clerk（前台职员）　　G：Guest（宾客）

C：早上好，怀特先生。Good morning, Mr. White.

G：早上好，我想检查一下我们后天将使用的多功能会议室的设备。Good morning, I want to check up the equipment of the multi-purpose meeting room we will use the day after tomorrow.

C：好的，我们为您预留了一个很大的会议大厅。您说是一个公司年会，对吧？Fine, we have reserved a large convention hall for you. You said that was a company annual meeting, right?

G：是的，你知道的，这是一家公司每年最重要的会议之一。Yes. You know, it is one of the most important meetings for a company every year.

C：当然，我相信我们能满足您的需求。Absolutely, I'm sure we can meet your needs.

G：那就太好了。你能现在带我去会议室看看吗？That will be great. Could you show me the meeting room right now?

C：当然了。With pleasure.

G：谢谢你。Thank you.

C：怀特先生，这里就是会议室，我们有高级的视听设备，并且中央舞台至少能容纳100人。Mr. White, here is the meeting room, and we have the superior audio-visual equipment and the central stage can hold 100 people at least.

G：你能打开这些设施吗？Could you turn on these facilities?

C：当然。您可以测试麦克风，并使用遥控器来控制。Sure. You can test the microphones and use the remote control to control them.

G：好的，舞台上有追光灯和激光灯吗？OK. Do you have chasing lights and laser lights on the stage?

C：是的，所有这些灯都是专业的。我想您会满意的。Yes, all the lights are professional. I think you will be satisfied.

G：听起来不错。非常感谢。Sounds good. Thank you very much.

C：不用客气。You are welcome.

补充阅读 Supplement Reading

会议室主要类型

一般的会议室包括主席台、听众区和发言区。部分会议室则不作明确区分，如圆桌会议室和会见式会议室。会场的布置类型可以是标准化的，也可以是个性化的。一般的标准化类型有：

剧院式

剧院式的摆放方式与电影院基本相同，正前方是主席台，面向主席台的是一排排的观众（听众）席，观众席座位前一般不设桌子。剧院式的布置适合于例会和大型代表会等不需要书写和记录的会议类型。

课堂式

课堂式与剧院式相似，不同的是课堂式的座位前方会摆放桌子以方便参会人员书写。也有一些剧院式会议室采用座椅边隐蔽式或折叠式写字台，为参会者提供方便。课堂式的布置适合用于专业学术机构举办的、具有培训性质的会议。

宴会式

宴会式由大圆桌组成，每个圆桌可坐5~12人。宴会式会议室一般用于中餐宴会和培训会议。在培训性会议中，每个圆桌只会安排6人左右就座，这样有利于同桌人的互动和交流。

鸡尾酒式

鸡尾酒式的会议室比较灵活，没有一个固定的模式。鸡尾酒会一般不安排座位或仅安排少量座位，大家拿取食物后可自由走动交流。鸡尾酒式会议室所能容纳的人数仅次于剧院式。

U 形

U 形会议室是指会议桌摆设成一面开口的 U 字形状，椅子放置在 U 字形办公桌周围；投影机可以放在 U 形的开口处。相对于同一面积的会议室，这种形式所能容纳的人数最少，一般适合小型的、讨论型的会议。

董事会形

董事会形也称中空形，会议桌摆成一个封闭的"口"字形状，椅子放置在"口"的外围。董事会形一般只适用于小型的会议。

除了以上常见的会场布置类型，还有 T 形、E 形、多 U 形等会议室。

按照会议室的规模，会议室可以分为中小型会议室和大型会议室等。

Main Types of Conference Rooms

The general conference room includes the rostrum, the audience area and the speech area. Some conference rooms do not make a clear distinction, such as round-table meeting rooms and meeting-style conference rooms. The layout type of the venue can be standardized or personalized. The general standardized types are:

Theater Style

The layout of the Theater Style conference room is basically the same as the cinema. The front is the podium, facing which is a row of audience (auditorium) seats, and there is generally no table in front of the audience seats. The theater layout is suitable for regular meetings and large representative meetings that do not require written notes or recording.

Classroom Style

The Classroom Style conference room is similar to the Theater Style. The difference is that there are tables placed in front of the seats to facilitate the participants to write. There are also some Theater Style conference rooms with hidden or folding writing desks to provide convenience for attendees. The Classroom Style conference room is suitable for training meetings held by professional academic institutions.

Banquet Style

The Banquet Style conference room is composed of large round tables, each of which can seat 5 to 12 people. The Banquet Style conference rooms are generally used for Chinese banquets and training meetings. In the training meeting, only about 6 people will be seated at each round table, which is conducive to the interaction and communication with others.

Cocktail Style

The Cocktail Style conference room is more flexible, without a fixed pattern. The cocktail party generally has no seats or only a small number of seats. After taking the food, people can walk around and communicate freely. The Cocktail Style conference room can accommodate a number of people secondary to that of the Theater Style.

U Style

The U Style conference room refers to the U-shaped conference table arranged in the shape of a U with one open side, and chairs placed around the U-shaped desk; the projector can be placed at the opening of U. Compared with the conference room of the same area, this form can accommodate the least number of people, which is generally suitable for small, discussion-type meetings.

Board of Directors Style

The Board of Directors Style conference room is also called a hollow shape, and the conference table is placed in the shape of the closed "mouth" word, and chairs are placed on the periphery of the "mouth". This style of conference room is generally only used for small meetings.

In addition to the above common types of venue layout, there are also T-shaped, E-shaped, multi-U-shaped and other types of conference rooms.

According to the size of the conference room, they can be divided into small, medium-sized and large conference rooms.

练一练 Activities

一、根据图片标注出汉语

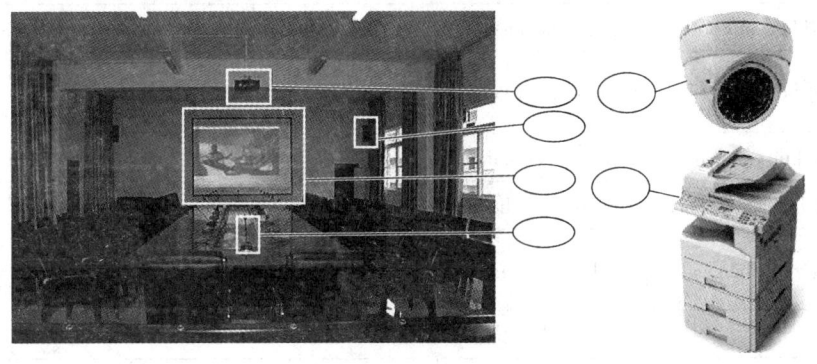

二、情景题

×××公司需要在你所在的酒店租用一间 50 人的会议室开年会，假定你是酒店的经理，请你对酒店相应会议室的设施及所能提供的会议服务内容作一个汉语介绍。

三、翻译下列句子

1. 您能为我们订一间多功能会议室吗？
2. 你们有能容纳 200 人的会议大厅吗？

3. 您需要哪些设施？
4. 您需要投影仪和电脑吗？
5. 大厅里有一个液晶屏幕。

Unit 2 会议接待服务 Conference Reception Service

导言 Preview

会议接待服务是指会议筹办方与主办方商谈、签订会议接待标准合同，对约定的事项提供全程的服务活动。会议接待贯串整个会议流程，涉及的服务范围广泛，包括会前工作、会中工作、会后工作三个环节，每个环节都囊括了众多的接待内容。

Conference reception service refers to the conference organizer negotiating with the sponsor, signing the standard contract of conference reception, and providing the whole process of service activities for the agreed matters. Conference reception runs through the whole conference process, involving a wide range of services, including pre-meeting work, in-meeting work and post-meeting work, and each includes a large number of reception matters.

词库 Word Bank

会议资料 Conference materials			
汉语 Chinese	英语 English	汉语 Chinese	英语 English
发言稿 fā yán gǎo	speech manuscript	广告牌 guǎng gào pái	billboard
报到册 bào dào cè	registration book	会议代表证 huì yì dài biǎo zhèng	conference representative certificate
会议指南 huì yì zhǐ nán	conference guide	会议礼品 huì yì lǐ pǐn	conference gift
会议日程 huì yì rì chéng	conference schedule	主办单位 zhǔ bàn dān wèi	sponsor
展板 zhǎn bǎn	display board	承办单位 chéng bàn dān wèi	organizer
常用词汇 Common vocabulary			
汉语 Chinese	英语 English	汉语 Chinese	英语 English
报到处 bào dào chù	check-in counter	与会者 yù huì zhě	attendant
文印室 wén yìn shì	printing room	调查表 diào chá biǎo	questionnaire
会标 huì biāo	conference logo	宴会 yàn huì	banquet
会务接待 huì wù jiē dài	conference reception	音箱 yīn xiāng	stereo
发票 fā piào	receipt	维修人员 wéi xiū rén yuán	maintenance personnel

常用句型 Useful Expressions

欢迎 Welcome

1. 欢迎光临喜悦大酒店，请问需要帮忙吗？Welcome to Xiyue Hotel. May I help you?
2. 女士/先生，您好，请进。Hello, madam/sir, come in, please.
3. 我是李华，我会负责接待您。My name is Li Hua. I will be responsible for receiving you.
4. 你们需要喝点咖啡吗？Would you like some coffee?
5. 希望您在这里过得愉快。I hope you will enjoy your stay here.

服务 Service

1. 您有什么吩咐？May I help you?
2. 我能为您做点什么？What can I do for you?
3. 如果您有其他需求，请随时与我们联系。Please contact us anytime if you have other needs.
4. 请您讲慢一点。Please speak slowly.
5. 请您再重复一遍好吗？Would you please repeat it?
6. 我们为您准备好了茶和点心，请享用。We have prepared tea and snacks for you. Please enjoy yourself.
7. 如果您对我们的服务满意，请填写我们的反馈调查表。If you are satisfied with our service, please fill out our feedback questionnaire.
8. 对不起，先生，这里不准抽烟。Sorry, sir, smoking is not allowed here.
9. 请问宴会什么时候举行？When will the banquet be held, please?

告别 Goodbye

1. 我们期待再次与您相见。We look forward to seeing you soon.
2. 感谢您的光临！Thank you for your coming!
3. 请慢走。Please take care.
4. 祝您愉快。Have a nice day.
5. 欢迎下次光临。Welcome to visit us next time.

情景对话 Situational Dialogues

对话 1 Dialogue 1 引导宾客 Guiding Guests

场景：一位前台职员正在引导宾客前往会议室。

Scene：A clerk is guiding a guest to the conference hall.

C：Clerk（前台职员）　　G：Guest（宾客）

C：您好，请问您需要什么帮助？Hello, what can I do for you?

G：您好，请问研讨会在什么地方？Hello, where is the seminar, please?

C：是今天下午三点的环境保护研讨会吗？Is it the environmental protection seminar at 3 p.m. this afternoon?

G：是的。Yes, it is.

C：您从左边的电梯上16楼，会有会议工作人员为您做指引。Take the elevator on the left to the 16th floor, and there will be the conference staff to guide you.

G：谢谢。Thanks.

C：不客气。You're welcome.

对话2 Dialogue 2 会场设备维修 Maintaining the Equipment of the Conference Hall

场景：一位酒店职员帮助一位宾客联系维修人员来维修会场的设备。

Scene：A hotel clerk helps a guest contact maintenance personnel to repair the equipment in the conference room.

C：Clerk（前台职员）   G：Guest（宾客）   M：Maintenance Personnel（维修人员）

G：您好，会议室的音响出了点问题，请帮我看看。Hello, there is something wrong with the audio of the conference room. Please help me to have a look.

C：请稍等，我打电话请维修人员过来检查一下。Please wait a moment. I'll call and ask the maintenance personnel to come and check it.

G：请尽快。As soon as possible, please.

（5分钟后 5 minutes later）

M：先生您好，请问您的音响哪里出了问题呢？Hello, sir, what's wrong with your audio?

G：您好，麻烦您帮我看一下左边的音箱，它没有声音了。Hello, please help me to check the stereo on the left, and there is no sound.

M：我检查一下，您稍等。I'll check it. Please wait a moment.

G：好的。OK.

M：噢，是连接线出了点问题，我来处理一下。Oh, there is something wrong with the cable. I will deal with it.

G：谢谢。Thank you.

（10分钟后 10 minutes later）

M：先生，音箱已经帮您修好了，抱歉给您带来了不便。Sir, the stereo has been repaired for you. Sorry for the inconvenience.

G：没关系，非常感谢。It doesn't matter. I really appreciate it.

M：您客气了，您还有其他问题要处理吗？You're welcome. Do you have any other problems to deal with?

G：没有了，谢谢。No more, thanks.

M：好的，祝您愉快。All right. Have a nice day.

对话3 Dialogue 3 复印服务 Copying Services

场景：一位宾客想要复印文件。

Scene：A guest wants to copy a document.

C：Clerk（前台职员）　G：Guest（宾客）

G：你好，请问酒店哪里可以复印文件呢？Hello, where can I copy the documents in the hotel?

C：女士，文印室在前面第二个房间。Ms, the printing room is in the second room ahead.

G：谢谢。Thank you.

C：不客气。You're welcome.

（在文印室 In the printing room）

C：您好，请问您需要什么帮助？Hello, what can I do for you?

G：你好，我想复印一下这份文件，用A4纸复印。Hi, I want to copy this document on A4 paper.

C：好的，您想复印多少份？OK, how many copies do you want?

G：十份吧。Ten.

C：请稍等……给您。Please wait a moment... Here you are.

G：谢谢，总共多少钱？Thank you. How much is it in total?

C：每张1元，一共10元。1 yuan per piece, and 10 yuan in total.

G：可以手机支付吗？Can I pay by mobile phone?

C：当然，您可以扫这个二维码支付。Of course, you could scan this QR code to pay.

G：已经付好了，谢谢。It's paid, thanks.

对话4 Dialogue 4 安排招待会 Arranging the Reception

场景：一位宾客正在询问前台职员招待会相关事宜。

Scene：A guest is asking about the reception at the front desk.

C：Clerk（前台职员）　G：Guest（宾客）

C：先生，您希望招待会什么时候开始？Sir, what time will you want the reception to start?

G：会议之后，5点半左右。After the meeting, around 5:30.

C：您想要什么水果？What kind of fruit would you like?

G：请准备一些苹果、香蕉、西瓜和葡萄。Please prepare some apples, bananas, watermelons and grapes.

C：那酒水需要哪些呢？And how about drinks?

G：请准备一些白葡萄酒、啤酒、果汁和酸奶。Please prepare some white wine, beer, juice and yogurt.

C：还要加点儿什么吗？Is there anything more to add?

G：就这些。That's all.

补充阅读 Supplement Reading

会议接待礼仪

（1）接打电话

接待人员在接打电话时要做到语言、态度、举止文明。要使用电话基本文明用语，如：您好、请、劳驾、麻烦、谢谢等，声调要愉悦，音量要适中，咬字要清楚。

接待人员主动给宾客打电话时，应在对方的工作时间内联系，尽量不要在节假日、用餐时间和休息时间给他人打工作电话（特别紧急时除外）。打国际电话时还要考虑时差。

电话礼仪提倡以短为佳，宁短勿长，通话的时间通常控制在三分钟之内。

（2）引路

如果是接待人员引导宾客，其应走在宾客的左前方一点的位置，遇到转弯时，应用右手示意，说声"请走这边"；如果是主人陪同宾客，应让客人位于自己的右侧，以示尊重，注意要并排走，不要落在后面。随同人员一般走在领导的两侧偏后一点或后面的位置。

（3）上下楼梯

上楼梯时，接待人员应让宾客、领导、女士优先，接待人员在后；下楼梯时，接待人员应在前，让宾客、领导、女士在后。

（4）乘坐电梯

乘坐电梯时，接待人员要先进电梯，再让宾客进入。电梯到达时，应让宾客先出电梯，接待人员此时应用手挡着电梯门，或按着电梯开门的按钮，防止门突然自动关闭，夹伤宾客。

（5）进出门口

进入门口时，接待人员应先把门推开，站在门口，用手示意，请宾客、领导、女士进入。出门时也是如此。如果接待人员是主陪，走到门口时，应用手示意，有礼貌地说声"请"。

（6）握手

①握手的先后次序

根据礼仪规范，握手时双方伸手的先后次序，应当在遵守"尊者决定"原则的前提下，具体情况具体对待。

在工作场合，握手时伸手的先后次序主要取决于职位、身份；而在社交、休闲场合，则主要取决于年龄、性别、婚否。

当宾客抵达时，接待人员应首先伸出手来与宾客相握，以示欢迎；在宾客告辞时，则应由宾客首先伸出手来与接待人员相握，以示再见。

②握手的力度和时间

握手时，为表示热情友好，应当稍许用力；与亲朋故旧握手时，所用的力量可稍大一些；而在与初次相识者及异性握手时，不可用力过猛。通常，与他人握手的时间不宜过短或过长。一般来说，握手的时间应控制在3秒钟以内。

（7）互递名片

接待活动中，在向对方赠送名片时应起立，双手递赠，以示尊重。在接受名片时也要用双手，接到对方名片后一定要看一遍，切不可不看一眼就装在衣袋里或拿在手上把玩，更不能把名片放在桌上，这些都是不尊重、不礼貌的行为。

Meeting Reception Etiquette

(1) Making Phone Calls

When making phone calls, the receptionist should be civilized in language, attitudes and behavior, and should use basic civilized language on the telephone, such as hello, please, excuse me, may I trouble you, thank you. The tone of voice should be pleasant, the volume should be moderate, and the words should be clear.

When calling guests, the receptionist should contact them during working hours and try not to call during holidays, meal hours and rest time (except in special emergencies). Consider the time difference when making international calls.

Telephone etiquette advocates that it is better to have a brief call than a long one, and the duration of the call should be controlled within three minutes.

(2) Guiding

If the receptionist is guiding the guest, he/she should walk on the guest's left side, slightly ahead, and when encountering turns, the receptionist should use the right hand to signal, and say "Please go this way"; if the host accompanies the guest, he/she should place the guest on the right side to show respect, walk side by side, and make sure not to fall behind. Accompanying escorts generally walk on either side of the leader, slightly behind or directly behind.

(3) Going up and down Stairs

When going up the stairs, the receptionist should stay behind and let guests, leaders and ladies go first; when going down the stairs, the receptionist should be in the front, and let guests, leaders and ladies walk behind.

(4) Taking the Elevator

When taking the elevator, the receptionist should enter the elevator first and then the guests. When the elevator stops, the guest should be allowed to get out of the elevator first. At this time, the receptionist should block the elevator door with his/her hand or press the button of the elevator to keep the door open, so as to prevent the door from closing automatically and pinching guests.

(5) Entering and Leaving the Door

When entering the door, the receptionist should push the door open first, stand at the door, with the hand signal, and then invite guests, leaders and ladies to enter. Similarly, the same goes when going out. If the receptionist is the main escort, when walking up to the door, he/she should give a signal and politely say "please".

(6) Shaking Hands

①The Order of Shaking Hands

According to the rules of etiquette, when shaking hands, the order in which the two sides reach out should be decided by the specific circumstances on the premise of abiding by the principle of the venerable's decision.

When shaking hands in the workplace, the order of reaching out depends mainly on the position status. In social and leisure occasions, it mainly depends on age, gender and marital status.

When guests arrive, the receptionist should first extend his/her hand to guests to welcome them; when guests leave, they should first reach out their hands to shake with the receptionist to say goodbye.

②The Strength and Time of the Handshake

When shaking hands, to show warmth and friendliness, you should use a bit of pressure; when shaking hands with friends and relatives, you can use slightly more force. But when shaking hands with someone you just met or with the opposite sex, do not use too much force. Usually, shaking hands with others should not be too short or too long. Generally speaking, the handshake time should be controlled within 3 seconds.

(7) Exchanging Business Cards

In reception activities, when presenting business cards to each other, you should stand up and present them with both hands to show respect. When receiving business cards, you should also use both hands. You should read it after receiving it. You must not put it in your pocket or play with it in your hand without looking at it. You can't put the business card on the table. These are all disrespectful and impolite behaviors to others.

练一练 Activities

一、将下列词语归类

发言稿　　　广告牌　　　报到册　　　主办单位　　　承办单位
展板　　　　会议代表证　会议指南　　会议日程

纸质材料：

参会人员证明：

宣传用品：

组织单位：

二、情景题

第二天 8308 会议室有一场重要的会议，你作为该会议室的服务生，检查了会议室，发现会议室中缺少报到册、会议日程、会议礼品，而且投影仪有问题。请将以上情况写出来上报给经理。

三、翻译下列句子

1. 欢迎光临喜悦大酒店，请问需要帮忙吗？
2. 我能为您做点什么？
3. 如果您对我们的服务满意，请填写我们的反馈调查表。
4. 对不起，先生，这里不准抽烟。
5. 欢迎下次光临。

Chapter 6　其他服务 Other Services

酒店为满足宾客的多种需求，会提供多种类型的服务，如医疗服务、购物、展览、打字复印、预订火车票和机票等。

In order to meet the various needs of guests, hotels will provide various types of services, such as medical services, shopping, exhibitions, typing and copying, booking train tickets and air tickets.

Unit 1　医疗服务 Medical Service

导言 Preview

酒店的卫生质量和卫生管理水平极其重要，定期消毒和清洁房间可以减轻客户的担忧，让他们感觉到更加安全和卫生。

The quality of hotel cleaning and hygiene management level are extremely essential. Regular disinfection and cleaning of rooms can alleviate guests' worries and make them feel safer and more hygienic.

为更好地满足宾客的需求，有些酒店会提供医疗卫生服务，如提供客房医疗服务、设置紧急医疗电话、提供医生咨询和药品紧急供应等。

In order to better meet the needs of guests, some hotels will provide medical and health services, such as providing room medical services, setting up emergency medical telephone numbers, providing doctor consultations and emergency medication supplies.

词库 Word Bank

身体部位 Body parts			
汉语 Chinese	英语 English	汉语 Chinese	英语 English
病人 bìng rén	patient	大腿 dà tuǐ	thigh
胃 wèi	stomach	小腿 xiǎo tuǐ	shank

续 表

心脏 xīn zàng	heart	手臂 shǒu bì	arm
呼吸 hū xī	breathe	肩膀 jiān bǎng	shoulder
牙齿（复数）yá chǐ（fù shù）	teeth（plural）	手指 shǒu zhǐ	finger

医疗 Medical treatment

汉语 Chinese	英语 English	汉语 Chinese	英语 English
医务室 yī wù shì	clinic	疼痛 téng tòng	pain
处方；处方药 chǔ fāng；chǔ fāng yào	prescription	头痛 tóu tòng	headache
药 yào	medicine	发烧 fā shāo	fever
药片 yào piàn	tablet	咳嗽 ké sou	cough
药丸/片 yào wán/piàn	pill	流血 liú xiě	bleed
止痛药 zhǐ tòng yào	painkiller	骨折 gǔ zhé	fracture
用量；剂量 yòng liàng；jì liàng	dosage	眩晕的 xuàn yùn de	dizzy
指示；说明 zhǐ shì；shuō míng	instruction	消化不良 xiāo huà bù liáng	indigestion
描述 miáo shù	describe	慢性病 màn xìng bìng	chronic disease

常用句型 Useful Expressions

询问病情 Inquire about the Patient's Condition

1. 您胃痛有多久了？How long have you had a stomachache?
2. 您什么时候开始有这种感觉的？Since when have you been feeling like this?
3. 您觉得眩晕吗？Are you feeling dizzy?
4. 您过去得过慢性病吗？Have you got any chronic diseases in the past?
5. 您以前经常头痛吗？Did you often suffer from headaches before?

提供医疗服务 Provide Medical Services

1. 让我听听您的心脏。Let me listen to your heart.
2. 让我给您量一下血压。Let me take your blood pressure.
3. 您应该尽快去医院。You should go to the hospital as soon as possible.
4. 明早验血前请不要喝水和进食。Please do not drink or eat before the blood test tomorrow morning.
5. 我相信您不久就会痊愈的。I'm sure you will recover soon.

服用药品 Take Medicine

1. 我们马上拿些止痛药来。We will bring some painkillers immediately.

2. 请遵医嘱服药。Please take the medicine according to the doctor's advice.

3. 每日三餐前服用一片，一日三次。Please take one tablet three times a day before meals.

4. 此药请不要空腹服用。Please do not take this medicine on an empty stomach.

5. 高烧不退时请服用退烧药，但每次间隔不能少于四个小时。When the fever does not go down, please take antipyretic medication, but the interval should not be less than four hours.

6. 多喝点水，别吃油腻和生冷食物，注意保暖。Drink more water, avoid greasy, raw and cold food, and keep warm.

照料病人 Care for the Patient

1. 我去给您倒点热水。I will bring you some hot water.

2. 您今天感觉怎么样？How are you feeling today?

3. 您需要再加条毛毯吗？Do you need another blanket?

4. 您想吃点什么？我帮您订餐。What would you like to eat? I'll help you order.

5. 您不舒服的时候就叫我。Call me when you feel unwell.

情景对话 Situational Dialogues

对话 1 Dialogue 1 医疗服务（1）Medical Service（1）

场景：一位宾客受伤了，正在寻求医疗帮助。

Scene: A guest was injured and is seeking medical help.

D：Doctor（医生）　　P：Patient（病人）

D：早上好。请坐。您怎么了？Good morning. Take a seat, please. What's wrong with you?

P：我刚刚摔倒了，小腿流血了。I fell over just now, and my shank is bleeding.

D：我来检查一下。您伤得不轻，需要到医院做进一步检查，我先为您止血。Let me check. You are badly hurt. You need to go to hospital for the further examination. I'll stop the bleeding first.

P：谢谢。Thank you.

对话 2 Dialogue 2 医疗服务（2）Medical Service（2）

场景：一位宾客身体不舒服，正在寻求医疗帮助。

Scene: A guest is not feeling well and is seeking medical help.

D：Doctor（医生）　　P：Patient（病人）

D：下午好，先生。您哪里不舒服？Good afternoon, sir. What seems to be the trouble?

P：我的胃有点儿疼。My stomach hurts a little.

D：从什么时候开始的？Since when?

P：今天吃完早饭疼起来的。It hurts after breakfast this morning.

D：您早餐都吃了什么呢？What did you eat for breakfast?

P：我喝了一杯豆浆，吃了一屉小笼包，还有一个茶叶蛋。I had a cup of soybean milk, a steamer basket of small steamed buns, and an egg boiled with tea leaves.

D：哦，听起来没什么问题。您还有其他不舒服的地方吗？Oh, that sounds fine. Do you have any other discomfort?

P：没有了。No more.

D：我先给您开点药缓解一下疼痛。如果吃了药一小时后还是不能缓解，请立刻来找我。I'll give you some medicine to relieve the pain first. If you still can't get relief after taking the medicine for an hour, please come to me immediately.

P：谢谢医生。Thank you, doctor.

对话3 Dialogue 3 医疗服务（3）Medical Service (3)

场景：一位宾客身体不舒服，正在寻求医疗帮助。

Scene: A guest is not feeling well and is seeking medical help.

C：Clerk（前台职员） G：Guest（宾客） F：Floor Attendant（楼层服务员）

C：您好，这里是前台，有什么可以帮您？Hello, this is Front Desk. May I help you?

G：你好，我是1213房间的客人。我头疼得厉害。可不可以请你帮我买些止痛药？Yes, I'm the guest in Room 1213. I have a bad headache. Could you please buy me some painkillers?

C：当然可以，您需要哪种止痛药？Certainly. What kind of painkiller would you like?

G：阿司匹林就可以。Aspirin is fine.

C：请稍等。一会儿楼层服务员会帮您把药送到房间。Just a moment, please. The floor attendant will take the medicine to your room soon.

（10分钟后 10 minutes later）

F：您好，女士，我是楼层服务员。我能进来吗？Hello, madam. I'm the floor attendant. May I come in?

G：请进，门没锁。Please come in. The door is unlocked.

F：女士，这是您要的阿司匹林。必要时服一片，但每次间隔不能少于4个小时。请遵照药品说明书服药。Madam, here is your aspirin. If necessary, take one tablet of the painkiller, but no more than once every four hours. Please follow the instructions.

G：非常感谢。Thank you very much.

对话 4 Dialogue 4 医疗服务（4）Medical Service（4）

场景：一位楼层管理员正在和医生沟通宾客的身体状况。

Scene：A floor attendant is communicating with a doctor about the condition of a guest.

F：Floor Attendant（楼层服务员）　D：Doctor（医生）

F：医生，她的情况怎么样？Doctor, how is she now?

D：没什么大问题，多睡觉，多喝水，不能吃刺激性的食物，休息两天就好了。There is no big problem. She needs to sleep more and drink more water. Do not eat stimulating food, and a few days later, she will recover.

F：医生，我现在能为她做点什么吗？Doctor, is there anything I can do for her now?

D：你可以给她倒一杯温水，再拿块湿毛巾过来。如果她有什么不舒服的地方及时联系我。You can give her a cup of warm water, bring a wet towel, and contact me in time if there is any discomfort.

F：好的，医生。谢谢您。Thank you, doctor.

对话 5 Dialogue 5 医疗服务（5）Medical Service（5）

场景：一位楼层管理员正在询问宾客的身体状况。

Scene：A floor attendant is asking the guest's physical condition.

F：Floor Attendant（楼层服务员）　G：Guest（宾客）

F：先生，您今天感觉怎么样？How are you feeling today, sir?

G：我今天感觉好多了，但还是感觉有点儿恶心。I feel better today, but I'm still a little sick.

F：您还没有完全恢复，记得多喝点水，别吃刺激性的食物，多休息，我相信您不久就会痊愈的。You haven't fully recovered yet. Remember to drink more water, don't eat stimulating food, and have more rest. I believe you will recover soon.

G：是的，你说得对。Yes, you are right.

F：好好休息，如果您有什么事，请给我打电话。Have a good rest. If you have anything else, please call me.

G：谢谢。Thank you.

补充阅读 Supplement Reading

提供医疗服务工作规范

1. 一般病症

（1）客人提出就诊要求：接到客人电话后，询问客人姓名、房号、性别和病情。

（2）协助就诊：电话通知医务室医生出诊，必要时亲自到房间协助就诊。

（3）记录：记录就诊处理情况以备查用。

（4）确认：亲自与客人联系，确保客人已与医生取得了联系。

2. 紧急病症（如心脏病、晕倒等）

（1）前往现场：接到报告后三分钟之内到达现场查看病情。

（2）组织抢救：通知酒店医生在三分钟之内到达，亲自打电话向急救中心求救。

（3）迎接医生：通知保安部领班，在医生到达时将其立即带到现场。

（4）护送病人前往医院：通知有关人员控制一部电梯，确保一名酒店医生同一名能够与客人进行语言沟通的酒店工作人员陪同病人前往医院。

（5）联络：保持与医院的联系，及时向酒店领导汇报客人病情。

Specifications for Providing Medical Services

1. General conditions

（1）Guest request: After receiving the guest's call, the clerk needs to ask the guest's name, room number, gender and condition.

（2）Assistance: The clerk needs to call the doctor in the clinic, and go to the guest's room in person when necessary.

（3）Records: The clerk needs to record the treatment situation for future reference.

（4）Confirmation: The clerk needs to contact the guest in person to ensure that the guest has got in touch with the doctor.

2. Emergency conditions (such as heart disease, fainting)

（1）Going to the site: The clerk needs to arrive at the site to check the condition within three minutes after receiving the report.

（2）Organizing rescue: The clerk needs to tell the hotel doctor to arrive within three minutes and personally call the emergency center for help.

（3）Meeting the doctor: The clerk needs to tell the foreman of the security department to bring the doctor to the scene immediately when he/she arrives.

（4）Escorting patients to the hospital: The clerk needs to inform the relevant personnel to control an elevator and ensure that a hotel doctor and a hotel staff member who can communicate with the guest accompany the patient to the hospital.

（5）Keeping in contact: The clerk needs to keep in touch with the hospital and report the guest's condition to the hotel manager.

练一练 Activities

一、请填写汉语名称

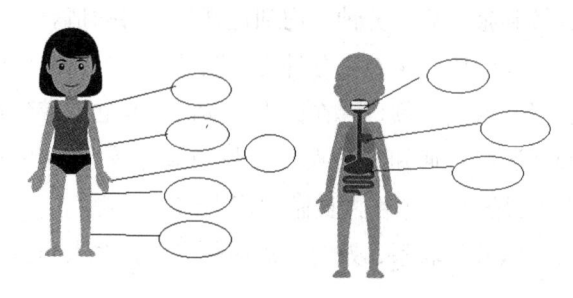

二、完成对话

一位母亲带孩子入住某酒店，第二天早上母亲发现孩子生病了，打电话向酒店前台寻求帮助。请根据以上情景，发挥想象完成对话。

三、翻译下列句子

1. 您过去得过慢性病吗？
2. 让我给您量一下血压。
3. 您应该尽快去医院。
4. 我们马上拿些止痛药来。
5. 您需要再加条毛毯吗？
6. 您不舒服的时候就叫我。

Unit 2　购物中心 Shopping Center

导言 Preview

酒店购物中心提供多种商品，包括服装、鞋帽、箱包、首饰等，可满足客人的不同购物需求，让客人在入住期间享受更多的乐趣。此外，酒店还提供多种购物服务，包括礼品包装、超市购物等，让客人在入住期间享受更多的便利服务。

The hotel shopping center offers a variety of goods, including clothing, shoes and hats, bags, jewelry, which can meet the different shopping needs of guests, making guests enjoy more fun during the check-in period. In addition, the hotel also provides a variety of shopping services, including gift packaging, shopping at the supermarket and others, so that guests can enjoy more convenient services during the stay.

词库 Word Bank

化妆品 Cosmetics			
汉语 Chinese	英语 English	汉语 Chinese	英语 English
洁面乳 jié miàn rǔ	liquid face wash	粉底液 fěn dǐ yè	liquid foundation
化妆水 huà zhuāng shuǐ	emollient water	眉笔 méi bǐ	eyebrow pencil
乳液 rǔ yè	lotion	睫毛膏 jié máo gāo	mascara
面霜 miàn shuāng	cream	眼影 yǎn yǐng	eye shadow
防晒霜 fáng shài shuāng	sunscreen cream	腮红 sāi hóng	blusher
香水 xiāng shuǐ	perfume	口红 kǒu hóng	lipstick
服装 Costume			
汉语 Chinese	英语 English	汉语 Chinese	英语 English
套装 tào zhuāng	suit	连衣裙 lián yī qún	dress
外套 wài tào	overcoat	半身裙 bàn shēn qún	skirt
T恤 T xù	T-shirt	套裙 tào qún	overskirt
卫衣 wèi yī	hoodie	睡衣 shuì yī	pajamas
衬衣 chèn yī	shirt	内衣 nèi yī	underwear
长裤 cháng kù	trousers	旗袍 qí páo	cheongsam
牛仔裤 niú zǎi kù	jeans	中山装 zhōng shān zhuāng	Chinese tunic suit
工艺品 Art work			
汉语 Chinese	英语 English	汉语 Chinese	英语 English
丝绸 sī chóu	silk	皮影 pí yǐng	leather-silhouette
剪纸 jiǎn zhǐ	paper-cut	木雕 mù diāo	wood carving
瓷器 cí qì	china	玉雕 yù diāo	jade carving
刺绣 cì xiù	embroidery	泥塑 ní sù	clay sculpture
中国结 zhōng guó jié	Chinese knot	年画 nián huà	New Year pictures
超市购物 Shopping at a supermarket			

续表

汉语 Chinese	英语 English	汉语 Chinese	英语 English
购物车 gòu wù chē	shopping cart	挑选 tiāo xuǎn	select
购物篮 gòu wù lán	shopping basket	称重 chēng zhòng	weigh
纸袋 zhǐ dài	paper bag	打包 dǎ bāo	pack
塑料袋 sù liào dài	plastic bag	结账 jié zhàng	settle accounts
折扣 zhé kòu	discount	购物小票 gòu wù xiǎo piào	shopping receipt

常用句型 Useful Expressions

购买化妆品 Buy Cosmetics

1. 您在找防晒霜吗？Are you looking for a sunscreen cream?

2. 这款乳液卖得很好。This lotion sells very well.

3. 这是我们的新款。您可以试用一下。This is a new model. You can try it out.

4. 这款粉底液的色号非常适合您。The color of this liquid foundation is perfect for you.

5. 这款口红的颜色是今年的流行色。The color of this lipstick is the popular color of this year.

购买服装 Buy Clothes

1. 您是想选一款套装吗？Do you want to choose a suit?

2. 这款连衣裙比较正式，适合出席晚宴、酒会等。This dress is more formal, which is suitable for attending dinner parties, cocktail parties, etc.

3. 我们有很多款T恤供您选择。We have many T-shirts for you to choose from.

4. 您平时穿多大尺寸的呢？What size do you usually wear?

5. 抱歉，这件外套在本店没货了，但是我们可以为您调货。Sorry, this coat is running out of stock at our store, but we can transfer another one for you.

6. 这件旗袍极具中国文化特色。This cheongsam is full of Chinese cultural characteristics.

购买工艺品 Buy Crafts

1. 这条围巾是100%蚕丝的。This scarf is 100% silk.

2. 中国茶叶闻名世界。Chinese tea is famous all over the world.

3. 我们提供精美的礼品包装服务。We offer exquisite gift packaging service.

4. 剪纸是中国传统手工艺品之一。Paper-cutting is one of the traditional Chinese handicrafts.

5. 这套瓷器是送礼的佳品。This set of china is a great gift.

6. 中国的"文房四宝"分别是笔、墨、纸、砚。China's "Four Treasures of the Study" are writing brush, ink, xuan paper and inkstone.

7. 您喜欢哪种类型的水墨画呢？What type of ink-wash painting do you like?

8. 这是一件1∶1还原的复制品。This is a 1∶1 scale replica.

超市购物 Shop at the Supermarket

1. 这些蔬菜都是今天早上刚刚运来的，非常新鲜。These vegetables were just shipped in this morning and are very fresh.

2. 您可以尝一下这款酸奶。You can try this yogurt.

3. 这里营业到晚上九点。It is open until 9 p.m.

4. 矿泉水在第二排的架子上。The mineral water is on the shelf in the second row.

5. 这是今天的特价商品，买一送一。This is a special offer for today. Buy one and get one free.

6. 我帮您打包。I'll pack it for you.

7. 您需要购物袋吗？Do you need a shopping bag?

8. 这是您的购物小票，请拿好。This is your shopping receipt, and please take it.

情景对话 Situational Dialogues

对话1 Dialogue 1 购物服务（1）Shopping Service（1）

场景：一位宾客在酒店购物中心购买化妆品。

Scene：A guest is buying cosmetics at the hotel shopping center.

C：Clerk（前台职员）　　G：Guest（宾客）

C：早上好，女士，有什么能帮您的吗？Good morning, madam. What can I do for you?

G：我想买些护肤品。I want to buy some skin care products.

C：您有想要购买的品牌吗？Do you have any brands that you want to buy?

G：没有，请给我推荐一款。No, please recommend one to me.

C：看您的肤质属于偏干型，推荐您使用这款水乳套装。它在补水的同时还能提亮肤色，非常适合您。You have dry skin, so I recommend you to use this hydrating toner and moisturizer set. It can hydrate and brighten your skin, which is suitable for you.

G：我可以试一下吗？Can I try it out?

C：当然可以。Of course.

G：不错，这个水乳套装多少钱？Good, how much does this hydrating toner and moisturizer set cost?

C：450元一套。450 yuan for a set.

G：好的，我要两套。有什么眼影盘推荐吗？OK, I want two sets. Do you have any eye shadow palettes to recommend?

C：有，我们刚刚到货了一款大地色眼影盘，适合日常妆容。您可以试一下。Yes, we have just received an earth-toned eye shadow palette, which is suitable for everyday makeup. You can have a try.

G：很好看，请帮我包起来。另外，我还想买一支口红。Very nice. Please wrap it up for me. In addition, I want to buy a lipstick.

C：您看这款口红怎么样？豆沙色今年非常流行。How about this lipstick? Cameo brown is extremely popular this year.

G：好的。请给我拿一支。Fine. Please get me one.

C：好的，您还需要别的吗？我们的护手霜今天打八五折，您要不要看一下？OK, do you need anything else? Our hand cream today is 15% off, and do you want to have a look?

G：不用了，谢谢。No, thank you.

C：好的，请这边结账。总共680元，我给您包起来。欢迎下次光临。OK, please check out here. It's 680 yuan totally. I'll wrap them up for you. Welcome to visit us next time.

对话2 Dialogue 2 购物服务（2）Shopping Service（2）

场景：一位宾客在酒店购物中心购买服装。

Scene：A guest is buying clothing at the hotel shopping center.

C：Clerk（前台职员） G：Guest（宾客）

C：下午好，我能为您做点儿什么吗？Good afternoon. Is there anything I can do for you?

G：我明天要去参加一个商务晚宴，我想挑选一个套装。I am going to attend a business banquet tomorrow. I want to pick out a suit.

C：您穿多大尺码？What size do you wear?

G：M码。M.

C：您可以试一下这套黑色的和这套蓝色的，试衣间在右边。You can try this black set and the blue set, and the fitting room is on the right side.

（过了一会儿 A few moments later）

G：这两套都不错。Both sets are pretty good.

C：是的，黑色套装更加端庄、正式，蓝色的会显得活泼一些。我更推荐您选择这套黑色的套装，显得您气质极佳。Yes, the black set is more dignified and formal, and the blue one is more lively. I recommend you to choose the set of black, which shows your temperament is excellent.

G：好的。请帮我包起来吧。Fine. Please wrap it up for me.

对话3 Dialogue 3 购物服务（3）Shopping Service (3)

场景：一位宾客在酒店购物中心购买手工艺品。

Scene：A guest is buying handicrafts at the hotel shopping center.

C：Clerk（前台职员）   G：Guest（宾客）

C：您好，能为您做些什么？Hello, what can I do for you?

G：我想选购一些中国的手工艺品作为礼物。能给我介绍一下吗？I want to buy some Chinese handicrafts as gifts. Can you introduce some to me?

C：剪纸、瓷器、丝绸制品、中国书画、文房四宝都是不错的选择。Paper cuttings, porcelain, silk products, Chinese painting and calligraphy, and the "Four Treasures of the Study" are all good choices.

G：什么是"文房四宝"？What are the "Four Treasures of the Study"?

C：文房四宝是由宣纸、毛笔、砚台和墨组成的书写用品，非常具有中国特色。They are writing supplies composed of a writing brush, ink, xuan paper and an inkstone, with Chinese characteristics.

G：很不错，我要两套。Very nice, please give me two sets.

C：我还建议您买些剪纸，种类丰富，纯手工制作，非常精美。I also suggest you buy some paper cuttings. Because they have a variety of types, and they are handmade and very exquisite.

G：我看一下。I'd like to have a look.

C：这里有花卉图案、生肖图案、人物图案的剪纸。There are flower patterns, zodiac patterns and figure patterns.

G：好的，我每个种类要一件。OK, I'll take one of each kind.

C：女士，我推荐您再看看这些瓷器，这儿有几套景德镇的优质瓷器，做工考究，值得收藏。Madam, I recommend you to look at the porcelain. Here are several sets of high-quality ones from Jingdezhen, which are well-made and worth collecting.

G：多少钱一套呢？How much for a set?

C：这套瓷杯750元，这套瓷碗630元。The set of porcelain cups is 750 yuan and the set of porcelain bowls is 630 yuan.

G：我要这套瓷碗。I want the set of porcelain bowls.

C：请这边付款。我为您提供礼品包装服务。Please settle your bill here. I will provide you with the gift packaging service.

G：谢谢。Thank you.

对话4 Dialogue 4 购物服务（4）Shopping Service (4)

场景：一位宾客在酒店超市购买水果。

Scene：A guest is buying fruits at the hotel supermarket.

A：Assistant（店员）　　G：Guest（宾客）

G：你好，请问购物车在哪儿？Hello, where is the shopping cart, please?

A：购物车在那边，您可以选择适合您的购物车类型。The cart is over there and you can choose the type of cart for you.

G：水果区在什么位置？Where is the fruit area located?

A：您一直走到后面再右转就到了。You walk to the back and then turn right.

（在水果区 In the fruit area）

G：请问猕猴桃多少钱？How much is the kiwi fruit?

A：猕猴桃每千克16元。The kiwi fruit is 16 yuan per kilogram.

G：这些橙子呢？What about these oranges?

A：橙子每千克12元。这些橙子又甜又多汁。Oranges are 12 yuan per kilogram. These oranges are both sweet and juicy.

G：我要几个猕猴桃和橙子。I want a few kiwis and oranges.

A：好的，我帮您称重、打包。OK, I'll weigh and wrap them for you.

G：你们有折扣吗？Do you give any discount?

A：是的，对于住店客人，我们可以打九折。Yes, for guests living here, we can give a 10% discount.

G：谢谢。Thank you.

A：您需要购物袋吗？塑料袋收费，纸袋免费。Do you need a shopping bag? Plastic bags are charged, and paper bags are free.

G：请给我纸袋。顺便问一下，你们最早几点营业呢？Please give me a paper bag. By the way, what time do you open at the earliest?

A：我们是全天营业的超市，如果您需要什么，可以随时过来。We are an all-day supermarket, and you can come here at any time if you need anything.

G：谢谢。Thanks.

补充阅读 Supplement Reading

中国是具有五千多年历史的文明古国，手工艺品种类繁多，技艺精湛，是中华文化的瑰宝，值得我们去传承和保护。

中国剪纸是一种用剪刀或刻刀在纸上剪刻花纹，用于装点生活或配合其他民俗活动的民间艺术。在中国，剪纸交融于各族人民的社会生活，是各种民俗活动的重要组成部分。

中国瓷器指的是中国制造的瓷器，在英文中"瓷器（china）"与"中国

（China）"同为一词。中国是瓷器的故乡，瓷器是古代劳动人民的一个重要的创造。

丝绸是中国的特产，中国古代劳动人民发明并大规模生产丝绸制品，更开启了世界历史上第一次东西方大规模的商贸交流，史称"丝绸之路"。从西汉起，中国的丝绸不断大批地运往国外，成为世界闻名的产品。

皮影戏，又称"影子戏"或"灯影戏"，是一种以兽皮或纸板做成的人物剪影表演故事的民间戏剧。表演时，艺人们在白色幕布后面，一边操纵影人，一边用当地流行的曲调讲述故事，同时配以打击乐器和弦乐，具有浓厚的乡土气息。

China is an ancient civilization with a history of more than 5,000 years. There are quite a few kinds of handicrafts with exquisite skills, which are the treasures of Chinese culture and are worthy of our inheritance and protection.

Chinese paper cutting is a kind of folk art that uses scissors or carving knives to cut patterns on paper to decorate life or cooperate with other folk activities. In China, paper cutting, which is an important part of various folk activities, integrates in the social life of people of all ethnic groups.

Chinese porcelain, refers to porcelain made in China. In English, "china" is the same word as "China". China is the hometown of porcelain, which was an important creation of the ancient working people.

Silk is a specialty of China. The ancient Chinese working people invented and produced silk products on a large scale, which opened the first large-scale trade exchange between the East and the West in the world history, known as the "Silk Road" in history. Since the Western Han Dynasty, Chinese silk has been shipped abroad in large quantities and becomes a world-famous product.

Leather-silhouette show, also known as "shadow play", is a folk drama made of animal skin or cardboard to perform stories. During the performance, the artists are behind the white curtain to manipulate the leather silhouettes, while telling the story in local popular tunes, along with percussion instruments and strings, with a strong local atmosphere.

练一练 Activities

一、请在以下每个分类中写出十个汉语物品名称。

　　化妆品

　　服装

　　工艺品

二、请用汉语介绍自己在酒店商品部向一位美国的顾客售卖图片中物品的过程，需要用到购物车、挑选、结账、购物小票等词语。

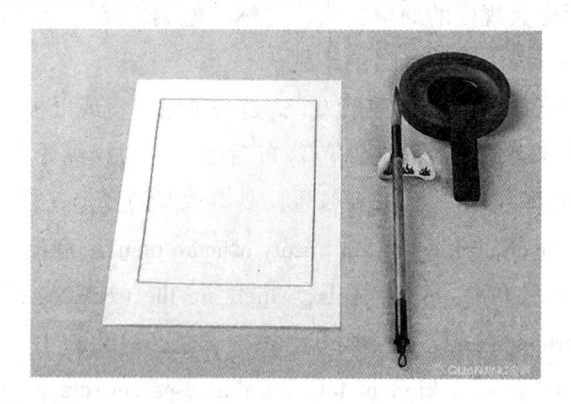

三、翻译下列句子

1. 这是我们的新款。您可以试用一下。
2. 您是想选一款套装吗？
3. 这款连衣裙比较正式，适合出席晚宴、酒会等。
4. 我们提供精美的礼品包装服务。
5. 矿泉水在第二排的架子上。
6. 您需要购物袋吗？
7. 这是您的购物小票，请拿好。

Unit 3　展览服务 Exhibition Service

导言 Preview

　　酒店展览服务，是指为商品流通、促销、展示、经贸洽谈、民间交流、企业沟通、国际往来等在大中型酒店举办的展览和会议。

　　Hotel exhibition services refer to exhibitions and conferences held in large and medium-sized hotels for commodity circulation, promotion, exhibition, economic and trade negotiations, non-governmental exchanges, enterprise communication, international exchanges, etc.

词库 Word Bank

常用词汇 Common vocabulary			
汉语 Chinese	英语 English	汉语 Chinese	英语 English
展览、展览品 zhǎn lǎn、zhǎn lǎn pǐn	exhibit	安排 ān pái	arrange
展厅 zhǎn tīng	exhibition hall	要求 yāo qiú	requirement
标准 biāo zhǔn	standard	包裹 bāo guǒ	parcel
展板 zhǎn bǎn	display board	展期 zhǎn qī	exhibition period
色标 sè biāo	color code	装饰 zhuāng shì	decoration
尺寸 chǐ cùn	size	展位 zhǎn wèi	stand
布展 bù zhǎn	exhibition arrangement	服务指南 fú wù zhǐ nán	service guide
观众 guān zhòng	viewer	邀请函 yāo qǐng hán	invitation
参展商 cān zhǎn shāng	exhibitor	展览主题 zhǎn lǎn zhǔ tí	exhibition theme

常用句型 Useful Expressions

1. 我们曾承接过多种大型的展览活动。We have undertaken a variety of large-scale exhibition activities.

2. 酒店提供完整、专业的展会服务。The hotel offers complete and professional exhibition service.

3. 我们的会议厅、多功能厅都可用作展厅。Our conference hall and multi-function hall can be used as exhibition halls.

4. 我们的展厅最多可容纳100个展位。Our exhibition hall can accommodate up to 100 booths.

5. 我们提供拆包服务。We offer an unpacking service.

6. 您对展厅的装饰有什么样的要求？What are your requirements for the exhibition hall decoration?

7. 在展厅入口处需要做多大尺寸的展板？What size of the panel should be made at the entrance of the exhibition hall?

8. 我们为参展商提供餐饮服务。We provide a catering service for the exhibitors.

9. 此次展览是什么方面的主题？What is the theme of this exhibition?

10. 展品易碎吗？Are exhibits fragile?

情景对话 Situational Dialogues

对话 1 Dialogue 1 展会服务（1） Exhibition Service（1）

场景：一位宾客正在和酒店前台职员沟通展会相关事宜。

Scene：A guest is communicating with a hotel clerk about the exhibition.

C：Clerk（前台职员） G：Guest（宾客）

G：你好，我下个月想在酒店举办一场为期三天的展会。Hello. I would like to have a three-day exhibition at the hotel next month.

C：请稍等，我帮您查一下这个时间是否可以预约。Just a moment, please. I'll check whether the appointment can be made at this time.

（过了一会儿 After a little while）

C：让您久等了，先生，下个月20日至25日我们的会议厅是空闲的，可以做展会。Thank you for waiting, sir. Our conference hall will be free from the 20th to the 25th of next month for the exhibition.

G：会议厅能容纳多少个展位？How many booths can the conference hall accommodate?

C：最多可以容纳150个标准展位。此次展览的是什么类型的展品？It can accommodate up to 150 standard booths. What kind of exhibits are on display?

G：是一些中国书画作品，都是非常名贵的。They are some Chinese painting and calligraphy works, which are very precious.

C：请您放心，我们会非常小心的。Please rest assured that we will be very careful.

G：谢谢。Thank you.

对话 2 Dialogue 2 展会服务（2） Exhibition Service（2）

场景：一位宾客正在和酒店前台职员沟通展会相关事宜。

Scene：A guest is communicating with a hotel clerk about the exhibition.

C：Clerk（前台职员） G：Guest（宾客）

C：请问此次展会的主题是什么？What is the theme of this exhibition, please?

G：是关于中国传统服饰方面的展览。It is about traditional Chinese clothing.

C：听起来特别吸引人。展品大概有多少件？Sounds particularly appealing. How many pieces are there?

G：180件左右。About 180 pieces.

C：那我建议您使用我们的多功能厅，可改造成适合主题的布局。Then I

recommend using our multi-function hall, which can be transformed into a layout suitable for the theme.

G：好的。除了展品，我们还需要一些展板做内容简介。OK. In addition to the exhibits, we also need some display boards to make content introductions.

C：没问题，您需要多少块展板？No problem. How many pieces of display boards do you need?

G：大概60块儿。我们还需要一个观展互动区。About 60 pieces. We also need an exhibition area for interaction.

C：我们可以将多功能厅中心舞台改造成互动区。The center stage of our multi-function hall can be transformed into an interactive area.

G：那太好了。That's great.

对话3 Dialogue 3 展会服务（3）Exhibition Service（3）

场景：一位宾客正在和酒店前台职员沟通展会相关事宜。

Scene：A guest is communicating with a hotel clerk about the exhibition.

C：Clerk（前台职员）　G：Guest（宾客）

C：您对展厅的布置有什么特殊要求吗？Do you have any special requirements for the layout of the exhibition hall?

G：是的。我们希望能用红色作为主题颜色。指示和引导标志也要清晰明了。Yes. We hope to use red as the theme color, and the instructions and guide signs should also be clear.

C：好的。我们会为您安排的。你们还需要用具有中国传统文化特色的元素点缀展厅吗？Fine. We will arrange it for you. Do you still need elements with traditional Chinese cultural characteristics to decorate the exhibition hall?

G：这真是个不错的主意。That is really a good idea.

对话4 Dialogue 4 展会服务（4）Exhibition Service（4）

场景：一位宾客正在和酒店前台职员沟通展会相关事宜。

Scene：A guest is communicating with a hotel clerk about the exhibition.

C：Clerk（前台职员）　G：Guest（宾客）

G：你们提供拆包服务吗？Do you provide the unpacking service?

C：是的，我们有非常专业的拆包人员。Yes, we have very professional unpackers.

G：拆包费用是多少？How much is the unpacking cost?

C：费用是由展品的大小和拆包的难易程度决定的，最低30元一件，最高200元一件。The cost is determined by the size of the exhibits and the difficulty level of unpacking, with a minimum 30 yuan and a maximum 200 yuan per piece.

对话5 Dialogue 5 展会服务（5）Exhibition Service（5）

场景：一位宾客正在和酒店前台职员沟通展会相关事宜。

Scene：A guest is communicating with a hotel clerk about the exhibition.

C：Clerk（前台职员） G：Guest（宾客）

C：展会期间是否需要在酒店住宿呢？Do you need accommodation during the exhibition?

G：是的，不过我们只在展会前一晚住宿，也就是5月6日晚上。Yes, but we only stay the night before the show, which is the night of May 6th.

C：您需要多少间房？How many rooms do you need?

G：20间标准间就可以。20 standard rooms are fine.

C：非常抱歉，5月6日的标间只有16间，可以把剩余四间换成大床房吗？I'm sorry, but there are only 16 rooms on May 6th. Can I exchange the remaining four rooms for big bed rooms?

G：好吧。请给我们安排安静点的房间。Alright. Please give us quiet rooms.

C：没问题。No problem.

G：酒店提供餐饮服务吗？Does the hotel provide a catering service?

C：您的住宿已经包含了自助早餐。我们还可以为参展者安排自助午餐，观展者也可以选择在我们的酒店大厅就餐。Your accommodation already includes a breakfast buffet. We can also arrange a lunch buffet for exhibitors, and visitors can also choose to eat in the lobby of our hotel.

G：自助午餐怎样收费呢？How to charge for the lunch buffet?

C：会展自助餐打85折，每人40元。The exhibition buffet is 15% off, 40 yuan per person.

补充阅读 Supplement Reading

展会流程

一、会前准备工作

（一）选择展会

1. 根据公司的产品及该阶段的营销策略，选择合适的展会；
2. 确定展会名称、时间、地点及组织方；
3. 和组织方联系，预订展位。

（二）筹备展会

1. 确定参展目标及展品；

2. 确定参展负责人、参展人员；

3. 安排展会筹备工作、筹备时间及相关负责人。

（三）展台策划

1. 联系展台搭建商并询价；

2. 告知展台设计要求；

3. 确定展板风格、制作商及费用；

4. 准备展板内容资料；

5. 设计展板，定稿后制作；

6. 确定布展时间及安排。

（四）展品及资料准备

1. 确定展品及重点展品；

2. 规划展品数量；

3. 列出清单交由储运部门准备；

4. 根据参展人员，确定名片数量；

5. 确定其他物品，如剪刀、胶带、笔、订书器等；

6. 清点展品内容及数量；

7. 装箱并托运。

（五）酒店预订

1. 视展厅位置，筛选酒店；

2. 询价，考察酒店环境及周边环境；

3. 确定参展人员及房间数；

4. 预订酒店。

（六）车票购买

1. 确定启程及回程时间；

2. 确定参展人员；

3. 购买或预订火车票和机票。

二、会中工作

1. 安排参展人员入住酒店；

2. 介绍产品，发放宣传资料及名片；

3. 回收客户登记表；

4. 展会结束后整理展品及资料并装箱托运；

5. 办理退房手续；

6. 返程。

三、会后工作

1. 书写总结报告，并开会讨论展会心得；

2. 整理客户资料，发给相关部门。

Exhibition Process

Ⅰ. Preparation work before the exhibition

1. Selecting exhibitions

（1）Selecting the appropriate exhibition according to the company's products and the marketing strategy at this moment；

（2）Confirming the exhibition name, time, location and organizer；

（3）Contacting the organizer, booking the booth.

2. Preparing the exhibition

（1）Confirming the exhibition targets and exhibits；

（2）Confirming the person in charge and the participants；

（3）Arranging the exhibition preparations, time and persons in charge.

3. Booth planning

（1）Contacting the booth builder for inquiry；

（2）Informing the booth builder of the booth design requirements；

（3）Confirming the style of the display board, the manufacturer and the cost；

（4）Preparing the contents and materials of the display board；

（5）Designing the display board, and making it after the final draft；

（6）Confirming the time of the exhibition and the arrangement.

4. Preparation for exhibits and materials

（1）Confirming the exhibits and key exhibits；

（2）Planning the number of exhibits；

（3）Submitting the list to the storage and transportation department for preparation；

（4）Confirming the number of business cards according to the participants；

（5）Confirming other items, such as scissors, tape, pens, staplers；

（6）Checking the content and quantity of the exhibits；

（7）Boxing and checking-in.

5. Hotel reservation

（1）Selecting the hotels according to the location of the exhibition hall；

（2）Inquiring, investigating the hotel environment and its surroundings；

（3）Confirming the number of participants and rooms；

（4）Booking the hotel.

6. Ticket purchase

（1）Confirming the departure and return time;

（2）Confirming the exhibitors;

（3）Purchasing or booking train tickets and air tickets.

Ⅱ. During the exhibition

1. Arranging the exhibitors to check in;

2. Introducing the products and distributing publicity materials and business cards;

3. Retrieving the customer registration forms;

4. Cleaning up the exhibits and materials, and then packing and boxing for shipment after the exhibition;

5. Handling the check-out procedures;

6. Returning.

Ⅲ. After the exhibition

1. Writing the summary report, and holding meetings to discuss the exhibition experience;

2. Organizing customer information and sending it to relevant departments.

练一练 Activities

一、请写出汉语

exhibit	service guide	exhibition arrangement
exhibition hall	standard	exhibition period
exhibitor	invitation	exhibition theme
decoration	viewer	requirement

二、翻译下列句子

1. 酒店提供完整、专业的展会服务。

2. 我们的会议厅、多功能厅都可用作展厅。

3. 我们的展厅最多可容纳100个展位。

4. 我们为参展商提供餐饮服务。

5. 展品易碎吗?

Unit 4　订票服务 Ticket Booking Service

导言 Preview

为方便宾客出行，一些酒店会提供预订火车票、机票、船票的服务。此外，一些酒店还会提供预订景区门票、展览门票等票务服务。

In order to facilitate guests to travel, some hotels will provide booking services for train tickets, air tickets and ship tickets. In addition, some hotels will also provide booking services for scenic spot tickets, exhibition tickets and other types of tickets.

词库 Word Bank

常用词汇 Common vocabulary			
汉语 Chinese	英语 English	汉语 Chinese	英语 English
预订 yù dìng	book	航班 háng bān	flight
机票 jī piào	air ticket	车次 chē cì	train number
火车票 huǒ chē piào	train ticket	座位 zuò wèi	seat
船票 chuán piào	ship ticket	过道 guò dào	aisle
出发 chū fā	depart	保险 bǎo xiǎn	insurance
到达 dào dá	arrive	身份证 shēn fèn zhèng	ID card
中转 zhōng zhuǎn	transit	日期 rì qī	date

常用句型 Useful Expressions

预订机票 Book Airline Tickets

1. 请您为我订一张到北京的机票，好吗？Will you please book an air ticket to Beijing for me?

2. 您想要哪一个航班？Which flight do you prefer?

3. 您想要直达的航班还是中转的航班？Do you want a direct flight or a transit flight?

4. 您想要靠窗的座位还是靠过道的座位？Do you want a window seat or an aisle seat?

5. 您什么时间出发？When do you set out?

预订火车票 Book Train Tickets

1. 请帮我预订两张从上海到广州的火车票。Please help me book two train tickets from Shanghai to Guangzhou.

2. 请核对一下您的信息。Please check your information.

3. 明天上午最早去杭州的火车是几点？When is the first train to Hangzhou tomorrow morning?

4. 我想要订往返票。I want to book a round-trip ticket.

5. 您需要购买保险吗？Do you need to buy insurance?

预订门票 Reserve Entrance Tickets

1. 请帮我预订参观故宫的门票。Please help me book a ticket to visit the Palace Museum.

2. 最近一场的话剧演出票是在后天晚上 7 点，需要我帮您预订吗？The latest drama performance is at 7 p.m. the day after tomorrow. Do you need me to book it for you?

3. 请提供您的购票信息。Please provide your ticket information.

4. 已经帮您预订了明天晚上 8 点在国家大剧院的两张话剧票。I have booked two tickets of the National Theatre at 8 p.m. tomorrow for you.

5. 请您注意演出地点距离酒店较远，请提前安排好时间。Please note that the performance location is far away from the hotel. Please arrange your time in advance.

情景对话 Situational Dialogues

对话 1 Dialogue 1 预订机票 Booking Airline Tickets

场景：一位宾客正在酒店预订机票。

Scene：A guest is booking an airline ticket at the hotel.

C：Clerk（前台职员）　G：Guest（宾客）

G：请帮我预订一张去深圳的机票，好吗？Could you book me a ticket to Shenzhen, please?

C：好的，太太，您想什么时候离开北京？Yes, madam. When do you intend to leave Beijing?

G：后天。The day after tomorrow.

C：那天有两个航班，一个是上午 10 点 20 分，另一个是下午 3 点 10 分。There are two flights available that day, one at 10:20 a.m., the other at 3:10 p.m.

G：请帮我订上午的航班吧。Please book the morning flight for me.

C：好的，请填一下您的信息。OK, please fill in your information.

对话 2 Dialogue 2 预订火车票 Booking Train Tickets

场景：一位宾客正在酒店预订火车票。

Scene：A guest is booking a train ticket at the hotel.

C：Clerk（前台职员）　　G：Guest（宾客）

C：您好，有什么可以帮您的吗？Hello, what can I do for you?

G：你好，我想预订两张从武汉到南京的火车票。Hello, I would like to book two train tickets from Wuhan to Nanjing.

C：请问您打算什么时间出发？When are you going to leave?

G：周五上午。Friday morning.

C：为您查到有多趟高铁和动车，且余票充足。There are many high-speed trains and bullet trains, and there are plenty of tickets left.

G：那就买上午8点25这个吧。Then buy the one at 8:25 a.m.

C：是两位成人吗？Two adults?

G：不是，我和我的儿子。No, it's me and my son.

C：您的儿子多大了？How old is your son now?

G：他今年7岁。He is 7 years old.

C：那您需要一张成人票和一张儿童票。请您填写一下身份信息。Then you need an adult ticket and a child ticket. Please fill in the identity information.

G：我应该在几点钟出发办理检票手续？When should I leave to check in?

C：您必须在早上7点前出发。You must leave before 7 a.m.

对话3 Dialogue 3 预约参观 Making Appointments

场景：一位宾客正在酒店预约参观中国国家博物馆。

Scene: A guest is making an appointment to visit the National Museum of China at the hotel.

C：Clerk（前台职员）　　G：Guest（宾客）

G：您好，我想预约参观中国国家博物馆，您能帮我约一下吗？Hello, I want to make an appointment to visit the National Museum of China. Can you help me with the appointment?

C：当然，您想什么时间去参观呢？Of course, what time do you like to visit?

G：越早越好。The earlier, the better.

C：请稍等。我来查一下。Please wait a moment. Let me check.

（2分钟后 2 minutes later）

C：女士，您可以预约本周四参观中国国家博物馆。开放时间是9:00—17:00。Ms, you can make an appointment to visit the National Museum of China this Thursday. The opening time is 9:00—17:00.

G：太好了，谢谢。博物馆在什么位置呢？Great, thank you. Where is the museum located?

C：中国国家博物馆在北京东城区东长安街16号。您可以乘坐地铁1号线或2号线前往。The National Museum of China is at 16 East Chang'an Avenue, Dongcheng District, Beijing. You can take Metro Line 1 or Line 2.

G：好的，那儿是我一直想去参观的地方。OK, it is the place that I've always wanted to visit.

C：中国国家博物馆现有藏品数量143万余件，涵盖古代文物、近现当代文物、艺术品等多种门类，在促进文明交流互鉴方面起到了非常大的作用。The National Museum of China has a collection of more than 1.43 million pieces, covering ancient cultural relics, modern and contemporary cultural relics, artworks and other categories, which plays a great role in promoting exchanges and mutual learning among civilizations.

G：听你这么说，我已经迫不及待想要去参观了。Hearing that, I can't wait to visit it.

补充阅读 Supplement Reading

中国国家博物馆是代表国家收藏、研究、展示、阐释中华文化代表性物证的最高历史文化艺术殿堂，负有留存民族集体记忆、传承国家文化基因、促进文明交流互鉴的重要使命。

中国国家博物馆现有藏品数量143万余件，涵盖古代文物、近现当代文物、艺术品等多种门类，藏品系统完整，历史跨度巨大，材质形态多样，涉及甲骨、青铜器、瓷器、玉器、金银器、钱币、佛造像、古籍善本、碑帖拓本、墓志、玺印、书画、雕塑、漆木家具、砖瓦石刻、珐琅器、玻璃器、丝织品、工艺品、老照片、民族文物、民俗文物、革命文物等等，具有独特鲜明特点，充分展现和见证了中华5000多年文明的血脉绵延与灿烂辉煌。

The National Museum of China is the highest historical, cultural and artistic palace representing the national collection and research, displaying and interpreting the representative material evidence of Chinese culture. It is entrusted with the important mission of preserving the collective memory of the nation, inheriting the national cultural genes and promoting the exchange and mutual learning of civilizations.

The National Museum of China has more than 1.43 million collections, covering ancient and modern cultural relics, contemporary cultural relics, works of art and other categories. The collection system is complete, as well as the historical span is huge, and the material forms are diverse, involving oracle bones, bronzes, porcelain, jade, gold and silverware, coins, Buddhist statues, rubbings of ancient books, rubbings of the tablets, epigraphs, royal seals, painting and calligraphy, sculptures, lacquer wood furniture, brick and tile stone carvings, enamel ware, glassware, silk crafts, artworks, old photographs, ethnic cultural relics, folk cultural relics, revolutionary cultural relics and so on. They have distinct and unique characteristics, fully demonstrating and witnessing the continuity and brilliance of Chinese civilization for more than 5,000 years.

练一练 Activities

一、请写出汉语

insurance   train ticket   arrive
air ticket   book   depart
transit   date   flight

二、请将下列句子翻译成汉语

1. Which flight do you prefer?
2. Afternoon flights preferably.
3. What time do I check in at the airport?
4. What time does the train reach Shanghai?
5. Do I need to change trains?

三、翻译下列句子

1. 请您为我订一张到北京的机票，好吗？
2. 您想要靠窗的座位还是靠过道的座位？
3. 请核对一下您的信息。
4. 您需要购买保险吗？
5. 已经帮您预订了明天晚上8点在国家大剧院的两张话剧票。

练一练参考答案

Chapter 1 前厅服务 Front Office Service

Unit 1 房间预订 Room Reservations

一、连线题

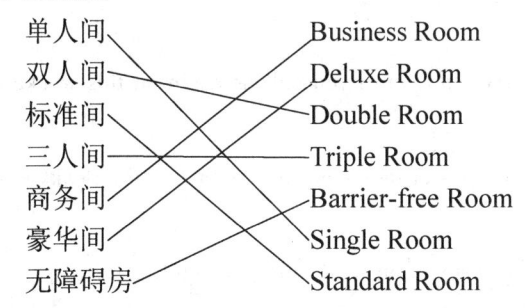

单人间 —— Single Room
双人间 —— Double Room
标准间 —— Standard Room
三人间 —— Triple Room
商务间 —— Business Room
豪华间 —— Deluxe Room
无障碍房 —— Barrier-free Room

二、请按照预订程序，将下面的句子排序

1. 您好，客房预订部，请问有什么可以帮助您？

2. 我想预订一个房间。

3. 要订在什么时候？您一行有多少人？

4. 4月16日到20日，只有我和我太太。

5. 4月16日到20日，请问您想预订哪种房间？

6. 双人间。

7. 请别挂断好吗？我来查看一下是否有空房间。（过了一会儿）让您久等了，先生。我们有空余的双床间，现在价格是每晚180美元，这样可以吗？

8. 好的，可以，我订了。

9. 谢谢您，先生。您能告诉我您的姓名和电话号码吗？

10. 没问题。我叫李军，电话是3242-5827。

11. 李军，电话是3242-5827。请问您，军是军队的军吗？

12. 嗯，是的，是军队的军。

215

13. 请问您4月16日大概什么时候到酒店？

14. 大约中午12点。

15. 李先生，因为现在是旺季，我们酒店预订只能保留到下午6点。

16. 好的，我知道了，我会在6点前到达。

17. 谢谢您，李先生。您已经在广州×××酒店办理了预订，从4月16日到20日，预住5天。您若不能如期到达，请务必在16日下午6点前通知我们。感谢您的电话，我们期待能为您服务。请问您还有其他问题吗？

18. 没有了。

19. 好的，您有任何需要再联系我们，再次感谢您，再见。

20. 再见。

三、翻译下列句子

1. I would like to reserve a room from April 5th to April 9th.

2. I'd like to book a single room with bath from the afternoon of October 4th to the morning of October 10th.

3. It's the peak season now. I'm very sorry, but could you call us again on this weekend? We may have a cancellation.

4. I am afraid we are fully booked for all types of rooms on that night. It's the peak season now.

5. Sorry, due to…, I have to cancel the reservation made in your hotel.

Unit 2　办理入住 Check-in

一、请选择对应的答案

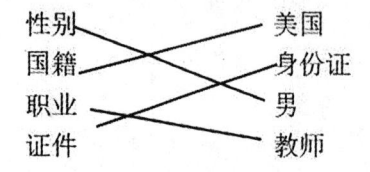

性别 —— 男
国籍 —— 美国
职业 —— 教师
证件 —— 身份证

二、请按照登记程序，将下面的句子排序

您好！请问您有预订吗？

是的，我有预订。

请出示一下您的身份证，我查一下订单。

李先生，预订信息显示，您是预订了一间标间，4月16日到20日，预住5天，是吗？

嗯，是的。

我给您登记了8215房间，房间在2楼，您可以向前走，有电梯。这是房卡，请您收好。早餐是早上五点到九点，如果您有问题可以拨打总台电话8888。

好的。

请您稍等，我给您登记一下，请您看摄像头（摄像头采集信息）。您需要预交押金1000元，押金收据退房时需要您出示。

请问您是划卡还是交现金？

好的，我划卡。

这是您的押金收据，请您收好。

好的，谢谢。

三、翻译下列句子

1. Please have a seat for a while. I'll help you with the check-in procedure.

2. Please give me your passport or ID card and credit card. I'll help you to fill in the form.

3. Give me your passport, please. We need it for registration.

4. I'll get the porter to take your luggage up.

5. The porter here will take your luggage and show you the way.

Unit 3 礼宾服务 Concierge Service

一、请写出以下名称

（行李箱）　　　（酒店行李车）

二、请排序

1. 将宾客乘坐的车辆引领至适当的停车位。
2. 主动上前为宾客开启车门，并用手挡在车门上方，以免宾客碰头。
3. 向宾客问好，表示欢迎。
4. 协助行李员卸行李，并确认件数，以免有遗漏。

5. 记下出租车的车号，引导车辆离开。

6. 及时拉开酒店大门，方便宾客进入大厅。

三、翻译下列句子

1. I'll send the luggage up by another lift.

2. Let me show you to your room. This way please.

3. Would you like me to call a taxi for you?

4. The voltage in your room is 220 volts.

5. You can store your valuables at the hotel's safe.

Unit 4　问讯服务 Information Service

一、请将下列句子翻译成汉语

1. A：我想兑换一些钱，请问银行在哪儿？

   B：请从这里上楼然后左拐，就在邮局旁。

2. 您可以在收银处兑换钱币。

3. 咖啡厅在二楼，全天供应快餐。

4. 您如果需要问讯什么事，可以打电话给前厅接待处。

5. 除了娱乐中心，我们在二楼还有一个健身俱乐部。

6. A：请问去餐厅怎么走？

   B：我亲自领你们去。

   A：请问咖啡厅在哪儿？

   B：径直走，穿过自助餐厅和餐馆，你会看到它就在前面。

7. A：到礼品商店，从这儿走，对吗？

   B：是的，沿着走廊走，走过报刊亭和图书馆就是商店。

8. A：我要找4号会议室。

   B：会议室都在休息厅对面，顺着右边走，走过电梯，上楼就是。

9. A：这里出租车的基价是多少？

   B：大约1公里1.2元，但是超过10公里以后加倍收费，并且晚上10点以后实行夜间收费价格。

二、翻译下列句子

1. The lifts are in the lobby near the main entrance.

2. Excuse me, where is the cashier's office?

3. By the way, could you please show me where the lift is?

4. Would you please tell me the daily service hours of the dining room?

5. Could you sell me two tickets for tomorrow?

Unit 5 总机服务 Operator Service

一、请写出汉语

an international call 国际电话

leave a message 留言

a paid call 付费电话

wake-up call service 叫早服务

connect/transfer 电话转接

hold the line 别挂机

二、请将下列句子翻译成汉语

1. 这是总机，我可以帮您吗？
2. 请问您要往哪个国家打电话？
3. 请问您要打哪个国家的电话？
4. 请您告诉我电话号码好吗？
5. 请问您的姓名和房号？
6. 您要我帮您接通电话吗？
7. 我可以问是谁在讲话吗？
8. 我马上为您接 333 号房。
9. 对不起，占线。您是等一会儿，还是过会儿再打过来？
10. 先生，没有人接电话，您是否需要留言？

三、翻译下列句子

1. Could you put me through to Room 618, please?
2. Sorry to have bothered you.
3. May I have extension two-one-one?
4. I'd like to make an international call.
5. I'm sorry. We can't find the guest's name on our hotel list.

Unit 6 外币兑换 Foreign Currency Exchange

一、连线题

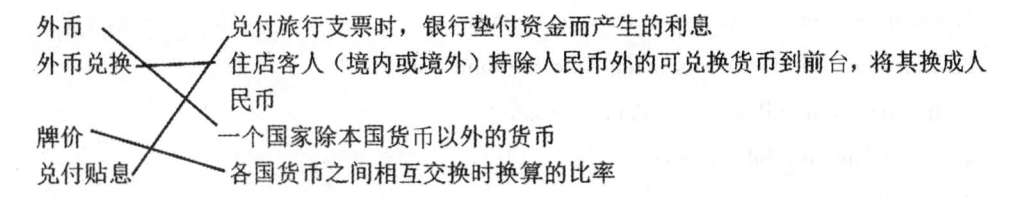

外币 —— 兑付旅行支票时，银行垫付资金而产生的利息

外币兑换 —— 住店客人（境内或境外）持除人民币外的可兑换货币到前台，将其换成人民币

牌价 —— 一个国家除本国货币以外的货币

兑付贴息 —— 各国货币之间相互交换时换算的比率

二、写出汉语

Euro 欧元　　　RMB 人民币　　　Franc 法郎　　　Pound Sterling 英镑

HK Dollar 港币　　Deutsche Mark 德国马克　　Japanese Yen 日元　　Thai Baht 泰铢

三、翻译下列句子

1. Could you fill out this form, please?

2. If we exchange large amounts, our cash supply will run out and we will be unable to oblige our other guests.

3. How much would you like to change?

4. Would you kindly sign your name and address on the exchange memo?

5. It's a free service.

Unit 7　办理离店 Check-out

一、请写出汉语

receipt 收据　　　　　swipe 刷卡　　　　　invoice 发票

bill 账单　　　　　　check out 退房　　　　service charge 服务费

PIN number 密码　　　pay the bill 结账

二、请将下列句子翻译成汉语

1. 早上好，前厅收银，有什么我可以帮您的吗？

2. 埃文斯小姐，您今天要退房吗？

3. 先生，您现在要退房吗？

4. 先生，您今天早上是否从房间冰箱里取过饮料？

5. 这是您的账单，请过目。

6. 您是不是检查一下，看您的账单是否正确？

7. 先生，您的行李是否已经拿下来了？如果没有，我将叫一名行李员帮您拿下来。

8. 我来把您的账单开出来。

9. 请问您今早是否使用过酒店服务设施或在咖啡厅用过早餐？

10. 谢谢等候，三天包括服务费在内一共是 470 美元。

三、翻译下列句子

1. I'm afraid you'll have to vacate your room by 12.

2. That charge is for drinks taken from the mini-bar.

3. In what form will your payment be made?

4. Can I have my bill, please?

5. Can I check out ahead of time?

Unit 8　处理投诉 Dealing with Complaint

一、请写出汉语
sorry 对不起　　　pardon 请原谅　　sorry to have incommoded you 给您添麻烦了
excuse me 打扰了　　regret 遗憾　　　apologize 道歉

二、请将下列句子翻译成汉语
1. 先生，出了什么问题？我能为您做些什么？
2. 这很少见，我会调查此事的。
3. 我再去给您重端一份上来。
4. 要不要我去把这道菜重做一遍？
5. 我去和厨师长商量一下，看看他是否能给予补救。
6. 非常抱歉，如果您愿意，我可以给您上点别的菜，当然这是本店免费赠送的。
7. 对不起，先生。请您原谅她，我们今天实在太忙了。
8. 很抱歉听您这么说，请相信我们一定会调查此事，我们的厨师长是很挑剔的。
9. 服务员，我太太冷得不行。
10. 也许您可以坐到那边的角落里，那里风小些。

三、翻译下列句子
1. If you get your luggage ready, we will move you to another room.
2. I'm sorry to hear that. We do apologize for the inconvenience. I'll have the shower fixed, the tub cleaned, the floor dried and toilet items sent to your room immediately.
3. We are sorry to inform you that we cannot do what you ask for.
4. You should respect our customs regulations.
5. What you have done is contrary to the safety regulations.

Chapter 2　客房服务 Housekeeping Service

Unit 1　清洁服务 Cleaning Service

一、朗读下列词汇
开关（kāi guān）
毛巾架（máo jīn jià）
水龙头（shuǐ lóng tóu）
浴缸（yù gāng）

熨洗（yùn xǐ）

空调器（kōng tiáo qì）

床垫（chuáng diàn）

浴室（yù shì）

二、角色扮演，两人一组，完成顾客要求服务员打扫房间的对话

（略，合理表达意思即可）

Unit 2　常规服务 Regular Service

一、将下列词汇匹配

(1) — (B)　　(2) — (E)　　(3) — (F)

(4) — (A)　　(5) — (D)　　(6) — (C)

二、将下列句子翻译成汉语

1. 抱歉打扰您，我现在可以清理房间吗？
2. 请再等 30 分钟好吗？
3. 就让东西放在那儿吧。
4. 这个房间看上去很不错。
5. 顺便问一句，这儿的自来水能喝吗？

Unit 3　洗衣服务 Laundry Service

一、将下列词汇匹配

(1) — (B)　　(2) — (D)　　(3) — (F)

(4) — (C)　　(5) — (E)　　(6) — (A)

二、根据语意排列句子顺序

A—D—F—G—E—B—C—H

Unit 4　维修服务 Maintenance Service

一、朗读下列词汇

用水冲洗　　yòng shuǐ chōng xǐ

滴下　　　　dī xià

维修　　　　wéi xiū

电工　　　　diàn gōng

设备工具　　shè bèi gōng jù

塞住了　　　sāi zhù le

二、翻译下列句子

1. The water tap drips all night long. I can hardly sleep.
2. The TV set is not working well.
3. Would you mind changing a room? The toilet is hard to repair today.
4. The toilet is stopped up.
5. I've locked myself out of the room. May I borrow a spare key?
6. What efficiency! Thanks a lot.

Unit 5　其他客房服务 Other Housekeeping Services

一、连线题

(1) — (E)　　　(2) — (B)　　　(3) — (A)　　　(4) — (F)
(5) — (C)　　　(6) — (G)　　　(7) — (D)

二、翻译下列句子

1. I'm out of toilet paper.
2. My toilet overflowed.
3. I'd like to use a safety deposit box.
4. Do you have any orange soda available?
5. Never mind, just add them to my bill.
6. There are some experienced babysitters in the babysitting center.

Unit 6　紧急事件 Emergency

一、紧急电话拨号填空题

紧急情况	电话号码
火警	119
生病急救	120
交通事故	122
紧急报警	110

二、翻译下列句子

1. My wife has slipped in the bathroom. She can't stand up.
2. I have a terrible headache.
3. Are you feeling better now?
4. Before the doctor arrives, is there anything I can do for you?
5. Does it hurt when I press here?
6. Don't panic! We'll help you get out of the building safely.

Chapter 3　餐饮服务 Food & Beverage Service

Unit 1　订餐和领位 Reservations and Seating Guests

一、连线题

(1) — (D)　　(2) — (C)　　(3) — (G)　　(4) — (F)
(5) — (A)　　(6) — (E)　　(7) — (B)

二、排列下列对话的顺序

K—J—F—B—C—E—N—A—M—I—D—G—L—H

Unit 2　点菜 Taking Order

一、连线题

(1) — (D)　　(2) — (G)　　(3) — (F)　　(4) — (A)
(5) — (C)　　(6) — (E)　　(7) — (B)

二、翻译下列句子

1. We have both buffet-style and à la carte dishes, and which would you prefer?
2. Please add some pepper to the soup.
3. Please take your time. I'll be back to take your order.
4. Are you ready to order, sir?
5. How would you like your steak done?
6. We have a wide range of vegetarian dishes for your choice.
7. Are you allergic to any particular food, sir?

Unit 3　中餐服务 Chinese Food Service

一、用汉语写出下图的菜名

A. 西红柿炒鸡蛋　B. 鱼香肉丝　C. 烧茄子　D. 火锅

二、连线题

(1) — (C)　　(2) — (A)　　(3) — (D)　　(4) — (F)
(5) — (G)　　(6) — (H)　　(7) — (B)　　(8) — (E)

三、翻译下列句子

1. It's a well-known delicacy in Chinese Cuisine.

2. It takes about 20 minutes to prepare the dish.

3. What is the most famous and popular dish in Sichuan Cuisine?

4. I am not used to chopsticks. Do you have knives and forks here?

5. This is our first trip to China. Will you recommend us some Chinese dishes?

6. Enjoy your meal!

7. What do you think of the food today?

Unit 4　西餐服务 Western Food Service

一、用汉语写出下图的菜名
A. 牛排　B. 水果沙拉　C. 薯条　D. 意大利面

二、连线题
(1) — (D)　　(2) — (F)　　(3) — (A)　　(4) — (G)

(5) — (B)　　(6) — (C)　　(7) — (E)

三、翻译下列句子

1. We'll get a piece of chocolate mousse cake.

2. Your meal is ready. Please enjoy your meal!

3. I'd like to order supper today and send to my room, please.

4. You can leave this tray outside your door.

5. This dish is quite delicious!

6. Are you ready to order now?

Unit 5　酒水服务 Drinks Service

一、写出下列酒的称谓
A. 啤酒　B. 红酒　C. 白酒　D. 鸡尾酒

二、连线题
(1) — (G)　　(2) — (F)　　(3) — (E)　　(4) — (A)

(5) — (D)　　(6) — (B)　　(7) — (C)

三、翻译下列句子

1. I'd like to try something new. Do you have any recommendations?

2. What would you like to drink? Try some Chinese Baijiu?

3. Which brand of beer would you like?

4. The best liquor in China is Maotai liquor, which is used for national banquets.

5. Would you care for an aperitif?

6. Yes, a nice bouquet when I smell it; and it tastes lovely!

Unit 6　结账 Settling the Bill

一、连线题

(1) — (D)　　(2) — (F)　　(3) — (A)　　(4) — (G)

(5) — (B)　　(6) — (C)　　(7) — (E)

二、根据语意排列句子顺序

C—G—E—F—B—H—D—A

Chapter 4　康乐服务 Health and Recreation Service

Unit 1　歌厅 KTV

一、朗读下列词汇

音响 yīn xiǎng　　音质 yīn zhì　　音色 yīn sè

麦霸 mài bà　　美声 měi shēng　　通俗 tōng sú

二、按照谈话顺序排列下列句子

C—F—A—E—G—B—D—H

Unit 2　水疗服务 SPA Service

一、用汉语写出下图的名称

A. 按摩床　B. 浴袍　C. 拖鞋　D. 毛巾

二、连线题

(1) — (F)　　(2) — (E)　　(3) — (A)

(4) — (B)　　(5) — (C)　　(6) — (D)

Unit 3　健身房 Fitness Center

一、朗读下列词汇

减肥 jiǎn féi　　健身 jiàn shēn　　曲线 qū xiàn　　伸展 shēn zhǎn　　热身 rè shēn

二、翻译下列句子

1. We all should warm up before doing some exercises.

2. Stretch your arms up.

3. Please show me your member card.

4. What about the water temperature and depth of the pool?

5. Then we have an excellent sauna, with a free supply of towels and soap.

Unit 4 美容院 Beauty Salon

一、连线题

(1) — (E)　　(2) — (D)　　(3) — (B)

(4) — (F)　　(5) — (C)　　(6) — (A)

二、翻译下列句子

1. I want to trim my moustache.

2. Would you like to have a shampoo?

3. How would you like your hair done, madam? Permanent, cold wave, or washed and styled?

4. I want a facial.

5. Have you taken a look at some of the new styles lately?

Chapter 5　会议服务 Conference Service

Unit 1 会议设备 Conference Equipment

一、根据图片标注出汉语

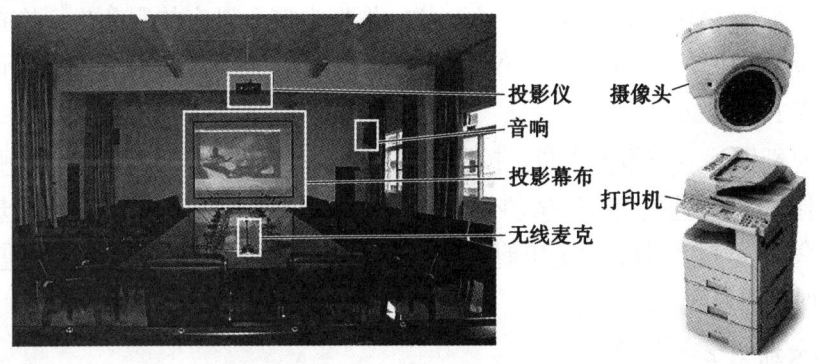

投影仪
音响
投影幕布
无线麦克
摄像头
打印机

二、情景题

×××公司需要在你所在的酒店租用一间50人的会议室开年会，假定你是酒店的经理，请你对酒店相应会议室的设施及所能提供的会议服务内容作一个汉语介绍。

×××公司×××先生，您好！这是我们酒店的50人会议室，我们的会议室宽敞明亮，好多家公司都在我们这里开会。我们的会议室配有投影仪、液晶显示屏，可以让参会人员全方位看到屏幕；同时我们这里配有无线麦克风、音响等，可以让会议室中每位参会人员清晰地听到发言人发言；角落配有复印机，可以及时为各位参会人员提供所需的复印服务。会议期间，我们会安排一名专业会议服务人员，为各位参会人员提供倒热水等服务。

三、翻译下列句子

1. Can you book a multi-function meeting room for us?

2. Do you have one convention room for 200 persons?

3. What facilities do you need?

4. Do you need a projector and a computer?

5. There is a LCD screen in the hall.

Unit 2　会议接待服务 Conference Reception Service

一、将下列词语归类

发言稿　广告牌　报到册　主办单位　承办单位　展板　会议代表证　会议指南　会议日程

纸质材料：发言稿 会议代表证 会议指南 会议日程

参会人员证明：报到册

宣传用品：广告牌 展板

组织单位：主办单位 承办单位

二、情景题

第二天8308会议室有一场重要的会议，你作为该会议室的服务生，检查了会议室，发现会议室中缺少报到册、会议日程、会议礼品，而且投影仪有问题。请将以上情况写出来上报给经理。

我作为8308会议室服务人员，按照酒店规定，提前一天对会议室进行例行检查。在检查过程中，我发现会议室中缺少报到册、会议日程、会议礼品，这些都是此次会议重要的会议资料，而且会议室中的投影仪有故障。明天这里将举行这一场重要会议，请经理及时沟通处理。

三、翻译下列句子

1. Welcome to Xiyue Hotel. May I help you?

2. What can I do for you?

3. If you are satisfied with our service, please fill out our feedback questionnaire.

4. Sorry, sir, smoking is not allowed here.

5. Welcome to visit us next time.

Chapter 6　其他服务 Other Services

Unit 1　医疗服务 Medical Service

一、请填写汉语名称

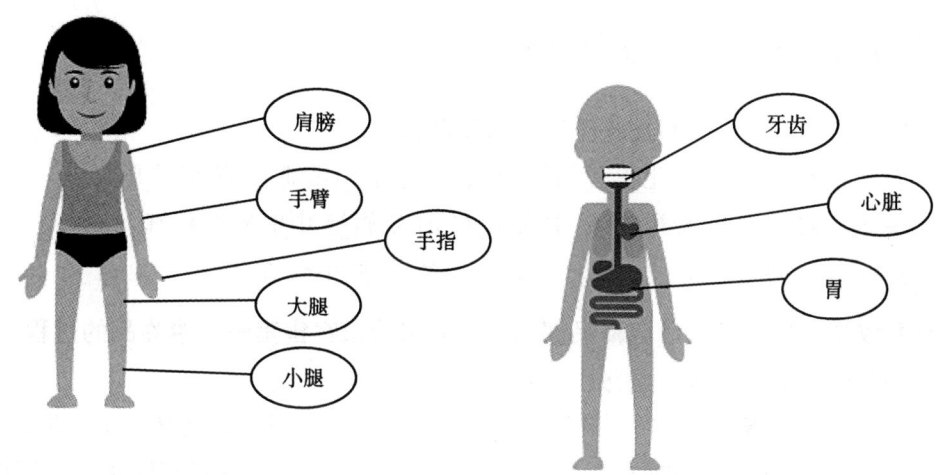

肩膀　手臂　手指　大腿　小腿

牙齿　心脏　胃

二、完成对话

C：（前台职员）　G：（宾客）　F：（楼层服务员）

C：您好，这里是前台，有什么可以帮您？

G：你好，我是1213房间的客人。我孩子发高烧了。可不可以请你帮我买些退烧药？

C：当然可以，您需要哪种退烧药？

G：布洛芬就可以。

C：请稍等。一会儿楼层服务员会帮您把药送到房间。

（10分钟后）

F：您好，女士，我是楼层服务员。我能进来吗？

G：请进，门没锁。

F：女士，这是您要的布洛芬。必要时服一片，但每次间隔不能少于4个小时。请遵照药品说明书服药。

G：非常感谢。

F：不客气，好好休息。如果您有什么事，请给我打电话。

G：谢谢。

三、翻译下列句子

1. Have you got any chronic diseases in the past?

2. Let me take your blood pressure.

3. You should go to the hospital as soon as possible.

4. We will bring some painkillers immediately.

5. Do you need another blanket?

6. Call me when you feel unwell.

Unit 2　购物中心 Shopping Center

一、请在以下每个分类中写出十个汉语物品名称。

化妆品　洁面乳　粉底液　化妆水　眉笔　乳液　睫毛膏　面霜　眼影　防晒霜　腮红

服装　连衣裙　半身裙　套裙　睡衣　卫衣　衬衣　内衣　旗袍　中山装　牛仔裤

工艺品　丝绸　皮影　剪纸　木雕　瓷器　玉雕　刺绣　泥塑　中国结　年画

二、请用汉语介绍自己在酒店商品部向一位美国的顾客售卖图片中物品的过程，需要用到购物车、挑选、结账、购物小票等词语。

您好！这是中国独有的文书工具，我们称它为文房四宝，就是"笔、墨、纸、砚"，这是非常有中国特色的物品，您可以带回一套作为纪念。这里有好几种，您可以随意挑选喜欢的款式，可以把这个放到您的购物车里与其他物品一起结账。结完账后，您可以拿着购物小票在前台换取一份精美的礼品。

三、翻译下列句子

1. This is a new model. You can try it out.

2. Do you want to choose a suit?

3. This dress is more formal, which is suitable for attending dinner parties, cocktail parties, etc.

4. We offer exquisite gift packaging service.

5. The mineral water is on the shelf in the second row.

6. Do you need a shopping bag?

7. This is your shopping receipt, and please take it.

Unit 3　展览服务 Exhibition Service

一、请写出汉语

exhibit <u>展览、展览品</u>　　service guide <u>服务指南</u>　　exhibition arrangement <u>布展</u>

exhibition hall <u>展厅</u>　　standard <u>标准</u>　　exhibition period <u>展期</u>

exhibitor <u>参展商</u>　　invitation <u>邀请函</u>　　exhibition theme <u>展览主题</u>

decoration <u>装饰</u>　　viewer <u>观众</u>　　requirement <u>要求</u>

二、翻译下列句子

1. The hotel offers complete and professional exhibition service.
2. Our conference hall and multi-function hall can be used as exhibition halls.
3. Our exhibition hall can accommodate up to 100 booths.
4. We provide a catering service for the exhibitors.
5. Are exhibits fragile?

Unit 4　订票服务 Ticket Booking Service

一、请写出汉语

insurance <u>保险</u>　　train ticket <u>火车票</u>　　arrive <u>到达</u>

air ticket <u>机票</u>　　book <u>预订</u>　　depart <u>出发</u>

transit <u>中转</u>　　date <u>日期</u>　　flight <u>航班</u>

二、请将下列句子翻译成汉语

1. 您想要哪一个航班？
2. 最好是下午的航班。
3. 我什么时候到机场办理登机手续？
4. 火车什么时候到达上海？
5. 我需要换火车吗？

三、翻译下列句子

1. Will you please book an air ticket to Beijing for me?
2. Do you want a window seat or an aisle seat?
3. Please check your information.
4. Do you need to buy insurance?
5. I have booked two tickets of the National Theatre at 8 p.m. tomorrow for you.

参考文献

[1] 上海旅游行业饭店职业能力认证系列教材编委会.饭店服务实用英语[M].北京:旅游教育出版社,2011.
[2] 创想外语研发团队.酒店服务业英语,看这本就够[M].北京:中国纺织出版社,2014.
[3] 刘延平,董亮.旅游英语口语[M].杭州:浙江大学出版社,2010.
[4] 李群.饭店服务英语[M].北京:北京理工大学出版社,2015.
[5] 冯岩岩.酒店实用英语[M].北京:对外经济贸易大学出版社,2010.
[6] 肖璇.现代酒店英语实务教程[M].北京:世界图书出版公司,2006.
[7] 陈江生.实用英语[M].3版.大连:大连理工大学出版社,2017.